EXECUTIVE'S POCKET GUIDE TO
ROI RESUMES
AND JOB SEARCH

LOUISE KURSMARK and JAN MELNIK

Executive's Pocket Guide to ROI Resumes and Job Search

© 2007 by Louise Kursmark and Jan Melnik

Published by JIST Works, an imprint of JIST Publishing, Inc.

8902 Otis Avenue

Indianapolis, IN 46216-1033

Phone: 1-800-648-JIST   Fax: 1-800-JIST-FAX   E-mail: info@jist.com

Visit our Web site at **www.jist.com** for information on JIST, free job search tips, book chapters, and ordering instructions for our many products! For free information on 14,000 job titles, visit **www.careeroink.com.**

Quantity discounts are available for JIST books. Have future editions of JIST books automatically delivered to you on publication through our convenient standing order program. Please call our Sales Department at 1-800-648-5478 for a free catalog and more information.

Trade Product Manager: Lori Cates Hand
Interior Designer: Marie Kristine Parial-Leonardo
Page Layout: Toi Davis
Cover Designer: designLab
Proofreaders: Gayle Johnson, Jeanne Clark
Indexer: Tina Trettin

Printed in the United States of America
11 10 09 08 07 06   9 8 7 6 5 4 3 2 1

Library of Congress Cataloging-in-Publication data is on file with the Library of Congress.

ISBN-13: 978-1-59357-333-1

ISBN-10: 1-59357-333-2

About This Book

Executives require exceptional job search strategies, resumes, and related documents to advance their careers, compete for the top C-suite opportunities, and present themselves effectively for board appointments. An expert approach, distinctive to senior-level professionals, is essential. And there must be a guaranteed return on investment (ROI). This book succinctly gives you the "keys to the board room" in preparing for and conducting an executive search that targets success.

Step-by-Step Strategies Presented with an ROI. Consistent with the theme of this book, every strategy proposed for implementation is accompanied by an easy-to-assess ROI to help you gauge the likelihood of success in *your search*. You'll find a step-by-step process outlined for each component of the job search—from how to create the compelling STAR stories in your resume—featuring Situation-Tactic-Action-Result—to developing cover letters that stimulate a response. You'll find all the tools needed to build your own professional bio as well as create distinctive Critical Leadership Initiatives documents. Need some assistance in refining your "elevator speech" or your job search e-mail messages? We'll give you the framework to craft exceptional ones! Curious whether a networking resume could be instrumental to your search? You'll learn how to not only create this tool, but develop a complementary networking card to help propel your search.

Problem-Solution Statements and Answers to the Most Vexing Questions. This book gives you the real answers to challenges faced by many executives; age, job-hopping, lengthy unemployment, underemployment, and many other tricky issues are addressed with candor and a solutions-focused approach. You'll find proven strategies for real-life concerns and many typical dilemmas. Easy-to-follow narratives are included to demonstrate how you can extract specific achievements and challenges from your experience and create copy for your own resume and cover letter that conveys the value-add you bring as a candidate. You'll find focused exercises, worksheets, and other tools to help you manage the process of writing your own resume materials as well as structuring your job search. Plus, you'll find a detailed timeline designed to accelerate your search and provide the parameters necessary to help ensure your success. Highly recommended actions are featured as "STAR Strategies" throughout the book.

A Return for Your Investment of Time. To maximize the value of this book's content, it has been strategically organized to take you efficiently through the job-prep and search process. You'll find short vignettes that demonstrate the most effective strategies for executives. Careful attention is paid to the key details unique to the senior-executive candidate. You will find techniques you can readily adapt to your own resume development or search challenges. And you'll find numerous, clear examples of each strategy or technique that you can tailor in crafting your own solution. Many best-in-class samples written by the top executive resume writers in the world augment the how-to portions interspersed throughout the book to give you the *what*, the *how*, and the *why* so that you can immediately implement leading-edge ideas in your own documents and job search.

Ready for Accelerated Success? The *Executive's Pocket Guide to ROI Resumes and Job Search* delivers the pragmatic, senior-level tools you'll need to confidently manage your own career, develop outstanding documents, and conduct a search campaign most likely to produce the results you desire. Your personal ROI is guaranteed as you embark on a plan incorporating the expert strategies and proven experience concisely presented in this book. *Carpe Diem!*

ACKNOWLEDGMENTS

We're grateful for the expert guidance of our editor, Lori Cates Hand. And we appreciate the opportunities to have assisted so many talented executives navigate their own career journeys.

DEDICATION

To our husbands, Bob Kursmark and Ron Melnik, who served as sounding boards, provided in-the-trenches perspectives, and willingly acted as occasional guinea pigs for our theories as they advanced their careers. And to our children, Meredith, Matt, Dan, Wes, and Stephen, who inspire us with their accomplishments as they lay the foundation for their own executive careers!

Contents

Introduction

Return on Investment. This is the theme that drives executive decisions around the globe. To make a compelling business case for any action, payback *must* exceed cost. From the executive's perspective, this is as true for personal career decisions as it is for corporate decisions.

The *Executive's Pocket Guide to ROI Resumes and Job Search* provides you with that same ROI. With its concise approach to typical executive situations, likely scenarios, and problem-solution statements, this guide tells you exactly what you need to know to maximize the results from your resume and job search efforts. Its emphasis on ROI and the bottom line means you will be able to quickly assess the applicability of a particular strategy, follow the easy-to-implement steps, and immediately position yourself for the most advantageous results. You will learn about the activities and career investments that are likely to produce the highest ROI—as well as those that offer lower dividends (for instance, posting your resume to general career Web sites such as Monster.com is not likely to generate a high ROI for executives).

Fundamental to any executive search campaign is the development of an exceptional resume crafted to demonstrate the future value you will bring to the next challenge. This book gives you strategies, examples, and solutions tailored precisely to the needs and concerns of executive job seekers.

As industry-leading professionals with private career-management practices catering to senior-level executives, we have a *combined 30+ years of experience* working with executive job seekers. Over the past decade alone, we have each consulted with hundreds of C-suite and upper- and middle-tier executives across a wide range of disciplines and industries. Key to our client-centric approach is a highly individualized methodology for working effectively with each client to provide maximum value and optimal results. Our approach always focuses on the ROI: Will this strategy produce the desired results in the most time-conservative and cost-effective means possible? Will this technique help the client to gain traction as a candidate within a desired target organization? Does this solution give the client the competitive edge to gain critical access—and then build momentum in his or her search campaign?

Collected here, in this comprehensive yet concise guide, are the best-in-class business practices for ROI resume development and job search strategies for executives. You will literally learn from the masters (we were the first two individuals in the world to earn the prestigious Master Resume Writer credential and are two of only about a dozen MRWs today). We give you the tools you need to successfully manage your own career—including leading-edge documents and time-proven strategies that work at the highest corporate levels.

What *ROI Resumes and Job Search* provides to propel your executive job search:

- Very specific details that focus on issues unique to senior executives

- Comprehensive scenarios showing the *what*, the *how*, and the *why*

- Readily transferable strategies you can immediately implement for greater value in your job search

- Proven solutions to actual problems

- Clear examples, including a professional array of resume samples, all focusing on executive ROI and demonstrating candidate value in a variety of interesting formats

- Complete vignettes of three executive career transitions from which you can draw numerous strategies

- FAQs, interspersed throughout crisp narrative, that give you immediate answers to your most pressing questions

- Stellar examples of STAR stories and complete instructions for developing your own

- Finally, a detailed index that will guide you to solid ROI answers and lucid examples to answer the key questions common to many executives and specific to you

Here's a quick chapter-by-chapter rundown of what you can expect in return for your investment of time:

Chapter 1, "Executive Resumes and Job Search," discusses the need for immediate impact in resumes and related documents. We explore a variety of executive-level search methods and strategies and provide a clear statement of the anticipated ROI for each. We cover networking, working with recruiters, and using Internet services, along with the topics of interviewing and negotiating. But, before you can take even the first steps in an aggressive executive search, you must have a well-developed, accomplishment-oriented, professionally branded executive resume.

This brings us to **chapter 2, "Develop ROI Content for Your Career Marketing Documents and Messages,"** where you'll find the heart and soul of this book: How do you translate what you've achieved into salient content that spells solution and success to the prospective employer? How do you demonstrate your value proposition? This section concisely details effective methods for developing material for your own branded resume and easy-to-implement strategies for achieving impact in your documents. You'll find liberal doses of thought-provoking Q&A designed to get at the root of your own success stories. Included is a formula for creating STAR stories (situation-tactic-action-result) to outline your top three or four contributions/accomplishments in each of your positions. Finally, we provide an easy-to-follow resume outline as a tool for capturing this critical content.

With a well-developed outline, you'll find the pointers in **chapter 3, "Executive Resume Writing Challenges,"** helpful in zeroing in on the best ways to incorporate your STAR stories, quantifiable achievements, and uniquely branded value propositions into your resume. You'll find recommendations for emphasizing or downplaying specific information, tactics for addressing any issues (concern about age, underemployment, lack of degree, and so forth), and practical strategies for developing the look and content of your resume. In an easy-to-reference "Special Situations" section, we discuss a number of dilemmas common to many executives—and answer each with expert advice and 1-2-3 solutions.

Beyond an exceptional resume, you'll be presented with a variety of executive tools in **chapter 4, "Additional ROI Documents,"** that can add tremendous value to your search process. These include scripting for "elevator speeches," impactful cover letters and e-mail messages, Critical Leadership Initiatives (an important pre-meeting and leave-behind paper), and other documents that may prove instrumental to your successful search.

Chapter 5, "Successful Transition Stories," provides inspiration, motivation, and know-how through the use of concise vignettes that clearly identify the problem and the solution. In snapshot format, you'll see how actual executives—perhaps with circumstances like your own—addressed specific challenges in their job search and successfully navigated the waters to their next big opportunity.

Chapter 6, "Gallery of Executive Career Documents," offers an exclusive selection of executive career documents depicting many of the strategies outlined in this book. You'll find materials written by the authors and samples culled from the best-of-the-best in the industry—other Master Resume Writers and Credentialed Career Masters from around the globe. Finally, if you want additional help and expertise, the appendix provides contact information for all of the executive resume writers who contributed to this book.

So what's the bottom line? You'll find this pocket guide to be loaded with salient information and proven strategies to help you effectively develop an executive resume and prepare for a successful search. Whether you are a seasoned and successful executive with a multi-decades track record, or an aspiring executive on a career track accelerated for rapid growth, you will derive exceptional results from the strategies embedded throughout *Executive's Pocket Guide to ROI Resumes and Job Search*. Let's get started!

Chapter 1

Executive Resumes and Job Search

"A wise man will make more opportunities than he finds."

—Francis Bacon

Impact is defined as "the power of making a strong, immediate impression." In comic book parlance, it's the *pow! bif! bam!* balloons that signal action, excitement, and a definite effect on the immediate future. That's impact, and that's what we want your resume and all of your career marketing documents to convey.

Why the need for such immediate impact? After all, you're not a cartoon superhero. As an executive, you won't go around saving the world or destroying evil geniuses. And a thoughtful, strategic approach, rather than a hasty rush to action, usually provides the best solution to complex business challenges.

Yet there are factors that make it imperative that your resume create a strong, immediate impression on your readers:

- **Busy executives:** Think of your own typical day at work and you'll understand that hiring managers, human resources professionals, executive recruiters, and networking contacts simply don't have the time to figure out who you are or what you can do for them. Your marketing documents must give them this vital information instantly.

- **Short attention spans:** Distraction and constant multimedia messages are a fact of modern-day life. If your documents require quiet, thoughtful contemplation for readers to understand your value, it's likely they'll move on to the next message before they can absorb this information from you.

- **An environment of constant change:** Today's fast-moving business climate requires us to change and adapt—constantly—to keep up. A vigorous tone and get-to-the-point messages will communicate that you thrive in this environment.
- **A glut of resumes:** A few mouse clicks and anyone can "blast" a resume to literally thousands of recruiters or apply to dozens of open positions. As a result, employers and recruiters are flooded with resumes. A low-impact, hard-to-understand resume gives them the excuse they need to weed you out.

Of course, you can't go around with cartoon balloons over your head announcing the *bam* results you can deliver—and we don't recommend adding a comic strip to your resume, either. So you'll need to find other ways to communicate the impact you will have in your next executive position.

Our ROI strategy is designed to do just that, letting decision-makers quickly learn that you have delivered business value in the past and are likely to do so in the future. And that promise of value—the return you'll supply on the investment of hiring you—will resonate at the highest executive levels of any organization.

In chapter 2, we walk you through the process of developing ROI content for your career marketing messages. And in chapters 3 and 4, you learn the tricks of the resume-writing trade, strategies that will enable you to create powerful resumes and other valuable documents to use during your job search.

But first we want to arm you with an action plan for putting all of these great materials to work. With a solid understanding of what to do and how to allocate your time, you can hit the ground running the minute you complete your documents.

ROI Search Strategies

Just as it makes sense for investors to seek the best return on their investment and for hiring authorities to choose the employees who can deliver the most value, we want you to select the search strategies that give you the best return on your expenditure of time, money, energy, and other assets at your disposal.

Not only that, we want you to have a clear understanding of how the strategies fit together, how you should schedule them into your week, and how you can move smoothly from one step to the next toward your ultimate goal.

Following is our recommendation for a fast-start, efficient, and highly effective six-week plan of initiatives that should generate a flow of opportunities and put you well on the way to your next job. Our primary focus is on the strategies that are most effective—as proven by our thousands of clients over the years and by any number of surveys taken to determine how people actually find jobs.

With each strategy, you'll find our recommendations for ROI-based resource allocation according to the effectiveness of that particular strategy. And we'll give you both a big-picture overview of the strategy and specific action steps to help you execute it quickly; easily; and with a clear understanding of the process, path, and expected results.

Putting it all together, we then provide a week-by-week plan of action that incorporates all of the strategies to kick your search into high gear right from the start. All too often, even savvy executives who are normally decisive and action-oriented find themselves feeling overwhelmed at the start of the complex—and sometimes all-new—endeavor of a job search. Our plan gives you the structure and control you need to jump into action.

Finally, sprinkled throughout the text in every chapter, you'll find our *STAR* Strategies. We coined this acronym to designate *Situation-Tactic-Action-Result* the insider secrets that will give you the fastest and best results from your efforts.

ROI value for each job search strategy is presented on the following scale:

> ★★★★ = maximum value
>
> ★★★ = reasonable value
>
> ★★ = limited value
>
> ★ = marginal value

STRATEGY #1: Networking

Different surveys provide slightly different numbers, but in every survey we've ever seen, network-
ing has consistently emerged as the number-one strategy for finding a new job. What this means, simply, is that most people—from 60% to 85%, depending on the survey—find their jobs through people they know or people they are referred to.

> ROI value: ★★★★
> Recommended resource allocation: 40%

Thus, it is to your definite advantage to activate your network and build new connections so that your contacts can point you to your next job opportunity.

✳ ✳

STAR Strategy: Prepare Before You Connect

Personal contacts—those you have now and those you'll develop during your search—are an incredibly valuable resource. Before you reach out, be sure that you're prepared to deliver the right message. Use the exercises in chapter 2 to prepare an introduction that is clear, concise, and value-focused.

Don't ask your contacts for a job; it's rare that they'll know of a perfect-fit opportunity. Instead, ask for their help, advice, specific information, ideas, or referrals. The better you can articulate who you are and the value you offer, and the more specifically you can ask for what you need, the more they'll be able to help you.

✳ ✳

ACTION ITEM: IDENTIFY AND ORGANIZE YOUR NETWORK.

❑ 1. Create a database of (ideally) 125 networking contacts, capturing as much contact information (e-mail address, phone numbers, physical address) as you can. To identify your network, consider the following categories, listed in the order that is typically *most valuable* for executives in transition:

- Closest friends and colleagues
- Past and present work colleagues, employers, and managers
- People who will serve as your professional references
- Other business contacts (vendors/suppliers, fellow board members)
- Association contacts
- Professionals (CPA, attorney, financial planner, banker, dentist, doctors, and so on)
- Neighbors
- Alumni connections
- Relatives
- Acquaintances (through kids, schools, church/temple, clubs)

❑ 2. Prioritize your contacts into five groups: your A (optimal), B, C, D, and E (least likely) prospects. Include 25 contacts per group. If you have significantly more than 125 contacts, add more groups or increase each group to 30 people.

❏ 3. Create an organizational system that will enable you to record and track your contacts, all of their leads and referrals, and your follow-up activities. Circling back to early contacts will give you another opportunity to connect for more ideas and show that you valued and acted on their suggestions.

ACTION ITEM: CONNECT WITH AND BUILD YOUR NETWORK.

❏ 1. Create a script and practice your introduction. (See chapter 2 for guidelines and ideas.) Be sure you are providing enough specific information so that your contacts will know how they can help you; your targeted research (described in Strategy #2) will provide critical information.

❏ 2. Initiate contact with your first group of 25. For best results and greatest efficiency, we recommend the **call-send-call strategy:** first contacting (or attempting to contact) each person by phone, then immediately following up by sending your resume with a short note, preferably by e-mail but by snail-mail if necessary. In your second call, a few days later, answer questions and glean ideas and recommendations from that contact.

❏ 3. Be sure to ask your contacts who they know—in your industry, at your target companies, or simply people who are well connected. In this way, you will steadily expand your network from your own circle of acquaintances to a broad and deep web of contacts.

❏ 4. Track all ideas, leads, and referrals and schedule your follow-up action.

❏ 5. Keep the ball in your court to stimulate the most and the fastest activity—whether it's a return phone call or contact with a new referral. Remember, your job search is the #1 priority for you, but not for most of the people in your network!

❏ 6. As you receive referral names, add them to your contact database and schedule them into your call-send-call activity chain.

❏ 7. Each week, launch a new phone campaign to your next group of 25; in this way, you'll reach all 125 contacts in just five weeks.

ACTION ITEM: PARTICIPATE IN STRUCTURED NETWORKING EVENTS.

These events, designed specifically for job seekers, can help you tap into a large network in your local area. It's important to attend the right events—those that include a good number of executive-level participants and emphasize productive activities for a swift transition. Avoid those that seem to be a "poor me" club of dispirited job seekers.

❏ 1. Identify events in your area—here are some places to find them:

- The "business events" section of your daily paper (usually posted once a week).

- Your local business journal.

- ExecuNet (www.execunet.com): In-person networking meetings, moderated by a career professional and often featuring a guest speaker, recruiter panel, or other helpful presentation, are offered in more than 40 cities around the nation. Look on the ExecuNet Web site under "networking" to find events near you. Membership is not required; however, in some cases non-members are charged a steeper meeting fee.

- Netshare (www.netshare.com): Grassroots, member-led meetings have sprung up around the country; you do not need to be a member to participate. Contact Netshare to see what's available in your area.

- Gray Hair Management (www.grayhairmanagement.com): There are chapters and networking events in 30 or more cities nationwide; membership is not required.

- Six Figure Jobs (www.6figurejobs.com): Live events are presented at least quarterly in major cities. Look on the Web site under "events" to find the schedule.

- Five O'Clock Club (www.fiveoclockclub.com): This organization offers a consistent program at locations nationwide. Before paying the modest membership fee, contact the organization to see whether meeting places are convenient for you.

- Large churches in your area that sponsor job clubs or support groups for people in transition. Some of these programs are large, vibrant, and well worth attending; others are too small or do not include enough executive-level participants to be truly valuable.

❏ 2. Try out several of the more promising meetings. Be prepared with your clear, concise, ROI-packed message and specific ways that the network can help you. Offer as many referrals and as much advice and support as you can. In networking, when you focus on giving, it's amazing how much you receive!

❏ 3. Select one or more groups to attend on a regular basis—typically once a week or once a month.

❏ 4. Use the group's database or participant list as an additional source for new contacts. Your participation in the group gives you an "in" that will warm up a cold call.

ACTION ITEM: NETWORK ONLINE.

Blogs, chat rooms, online databases, and other exchanges can create a "virtual community" and good source of leads and referrals. As with in-person networking, you will need to find the forums that are most appropriate for you and most helpful.

☐ 1. Research online networks. Some good starting places:

- ExecuNet (www.execunet.com): Membership is required to join interactive online networking groups.

- LinkedIn (www.linkedin.com): A large and rapidly growing member base of high-level professionals provides an excellent referral network, provided you can connect to them via people you know. There are other business-networking services on the Internet, such as Ryze and Ecademy, that you might want to check out as well. These services are free.

- Jobster (www.jobster.com): An innovative service designed to let companies attract passive and hard-to-source candidates through networks and recommendations.

- Online networking organizations for your profession: Good examples are the Financial Executives Networking Group (www.thefeng.org) and the Marketing Executives Networking Group (www.mengonline.org).

- Professional associations related to your profession or industry.

- Blogs that are read by decision-makers in your industry.

☐ 2. Schedule time weekly to visit your preferred sites. For blogs/chat rooms, ask questions; post advice and suggestions; and establish a visible, credible identity. As appropriate, follow up directly with individuals to explore areas of mutual interest and possible job opportunities. With online networking sites, you can be more direct and ask for specific help, such as a connection to a company or an individual related to your job search.

✳ ⁝ ✳ ⁝ ✳ ⁝ ✳ ⁝ ✳ ⁝ ✳ ⁝ ✳ ⁝ ✳ ⁝ ✳ ⁝ ✳ ⁝ ✳ ⁝ ✳ ⁝ ✳ ⁝ ✳ ⁝ ✳ ⁝ ✳

STAR Strategy: Create a Support and Accountability Team

As a key part of your networking strategy, we recommend that you recruit a small team of people to give you feedback and support for the duration

(continued)

(continued)

of your search. Your team might include your spouse, close friends or business colleagues, your financial advisor, fellow board members, or other professionals. You might even want to hire a professional career advisor or coach for objective, expert guidance. (See the appendix for resources.)

Your team members should possess a positive attitude and genuinely care about you and your success. However, they should not be "yes people," agreeing to everything you suggest; you should be able to rely on them for honest opinions and fresh perspectives.

To keep your team motivated and engaged, ask them to keep you accountable for performing your action items and doing what you say you are going to do. Knowing that you have to report in at your weekly coffee meeting or Monday-morning check-in will give you the task orientation that is so critical to persevering in your job search, which can be repetitious, tiring, and even dispiriting (hearing all those "no's" before you get to one "yes").

★ ∶★ ∶★ ∶★ ∶★ ∶★ ∶★ ∶★ ∶★ ∶★ ∶★ ∶★ ∶★ ∶★ ∶★ ∶★ ∶★ ∶★ ∶★

STRATEGY #2: Targeted Search

What do we mean by targeted search? Simply, you research, identify, and pursue *specific target companies* that are a good fit for your expertise and interests. As we will explain in chapter 2, for best results—a swift and successful search—you must first articulate your target and sharply define your "selling points" that will appeal to your prime audience (the decision-makers at your target companies).

> ROI value: ★★★★
> Recommended resource allocation: 35%

Done correctly, the exercises we outline in chapter 2 will paint a complete picture of the type and size of company where you want to work. You'll have identified specific industries and geographic regions and given some thought to the culture that is most appealing to you. Then it's time to match these criteria with the companies that represent your prime targets.

Targeted search activities go hand in hand with networking activities, which were described in Strategy #1. The better you can define to your networking contacts what you are looking for—industries, organizational size, and even specific company names—the better they'll be able to help you. Combined, these two key strategies—networking and targeted search—should consume at least 75 percent of your time, energy, and other resources.

* : *

STAR Strategy: Maintain a Tight Focus for Best Results

You might think that narrowing your search to selected targets will harm rather than help. After all, isn't it better to be open to what's available, and aren't you qualified to work at a variety of functions and in multiple industries?

In fact, the opposite is true. The tighter your focus, the easier it is for contacts to understand what you want and refer you appropriately. A sharp focus also allows your contacts to maintain a clear mental image of "who you are" and how they can best help you. Not only that, but by clearly articulating a precise target, you portray yourself as decisive, visionary, and results-focused—exactly the qualities companies are looking for in executives.

* : *

When you have completed the prep work of defining your ideal next position (again, this process is outlined in chapter 2), you can begin to match the target to specific companies. Start with a large list and follow the action items to narrow down all of the possibilities to a manageable number of good-fit organizations.

ACTION ITEM: IDENTIFY TARGET COMPANIES.

☐ 1. Start with competitors to your most recent employer and other past employers, where your direct experience and competitive information will be of value.

☐ 2. Consider your employers' vendors and alliance partners, who will value your industry knowledge and ability to lead them to new channels or new markets.

☐ 3. Read the business section of your daily paper and your city's or region's business journal. Look for companies that have good ideas, new market opportunities, or aggressive growth plans and where your expertise can help them achieve their goals.

☐ 4. Expand your search beyond your local area to national and international business news articles. We strongly suggest using a news aggregator or RSS reader to make this task easier, faster, and more efficient. You can find a list of recommended aggregators at http://blogspace.com/rss/readers. A more extensive list is available through Wikipedia (http://en.wikipedia.org/wiki/List_of_news_aggregators).

☐ 5. Explore other online resources, such as the following:

- www.fortune.com for information on present and past members of the Fortune 500

- www.hoovers.com for vast information on public companies

- www.dnb.com for extensive business data, including lists of companies sorted by SIC code

- www.zoominfo.com and www.google.com for information on specific individuals at your target companies

- Other sites and resources that you can find through search engines or through links from the above-mentioned sites

Some of these in-depth resources require fee-paid membership; you might, however, be able to tap into them for free via your college or university career center, which is generally available to alumni as well as current students.

☐ 6. Visit, call, or e-mail the reference librarian at your local library. (The downtown/main library may offer more comprehensive search services than a small branch library.) A reference librarian is a treasure-trove of knowledge and can help you find directories, news articles, annual reports, financial information, and other resources that will help you identify and ultimately pare down your list of target companies.

ACTION ITEM: THIN YOUR LIST.

☐ 1. Collect information on your "possible" companies and measure it against your target. You can use all of the sources in the preceding action item and also visit each company's Web site. Any or all of these criteria—and more—might come into play:

- Geographic location (headquarters, international locations, production sites, branches, and so forth)

- Size of company

- Growth plans

- Reputation of CEO and top executives

- Legal and/or financial difficulties

- Products (current and projected)

- Markets (current and projected)

- Recent history such as changes in leadership

- Company mission and values

- Industry outlook (contracting or expanding?)
- Opportunities in the market; threats or challenges to achieving desired results

☐ 2. Be particularly alert to business opportunities that you identify as a result of your research and where your skills, experience, knowledge, and track record will be of value. It is vital to employ this information when approaching the company, to convey that you understand their business and can help them achieve their goals.

☐ 3. Create a "short list" of companies that are your prime targets. Keep all of your notes, however, even for companies that don't make the cut; you will revisit, fine-tune, and expand your target list throughout your search as you learn more about your target companies and their culture, people, and potential.

☐ 4. Be 100 percent sure that your objective is achievable and your targets are a good fit *before* you launch an aggressive targeted search. Ask your closest contacts to give you feedback on your targets. Share with them your ideal position information and ask whether it's realistic. Solicit their input into your decision-making as you narrow the list.

ACTION ITEM: INCORPORATE YOUR TARGET LIST INTO YOUR NETWORKING STRATEGY.

Your goal in every networking interaction is to gain a lead or connection to a person at a target company or in a target industry. To do this, you need to educate your contacts about your targets.

☐ 1. When possible, ask for a specific resource: "I'd love to get an introduction to Chris Anderson, CFO at Acme Holdings."

☐ 2. Use examples: "I'm looking for a company *like* Worldwide Widgets." This is more meaningful to most people than "a company with $300 million in sales in a traditional manufacturing industry."

☐ 3. Consider creating a one-page document that includes a very brief summary of your qualifications along with your top target companies. You can hand this out at networking meetings or forward it to your circle of contacts so that they'll better understand what you are looking for and how they can best help you. You can see an example of this one-page handout in chapter 4.

ACTION ITEM: CONSIDER A DIRECT-MAIL CAMPAIGN.

Particularly if you are targeting small to midsized companies in one or a few specific geographic locations, a broadcast letter campaign can produce great results. In general, you should send the letter to a large number of companies, so such a campaign can be a significant investment; but it might enable you to reach decision-makers at a time and in a format that will catch their attention.

☐ 1. Compile or purchase complete contact information for the appropriate senior executive at each target company.

☐ 2. Mail-merge the data with an appropriate cover letter, one that identifies with the company's challenges and positions you and your expertise as a solution.

☐ 3. Either send them all at once, as a "mail blast," or send them in batches of 25 to 50 per week that you will follow up with a phone call.

☐ 4. Print your letters and resumes on high-quality paper and send them via standard U.S. Mail.

You can get help with this action item. For complete services, from data selection to letter preparation, we recommend these two trusted resources: Pro/File Research (www.profileresearch.com) and JobBait (www.jobbait.com). You might also consider using a virtual assistant or secretarial service to manage the mail-merge, printing, and mailing.

STRATEGY #3: Executive Recruiters

Recruiters, also known as "head-hunters," can be an excellent resource during your executive job search. After all, they special-

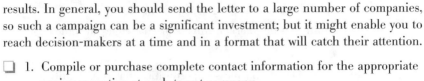

ROI value: ✱
Recommended resource allocation: 10%

ize in placing mid- to senior-level executives in jobs at companies of all sizes, and it stands to reason that they are always looking for good candidates just like you to fill those positions.

We have found, however, that misconceptions abound regarding the role and value of executive recruiters. When considering this strategy, keep these facts in mind:

• **Recruiters work for their client (the employer), not for you.** This means that the commonly held belief that recruiters will "find a job for you" is false. This can be a rude awakening to high-performing executives who assume they will be a hot property for recruiters.

• **Recruiters work to fill tightly specified openings.** Thus, it's fruitless to think you can convince a recruiter that you can do the job if you don't have the precise background for which he or she is searching. When hired to find candidates with "a-b-c" credentials, that's precisely what a recruiter must deliver.

You will be most attractive to recruiters if you are looking for the same type of job you've held previously, in the same industry. Again, recruiters need to fill specs. If the spec says a "financial executive with 10 years of experience in manufacturing, preferably automotive," you can rest assured your 10 years in technology services will not be a good fit. Most often, recruiters seek individuals with a strong background in a specific industry.

Regardless of the rigid nature of most recruiter assignments, there are some things you can do to make this strategy an effective part of your search. Just be sure you are not over-relying on recruiters; we recommend that you spend no more than 10% of your resources on this channel.

ACTION ITEM: RECONNECT WITH PERSONAL RECRUITER CONTACTS.

Chances are, you've had contact with recruiters in the past. Maybe you hired them to find executives for your company. Perhaps you were called on a semi-regular basis by recruiters in your industry or were even recruited for one or more of your past positions. The best time to build a relationship with a recruiter is when you're *not* looking for a job; if you've done this, now it's time to tap into those contacts.

1. Using the same call-send-call strategy as we recommend for all of your networking contacts, reach out to the recruiters you know and ask whether they have any suggestions—perhaps they can consider you for an open position or refer you to another recruiter who is a better fit for your background.

2. Periodically update your recruiter contacts with the progress of your search, updates to your resume, or specific target information that will help them fit you to opportunities they have or know about.

ACTION ITEM: IDENTIFY AND CONTACT THE RIGHT RECRUITERS.

Keeping in mind that recruiters don't work exclusively for you, neither should you limit yourself to one or even a handful of recruiters. Although we don't suggest that you blast your resume to every recruiter under the sun, we do recommend that you get your resume into the databases of the *right* recruiters. This means recruiters who specialize in placing people with your background, at your level, in your target industries.

1. Evaluate executive recruiter mass-distribution services to find which one gives you the options that are best for you. For example, can you pinpoint specific industries? Select retained-only recruiters? Include your resume as a Word attachment rather than as a text-only file?

Looking at several services will give you the data you need to make an informed decision. Following are several services that we like:

- Executive Agent (www.executiveagent.com)
- Pro/File Research (www.profileresearch.com)
- Resume Machine (www.resumemachine.com)

❏ 2. Consider using additional resources to obtain recruiter names for your own e-mail campaign or other contact strategy.

- Kennedy Directory of Executive Recruiters: Hard-copy format of the original "red book" for executive job seekers. Can be ordered online at www.kennedyinfo.com.

- Pro/File Research (www.profileresearch.com): Data and services totally customized to your specific needs.

- Resume Machine (www.resumemachine.com): By choosing the "self-managed campaign" option, you'll receive data lists that you can use to mail-merge multiple documents or pursue individually by phone, fax, or e-mail.

- Select Recruiters (www.selectrecruiters.com): Source for download-able data from the *Kennedy Directory of Executive Recruiters*.

- SearchSelect (www.kennedyinfo.com/js/ss.html): Annual subscrip-tion to the online version of the *Kennedy Directory of Executive Recruiters*.

ACTION ITEM: POST YOUR RESUME.

For executive job seekers, we don't recommend posting your resume on Monster, Yahoo! HotJobs, CareerBuilder, or other mass-market sites; it's just not an effective strategy for drawing the right kind of contacts. However, as part of your recruiter strategy, you might want to post your resume in the databases of top recruiters and, as appropriate, on the Web sites of professional associations for your field. This passive strategy can put your documents in the right place at the right time. Just keep in mind that the odds are low that you'll find a job this way, so don't rely on a posting as your *only* or even *primary* strategy.

❏ 1. Identify the sites and recruiting firms that are right for you and follow their (detailed) instructions for posting your resume and profile to their database. In addition to these "top-three" executive recruiting firms, review Web sites of your professional associations to see whether a resume-posting service is available.

- Heidrick and Struggles (www.heidrick.com)
- Korn/Ferry International (www.kornferry.com)
- Spencer Stuart (www.spencerstuart.com)

✳ ∶ ✳ ∶ ✳ ∶ ✳ ∶ ✳ ∶ ✳ ∶ ✳ ∶ ✳ ∶ ✳ ∶ ✳ ∶ ✳ ∶ ✳ ∶ ✳ ∶ ✳ ∶ ✳ ∶ ✳ ∶ ✳ ∶ ✳

STAR Strategy: Build Recruiter Relationships When You're Not Looking for a Job

Although this STAR Strategy won't help you now, make note of it for your future career management. When you are employed and not looking for a job, look for opportunities to build relationships with recruiters. You can do this best by being a resource to them—by referring them to good job candidates when they have a specific need.

You might also be in the position to retain a recruiter to conduct a search for your company. You hold the power in that relationship and can leverage it for your long-term advantage. Then, when you are again in a job search, the recruiters who are already part of your network will be much more helpful to you than those you don't know.

✳ ∶ ✳ ∶ ✳ ∶ ✳ ∶ ✳ ∶ ✳ ∶ ✳ ∶ ✳ ∶ ✳ ∶ ✳ ∶ ✳ ∶ ✳ ∶ ✳ ∶ ✳ ∶ ✳ ∶ ✳ ∶ ✳ ∶ ✳

STRATEGY #4: Published Leads

Whether posted online or published in a newspaper, business journal, or professional associa-

ROI value: ✳
Recommended resource allocation: 10%

tion magazine, published leads represent an obvious avenue for you to pursue during your job search. Your application can give you an entrée into your target companies, or others you haven't yet identified, and can put your resume into the databanks of executive recruiters.

The upside to published leads is that they're easy to find and easy to respond to. The downside is that everyone else knows about them, too; thus, your chances of gaining an interview—even when you match the stated requirements to a "T"—are quite slim. After all, the employer has dozens or hundreds of resumes to review and needs to quickly weed out candidates to keep the search to a manageable size. Any excuse to eliminate you from contention helps in this scaling-down process.

Given this scenario, we recommend that you respond to published ads in a manner that's quick and efficient, and leaves most of your time for networking and targeted search activities. Here's how to do it.

ACTION ITEM: IDENTIFY THE BEST SOURCES FOR PUBLISHED AND POSTED ADS.

❏ 1. At the start of your search, spend some time reviewing various sites for executive job postings and see which have the greatest number of appropriate listings. Bookmark these sites and return periodically to review and respond to postings. (In addition to your own research, see our suggestions for executive sites in Strategy #5. Some require fee-paid membership.)

❏ 2. Identify publications that list appropriate openings. In addition to professional journals and business journals, we suggest that you regularly review the Sunday newspaper for the largest city close to you, as well as other cities that are key targets.

ACTION ITEM: CREATE AN EFFICIENT PROCESS FOR AD RESPONSES.

❏ 1. Once per week, dedicate time to review all of your identified sources, select appropriate postings, and quickly respond.

❏ 2. Write a template cover letter that you can rapidly adapt for individual ads. Spending hours composing a custom-crafted letter for each ad is not a wise investment of your time, given the relatively low rate of response you can expect.

❏ 3. Create an easy-to-manage process for storing the ads with a note as to when you responded and perhaps a copy of your cover letter.

❏ 4. If an ad appears for one of your target companies, in addition to responding through formal channels, redouble your efforts to connect with someone at that company—preferably the hiring manager or other senior executive.

STRATEGY #5: Internet Job Sites and Services for Executives

The Internet abounds with fee-based sites and services targeted to senior executives. Many of

ROI value: ✱
Recommended resource allocation: 5%

these services are excellent, and we recommend that you consider joining one or several as part of your integrated job search. In addition to job postings, you might find such services as recruiter distribution, resume posting, virtual networking, teleclasses and webinars, complimentary review of your resume, newsletters and other publications, and any number of additional services to help you become more knowledgeable about and proficient in the skill of executive job search.

We have both been affiliated with several of these sites, serving as a resource to members, hosting seminars and meetings, and writing articles. So we might be biased! But we have been impressed with the quality and expertise they provide to their members.

Two cautions: Don't rely on this as your only strategy, and thoroughly investigate fees and services before joining.

ACTION ITEM: INVESTIGATE AND JOIN ONE OR MORE APPROPRIATE EXECUTIVE CAREER SITES.

☐ 1. Start with our list of recommended sites, presented here in alphabetical order, and see which one seems to offer the best package of services to fit your needs. (See the appendix for additional sites.)

- Bluesteps (www.bluesteps.com): A membership site affiliated with the Association of Executive Search Consultants.

- ExecuNet (www.execunet.com): One of the longest-established executive career services, founded in 1988 and going strong.

- Executive Registry (www.executiveregistry.com): From Kennedy Information.

- The Ladders (www.theladders.com): Multi-site source for $100K jobs, for both general and specific functional areas.

- Gray Hair Management (www.grayhairmanagement.com): Nationwide network of senior executives.

- Netshare (www.netshare.com): Specializing in senior executive job listings and services.

- RiteSite (www.ritesite.com): Founded by John Lucht, author of *Rites of Passage at $100,000+*.

☐ 2. Sign up with your chosen site and maximize your ROI by investigating and taking advantage of the full range of services.

☐ 3. One of your primary activities on these sites will be to search for and respond to job postings, as discussed in detail in Strategy #4.

✴ ✴

STAR Strategy: A Five-Pronged Approach

For best results, implement all five of our recommended strategies simultaneously, as outlined in the six-week plan in table 1.1. Multiple vigorous

(continued)

(continued)

efforts will yield the best results and help you avoid mistakes such as these that derail or prolong many executive job searches:

- Reliance on just one method

- Overdependence on less-effective search methods such as posting your resume or responding to online postings or want ads

- Belief that a recruiter will find a job for you, thinking that all you have to do is send your resume to a few headhunters and wait for the opportunities to roll in

- Abandonment of all other activities when you are pursuing a "hot" prospect or when a job offer appears imminent

- Assumption that some people in your network can't or won't help you

SIX-WEEK PLAN

Hit the ground running with our six-week plan to create a strong foundation and energetic momentum for what is likely to be a three- to nine-month search. Our methodical approach will train you in all of the critical aspects of searching for a new executive position, and you'll be able to redeploy them as needed for the remainder of your search.

TABLE 1.1: THE SIX-WEEK PLAN

Week	Action
1	*ROI Message:* Develop ROI material, resume and addendum materials, template cover letters, and 30-second introduction.
	Targeted Search: Define your target market— industry, company size and type, and specific companies.
	Physical Preparation: Review and refresh your appearance and wardrobe for both business-casual meetings and formal interviews.
2	*Networking: A* contacts (call-send-call; see Strategy #1).

Week	Action
	Networking: Follow-up activities with leads generated through *A* group.
	Targeted Search: Continue to refine your target market, adding and deleting companies through information you develop via research and your personal contacts.
	ROI Message: Practice telephone-screen interview replies and initial salary-screening responses.
	Networking: Research structured networking events in your area and schedule or attend as appropriate.
	Recruiters: Connect with personal recruiter contacts.
	Recruiters: Execute recruiter mass e-mailing.
	Published Leads: Once per week, review all of your sources and respond with a quickly edited cover letter and your resume.
3	*Networking: B* contacts (call-send-call).
	Networking: Follow-up activities with leads generated through *A* and *B* groups.
	Targeted Search: Continue to refine your target market.
	ROI Message: Practice interview skills; be sure you are fully prepared to deflect salary questions in a polished and professional manner.
	Published Leads: Respond with a quick cover letter and resume.
4	*Networking: C* contacts (call-send-call).
	Networking: Follow-up activities with leads generated through *A, B,* and *C* groups.
	Targeted Search: Continue to refine your target market.
	Targeted Search: Launch a direct-mail campaign if this strategy makes sense for you.

(continued)

(continued)

Week	Action
	ROI Message: Critically evaluate your interview performance and spend some time on preparation/improvement as needed.
	Published Leads: Review sources and respond with a quick cover letter and resume.
5	*Networking:* D contacts (call-send-call).
	Networking: Follow-up activities with leads generated through *A*, *B*, *C*, and *D* groups.
	Published Leads: Review sources and respond with a quick cover letter and resume.
	Targeted Search: Continue to refine your target market.
	ROI Message: Prepare for second (more in-depth) interviews, factoring in what you've learned about the company during your research activities.
6	*Networking:* E contacts (call-send-call).
	Networking: Follow-up activities with leads generated through *A*, *B*, *C*, *D*, and *E* groups.
	Targeted Search: Continue to refine your target market.
	Published Leads: Review sources and respond with a quick cover letter and resume.
	ROI Message: Review and practice salary-negotiation skills.

ANALYZE YOUR PROGRESS AND KEEP MOVING FORWARD

The six-week point is a good time to step back, review what you've done, and reflect on how well you're progressing. By this point, you should be scheduling both formal interviews and informal networking discussions at least 3 to 10 times per week. You should have a broad and deep web of contacts, have penetrated several of your target companies, and be adept at communicating your ROI messages in networking situations and interviews.

Now, keep that momentum going by repeating the appropriate steps in the Six-Week Plan until you convert those meetings to interviews, and those interviews to offers.

If, on the other hand, your progress has stalled or has never gotten off the ground, it's time to take a critical look at what you are doing, what you are saying, and how you are being perceived by your many audiences. We believe in taking a problem-solution tack, evaluating precisely where the sticking point occurs and fixing the problem at that point.

Here are some of the typical problems we see, along with our recommended solutions.

PROBLEM: NOT GENERATING ENOUGH LEADS, REFERRALS, AND MEETINGS

Solutions:

- Step up your networking activities: Make more calls, attend more meetings, and reach out to more people.
- Sharpen your focus and hone your ROI message so that your network understands who you are and how to help you.
- Put in the time: If you are spending just an hour or two a week on your job search, it's tough to generate substantial activity.
- Review all of the recommended strategies in this chapter and see where you could be more diligent. Most often, we find that job seekers are focusing on the easy-but-ineffective strategies (responding to published leads) and skimping on the more challenging but indisputably more effective activities (networking and targeted search).

PROBLEM: GETTING MEETINGS, BUT NO INTERVIEWS

Solutions:

- Be more assertive in your meetings. If you sense there might be a need for your services, say, "I think there is a fit here for me. Who do you suggest I speak with to get to the next step?"
- Be more direct in your networking. Don't be afraid to ask, "What companies do you know that are expanding? Who do you know at Worldwide Widgets?"
- Sharpen your focus and polish your ROI message so that your contacts can relate your value to an identified need and can easily describe/ recommend you to others.

PROBLEM: YOU ARE IN LIMBO, CONSTANTLY WAITING FOR RESPONSES THAT ARE SLOW TO ARRIVE... IF THEY ARRIVE AT ALL

Solutions:

- As we recommended earlier, keep control over the networking process by offering to make connections directly rather than waiting for your contact to do it.
- At the end of each interview, be sure you are clear about the next steps, when you can expect to be contacted, and what to do if you don't hear by that date.

PROBLEM: NOT ADVANCING BEYOND THE FIRST OR SECOND INTERVIEW

Solutions:

- Review, refine, and practice your ROI messages; be sure that every interview response communicates how you can solve business challenges.
- Get feedback from your "accountability team" with regard to your interview answers.
- Ask a trusted friend or department-store personal shopper to review your appearance and be sure you are conveying a tip-top executive presence.
- Sharpen your focus to be sure you are not interviewing for jobs that are not a good fit for your skills, expertise, and passions.

PROBLEM: REACHING FINALIST STATUS, BUT NEVER EARNING THE OFFER

Solutions:

- Review all of the solutions for the preceding problem.
- Relax! If you are getting everything but the offer, you are doing many things right, and it is just a matter of luck and timing until the right job rolls around.

PROBLEM: NOT SUCCEEDING DESPITE MONTHS OF HARD WORK IN A FOCUSED SEARCH

Solutions:

- For executives who are action-oriented and solution-focused, the lack of clear direction in job search can be frustrating. You know, in general, what you have to do, but the ROI from each activity is not always clear. To help your mind-set, establish aggressive and definable goals each week—number of calls, number of networking meetings, number of interviews—and check them off as you complete them. You'll derive a small feeling of satisfaction while, in the larger picture, propelling your search.

- Again, relax. (We know it's easier to say than to do.) Job search *always* takes longer than people expect. As long as you are directing a dynamic search, consistently generating leads and interviews, and presenting yourself well during the interview process, you can be confident that your search is on the right track.

STAR Strategy: Consider Hiring a Coach or Career Agent

As we've discussed in this chapter, it's entirely practical to manage your job search on your own. You can learn the steps and manage the processes. But you might be able to accelerate your search and outsource some of the "grunt work" by hiring a career coach, interview coach, executive coach, career agent, targeted search expert, virtual assistant, or another professional service provider who has expertise in executive career transitions.

We especially recommend coaching assistance when you are dealing with a difficult or unusual termination situation; when you are trying to cross over to a new industry or new function; when you feel less than confident about your presentation/interviewing skills; when you are uncomfortable at the prospect of networking; when you are searching while still employed (your time for your search will be extremely limited); when you are a senior executive accustomed to handing over the detail work to an assistant; or when your search has gone on with limited productivity for more than three months.

When discussing your needs with potential coaches, be clear about what you want and make sure you thoroughly understand what they provide and what their fees are. Acknowledge that you must play a part in every process (in reality, a coach can't handle the entire job search for you), and be sure each prospective coach has experience working with executives.

See the appendix for our recommended resources.

Chapter 2

Develop ROI Content for Your Career Marketing Documents and Messages

"This above all: to thine own self be true."

–*William Shakespeare*, Hamlet

In chapter 1, you learned recommended job search strategies, specific tactical action plans, and a six-week program of activities to create fast-moving momentum for your executive transition. Examining a variety of tools and projected return on investment for each, we repeatedly recommended that you pack your resume, cover letters, networking interactions, and interviews with ROI content that will convey your value. In this chapter we give you the detailed how-to techniques for translating what you have achieved into powerful content for use in your career marketing documents and messages, to demonstrate your value proposition to a prospective employer or recruiter.

In this chapter, you'll also learn how to use the STAR formula to develop powerful stories for use in your resume and related documents as well as during interviews. Following our step-by-step guidelines, you'll actually develop three to five STAR stories that succinctly tell the *S*ituation, *T*actic, *A*ction, and *R*esult. This approach extracts the maximum value from each of your key accomplishments and creates substantiated sound bites that are crucial to convey to decision-makers. Using this foundation, you can go on to develop additional STAR stories for all of your significant career accomplishments.

GETTING STARTED: ANSWER THREE CRITICAL QUESTIONS

In our private practices, we like to lead off client consultations with several critical questions that get at what drives our clients. Consider these three topics:

1. **Describe your ideal next position:**
   - What title would that job have?
   - In what industry would it be?
   - What type and size of company would be desirable?
   - What challenges or opportunities might exist?
   - Are you willing to relocate?
   - What expectations do you have relative to compensation?

2. **What do you want to do?** Sounds pretty basic, doesn't it? But to best respond to this question, think of those skills you absolutely must use to derive greatest satisfaction from your next job.
   - Are you happiest when you are hands-on?
   - Do you enjoy managing multiple sites remotely?
   - Do you want an organization that is flexible, adaptive, and ready to rally to the new vision you instill?
   - Do you love international travel?
   - Or have you played road warrior far too long in your most recent career moves and seek a little less travel/more stability for yourself and your family?
   - Can you look back on your career and see that you were happiest when you were faced with seemingly insurmountable challenges— and successfully turned things around?
   - Do you get bored easily?
   - If you join a well-run organization that simply turns over the reins to you and doesn't support new initiatives, will you be stir-crazy in 18 months?

3. **What are your signature strengths?**
   - For what areas of strength are you best known?
   - For what "hard" skills have you been consistently recognized over the course of your career?
   - What are those "signature capabilities" that you're really good at?
   - What are the distinctions in your background and skill set that you think will prove most interesting (in other words, most transferable or desired) by subsequent employers?

- What are some of the reasons you've been recruited or hired in the past?
- What capabilities have led to your greatest business successes?

CAVEAT: This question is not meant to elicit your attributes (for example, hardworking, organized, self-motivated, and so on). What you want to define are those skills you possess that are critical to the performance of your target position. Here are some examples to prompt you:

- Building high-performing teams
- Identifying profitable new markets for existing products or services
- Improving manufacturing yield and team productivity while cutting costs
- Driving business-to-business sales of complex services

Sample Answers to the Three Critical Questions

Here's how this exercise might look for a senior-level marketing director.

Describe your ideal next position.

"Depending on the organization's size, I'd want to be at either a director level or the vice president of marketing. If it's a larger company, this could be divisional. I'd want to be challenged by the opportunity to grow the company (or division) to the next level—whether this means turning around an underperforming organization, continuing to advance an already producing operation, or effectively launching a new business unit or division."

What do you want to do?

"I need to be in a role where I can really shape the organization—to create greater value, produce higher returns. I'm especially energized by opportunities to do more. If revenues of a product line have stagnated at a 25 percent market share for several years (or, worse, continually eroded on, say, a heritage brand), I want to turn the line upside down, always retaining the signature strengths, and architect ways to boost this to 40 or 50 percent."

What are your signature strengths?

> "I'm a true visionary. Overused term, I know, but it defines at all levels what I bring to the table. I'm a creator—I see opportunities where others have long since moved on to something else. Perhaps even more importantly, I create opportunities of significant impact to the company and to the bottom line. I'm recognized for consistently combining these things—I have creative vision—and implementing initiatives that have far-reaching strategic importance. I'm equally comfortable leveraging an organization's strengths for both the short term and the long term."

In those three response paragraphs for our senior-level marketing director is the genesis of how the position paper (the resume) can best be crafted. In chapter 5, "Successful Transition Stories," we'll show how these responses were woven into an actual resume. And here is the key takeaway of this entire chapter:

If you do nothing else, when you sit down to capture your own responses to these seemingly simple questions, *be authentic*. Think critically (but positively) about yourself and your contributions. Be as expansive as you wish—but keep coming back to the three critical questions and try to get down on paper what really drives you.

The purpose of this exercise is to assess, extract, and capture your signature strengths. For some people, it is one of the most difficult exercises in the career transition process. However, virtually everything else that you'll be doing stems from this critical information. It doesn't make sense to start your search until you can define—precisely and uniquely—who you are, what you want to do, and the skills and performance traits that distinguish you.

EXERCISE 1: Articulate Your Target and Capture Your Signature Strengths

The following exercise will help you answer three critical questions.

Describe your ideal next position.

This is the easiest of the three questions for most executives to answer. In addition to the ideas suggested earlier, consider the following in crafting your reply:

- Organization size.
- Span of control.
- Geography (both for the company/division/operation and where you want to live).
- Scope: local, regional, national, or global?
- Do you want multi-divisional or multi-plant responsibility?
- Single or multiple sites?
- Exactly how important is title to you? (Be honest.)
- Will you consider—or even prefer—the challenge of a startup? If the answer is yes, this points to a different skill set, perhaps more entrepreneurial, that you might want to expand on, thus opening the door to additional opportunities.
- What kind of environment and culture do you prefer?
- What are your compensation expectations?

All of these factors point toward the position that is the best fit for you at this particular stage of your life and your career.

1. Describe your ideal next position.

_____

_____

_____

_____

_____

_____

_____

_____

_____

_____

What do you want to do?

A good way to get started on this question is to think in reverse: If you weren't able to do certain things in your next position (or perhaps even currently), would you be unhappy or unfulfilled? What are those skills?

(continued)

(continued)

For example, if you are targeting a presidential or even divisional GM level, do you want to be able to still touch customers, be involved in specific client interactions, or keep your "finger on the pulse" of exactly what's going on within the sales and marketing organization? In a smaller, more entrepreneurial organization, this is likely to be very possible. In a large, multi-conglomerate corporation, you may find yourself missing that ready ability to make a difference and feel a surge of excitement from occasionally being out there on the front lines.

In instances where we've worked with executives who've grown out of the engineering ranks, it's sometimes difficult to leave totally behind an involvement with R&D and the opportunity to add value in the design and launch of a new product. That may resonate with you—and be something important to identify as a skill area that you want to use in your next position. Perhaps cultivating strategic alliances is a real strength—and something that creates energy for you and the organization. Remember, you must be authentic. Your "what do you want to do" statement should reflect those activities that are most important to you, not those that you *think* will be most prominent in the job or the level to which you aspire.

2. What do you want to do?

_____

_____

_____

_____

_____

_____

_____

_____

What are your signature strengths?

Possible ideas include the following:

- Leadership
- Ability to identify, cultivate, and retain talent
- Communication skills

- Ability to develop people
- Team-building
- Networking skills
- Ability to spot emerging opportunities

Do these qualities describe you?

- Highly focused
- Results driven
- Inspirational

Or, looking at it in another way, do you see yourself as a...

- Rainmaker
- Leader by example
- Consensus builder
- Motivator
- Creator
- Mentor
- Marketing genius
- Deal broker
- Turnaround expert
- Innovator
- Idea generator
- Master at leveraging organizational strengths

The key is to identify what really separates you from anyone else at this level...what you know *to be true about yourself.* Some executives find it useful to consider how others have described them—in letters of commendation, "atta-boys," and performance reviews and evaluations. What truly distinguishes you and your leadership/management style? *What really defines you from the standpoint of the value you have added?*

3. What are your signature strengths?

_____

_____

_____

(continued)

(continued)

_____

_____

_____

_____

_____

_____

✶ ⁞ ✶ ⁞ ✶ ⁞ ✶ ⁞ ✶ ⁞ ✶ ⁞ ✶ ⁞ ✶ ⁞ ✶ ⁞ ✶ ⁞ ✶ ⁞ ✶ ⁞ ✶ ⁞ ✶ ⁞ ✶

STAR Strategy: Locate Target Positions

To help inspire you in the process of identifying your career target, what you'd like to do, and signature strengths, consider sleuthing on the Internet to locate several possible targets (even if all the criteria do not fit). It's not essential that these be positions you'd actually consider; rather, such listings may provide key information for focusing your resume and cross-checking qualifications. Good sites for executive job postings include www.execunet.com, www.netshare.com, www.6figurejobs.com, and www.monster.com.

✶ ⁞ ✶ ⁞ ✶ ⁞ ✶ ⁞ ✶ ⁞ ✶ ⁞ ✶ ⁞ ✶ ⁞ ✶ ⁞ ✶ ⁞ ✶ ⁞ ✶ ⁞ ✶ ⁞ ✶ ⁞ ✶

The time and effort you devote to answering these three "target/signature strength" questions will pay large dividends later in the resume-writing process (and, in fact, in every stage of your career transition). For the resume, your responses will come into play when identifying keywords, target titles, and select components of your qualifications profile. They'll also prove useful in developing the content of your letters of introduction and traditional-but-innovative cover letters. And you'll find them essential in crafting your introductions to networking contacts and potential employers.

✶ ⁞ ✶ ⁞ ✶ ⁞ ✶ ⁞ ✶ ⁞ ✶ ⁞ ✶ ⁞ ✶ ⁞ ✶ ⁞ ✶ ⁞ ✶ ⁞ ✶ ⁞ ✶ ⁞ ✶ ⁞ ✶

Elevator Speeches and Power Introductions

Your 30-second introduction (often referred to as an "elevator speech," a term coined to reflect the amount of time you might typically spend ascending multiple floors in an elevator and running into an old contact who has asked for a quick update on "what you've been up to") combines signature strengths with actual experience and, in the case of a job seeker, puts a forward-thinking spin on what you'll do next.

For instance, consider the following elevator speeches for various professionals. These might be used on the phone (after the initial greeting) or at networking events or adapted for more casual encounters—maybe even in an elevator!

Sample 1: "I'm a senior operations management professional in the manufacturing field with a track record of restoring profitability and achieving significant growth initiatives. For the past 17 years, I have produced exceptional results for three organizations: a privately held high-tech composites company, a startup injection-molding plastics company, and a publicly traded $1 billion electronics component manufacturer. I'm targeting opportunities where I can add value through improved operations management, implementation of lean manufacturing methods, and a practiced approach to cross-training and optimal staff alignment."

Sample 2: "For nearly 20 years, I have managed high-growth pharmaceutical and medical device manufacturing companies. I have led executive management teams to achieve exceptional results in market share and overall profitability. As a CEO or president, I bring a hands-on style of leadership to a company—quickly identifying key organizational members and determining areas of strength, opportunity, and outage. I'm skilled in creating vision, stretching a company's competencies, and orchestrating new product launches and market-expansion plans that consistently garner added revenue streams. My goal is to leverage these strengths in a new opportunity that demands an innovative, collaborative leader and rainmaker."

Sample 3: "What I do is jump-start revenues for new technology companies. I'm equally proficient developing the strategic marketing plan—everything from market positioning and product development to branding through advertising and sales—and delivering the presentation to make the sale to key accounts. In the past 10 years I have led the marketing function for three startups, in each case building revenues from virtually zero to as much as $10 million in two or three years. Once revenues are established, I build strong teams and disciplined processes for efficient operations and sustained growth. The challenge of creating a new market for a new product is exciting and something that I'm looking for in my next position."

(continued)

(continued)

(See chapter 4, "Additional ROI Documents," for additional examples of traditional and expanded elevator speeches. Note that the content of these power introductions can frequently be used in e-mail cover notes to recruiters and hiring authorities.)

★ : ★ : ★ : ★ : ★ : ★ : ★ : ★ : ★ : ★ : ★ : ★ : ★ : ★ : ★ : ★ : ★ : ★ : ★

CREATE ROI CONTENT FOR YOUR RESUME

For now, set aside your elevator speech and the results of the three exercises you completed in Exercise 1. This is the same approach we use when working with our executive clients in developing their resumes and other job search documents. This important information will come into play when you're actually writing your resume. First, however, you will develop powerful raw material that is truly the heart and soul of your resume: what you've achieved, what you've produced, and forward-thinking examples that predict *what value you'll bring in a subsequent position.*

After all, you can talk all you like about what you want, what you're good at, and how others perceive you, but to be credible you'll need to offer proof—what you've accomplished in the past using your signature skills and tackling the challenges that delight you.

Tell the Story (It STARs You)

The art of writing an executive resume is often likened to storytelling with a purpose. Your goal? To select and present examples that give a snapshot overview of the influence you've wielded, the quantified results you've produced, and the know-how behind your most significant initiatives.

To maximize the impact of everything you're writing, we recommend that you consciously look at any examples you are considering using on your resume through the lens of "What are my signature strengths? (You might refer to the target/signature strength exercises from earlier in this chapter.) Does this story support that strength and illuminate for the reader exactly what challenge I faced, what initiatives I planned, what actions I took, and what outcome I delivered?"

This is the STAR approach to resume writing (Situation-Tactic-Action-Result). Start with what you consider to be your top two or three "career-defining" achievements. For this stage, we recommend you tell your story in narrative fashion. Don't worry about the resume or try to use "resume language" at this point. The stories you select should be relevant to your current goals and reflect your signature skills and leadership strengths. Be certain they are not too dated; it's okay to go back in time for one or more stories, but do bring the timeline forward and include others that are more recent in nature. In the pages following this exercise, you will find five completed examples of STAR stories for executives in a variety of fields.

EXERCISE 2: Write Your STAR Stories

Here is the four-step process to use in crafting your own STAR stories.

1: Situation

What is the challenge you faced? What was the opportunity presented? It doesn't necessarily have to be a negative—a problem; it could be an opportunity that you perceived or was presented to you, such as an underoptimized sales avenue or unexplored distribution channel—maybe a product launch in a new vertical market, country, or continent. At this stage in the exercise, provide as much detail as possible in *quantifying* the challenge or opportunity and describing the situation.

The emphasis on *quantify* is deliberate: It's not enough to say that you were challenged to "grow market share"; you need to share the specific expectations ("challenged to increase market share that had stagnated at 15% for 5 years"). Later, you will quantify what you actually accomplished, measured against this expectation. Numbers are easily grasped and readily communicated, and present verifiable evidence of your achievement.

When describing the situation, your goal is to put your readers or listeners "in the picture" so that they thoroughly understand the context before you start talking about what you did.

What challenge or opportunity did you face?

_____

_____

_____

_____

_____

_____

(continued)

(continued)

_____

_____

_____

_____

2: Tactic

In this part of your STAR story, give your readers and listeners insight into how you solve problems. How do you attack a situation? What resources do you bring to bear? What kind of planning process do you find most effective when facing a challenge or opportunity? Describe what you did in this particular instance to position yourself for a positive outcome.

What tactics did you use to achieve success?

_____

_____

_____

_____

_____

_____

_____

_____

_____

3: Action

This is usually easy to describe. What did you actually do? Descriptive action verbs that can often lead these statements include the following:

Led

Quarterbacked

Orchestrated

Spearheaded

Drove

Managed

Implemented

Reengineered

Although it's important to provide enough detail to fully describe your activity, don't get bogged down in the minutiae of a project or too many tactical steps.

What did you actually do?

_____

_____

_____

_____

_____

_____

_____

_____

_____

_____

4: Result

Here's the bottom line: What happened? What were the results of steps 1, 2, and 3? What success was realized? What foundation was established going forward? Did you achieve any awards (internal to the organization or industry-wide), formal recognition, or commendation?

Here, again, it's essential that you quantify your results wherever possible, in percentages or absolutes; without these hard numbers, your stories will lack credibility. Think broadly about both specific measurable outcomes and the less-definable but no less important results. And, whenever possible, look long-range toward the strategic impact of your actions. For example, perhaps you can demonstrate that you were

(continued)

(continued)

instrumental in positioning your company for long-term success or avoiding a significant problem that plagued your industry.

What were your results?

_____

_____

_____

_____

_____

_____

_____

_____

_____

Additional STAR Story Blanks

1: Situation

_____

_____

_____

_____

_____

_____

_____

_____

_____

2: Tactic

_____

_____

_____

_____

_____

_____

_____

_____

3: Action

_____

_____

_____

_____

_____

_____

_____

_____

4: Result

_____

_____

_____

_____

(continued)

(continued)

1: Situation

2: Tactic

_____

_____

3: Action

_____

_____

_____

_____

_____

_____

_____

_____

4: Result

_____

_____

_____

_____

_____

_____

_____

1: Situation

_____

_____

(continued)

(continued)

2: Tactic

3: Action

4: Result

1: Situation

(continued)

(continued)

2: Tactic

_____

_____

_____

_____

_____

_____

_____

_____

_____

3: Action

_____

_____

_____

_____

_____

_____

_____

_____

4: Result

_____

_____

_____

_____

_____

_____

_____

_____

_____

Sample STAR Stories

In this section you'll meet five senior-level executives—each telling a STAR story in their own words that reflects one significant accomplishment each. Just as you will, each of these executives will ultimately have three to five STAR stories, maybe more, *for each of their past positions*, from which they will select highlights to relate during interviews, include in their resumes, and perhaps incorporate into the Critical Leadership Initiatives document that we will discuss and recommend in chapter 4.

As you will see, any one of these STAR stories makes for great reading and storytelling—in an autobiography or even in an in-depth interview. But it's clearly impractical to present nearly a full page of narrative for one key success story as part of a resume. That's where judicious editing and careful writing will enable you to present an impactful STAR story on your resume in just a few lines.

Following each case, you will see an example that illustrates how the Situation-Tactic-Action-Result story could be framed in a powerful bullet point on that individual's resume.

It's important to note that a single STAR story *might* result in several different bullet points reflecting various key strengths. For example, one STAR story might be dissected to illustrate multiple signature skills such as driving revenue growth, empowering staff, and developing innovative marketing strategies. Your STAR stories are truly the stuff from which a great resume and a compelling interview are made!

As you read these examples, we hope you'll be inspired and consider *your unique background* and the many key stories you will tell about your achievements.

CASE 1: GEORGE TOMCZAK

Background: George is a 52-year-old CFO hired 12 months ago by Jones, Inc., a multimillion-dollar, multi-site manufacturer in the semiconductor industry. He is specifically tasked with reining in the finance-and-admin organization, eliminating duplication of resources, and establishing a smooth-running team.

1: Situation

Following costly acquisition of a larger competitor (immediately before I was hired), Jones was cash-poor, key customers were complaining about improperly applied credits and inaccurate invoicing, there was excessive overhead in the finance and administration departments, and organizations were working at cross-purposes with no integration between Jones' former finance organization and the "new" group. The company president was employing a hands-off approach to assimilation.

2: Tactic

My first step was to assemble a team comprising the comptrollers of the original company and the acquired company and bring in my best IT resource and several of the top accounting and admin resources from both groups to analyze and discern the optimal systems from both organizations. I developed a vision and ensured everyone was clear on the desired outcome. Everyone also understood that in the new landscape, only the best talent and resources would remain.

3: Action

The team mapped out a strategy, determined the technology necessary to implement a complete assimilation, and developed a timeline for execution. I drove the process with specific success milestones and recalibration as necessary.

4: Result

In less than six months, I established a single finance-and-admin team that supports all of the company's operations efficiently. I effectively preserved relationships with strategic customers by aligning finance staff with key accounts and implementing new terms and conditions that benefit customers and Jones alike. I pared close to $1 million in overhead costs by creating one team; some resources were hired in other company departments, some took advantage of favorable early retirement offers, and underperforming staff were released to seek work elsewhere. The new finance team is focused on a forward direction to support a turnaround in the company's financial direction.

Sample STAR Statement for Resume

- Synthesized finance and administration department supporting merger of two organizations; streamlined operations and improved overall efficiency by instituting key controls to eliminate duplication of resources. **Result:** Generated $1M in overhead savings.

CASE 2: SARAH GENOVESE

Background: Sarah is a 41-year-old senior hospital administrator managing the emergency department of a large Midwestern hospital. She's been in the field for more than 15 years, working her way up from assistant director to director of AVP to, now, vice president, recruited to a new facility with each promotion. She's been brought on board as VP to standardize emergency medical care, synthesize procedures, and develop a plan of action that ensures quality and profitability.

1: Situation

Midwest Medical Center has more than doubled its physical size in the past few years and nearly tripled its professional and administrative staff. I was hired to evaluate overall operations and instill new policies to boost poor patient satisfaction metrics, address continued lack of profitability despite increase in outpatient procedures, and turn around faltering staff morale. Patient surveys conducted over the past two years revealed scores in the 1.5 to 2.25 range (1 being the lowest rating, 5 being the highest). The emergency department, which had increased in utilization commensurate with the increase in overall facility size, had suffered decreases in overall margin the last three years to the point of hitting an all-time low the year before I was hired. Staff morale was considered poor, absenteeism was up significantly (30 percent over the previous year), and turnover was nearly 25 percent—higher even than the 20 percent that is considered standard for our industry.

2: Tactic

I recognized that a focus on the community was missing from the center's mission statement and that this could prove key to turning around patient perception of the facility as a whole. I also observed a common problem with expansion without a cohesive plan—no one was paying attention to overall allocation of resources and fiscal accountability.

3: Action

First, I pulled together the Director of Emergency Nursing (a veteran with a real understanding of what was needed in terms of clinical care), several physicians, and key representatives of both nonprofessional and clerical staff to brainstorm and iden- tify an optimal way to deliver patient care in a relatively new, state-of-the-art facility. They were initially given no parameters and charged with creating the best plan possible to ensure quality and service objectives. All factors were taken into account—from risk management and community image to improved utilization of emergency department services. Equal attention was paid to processes for ensuring effective coding and documentation to capture highest reimbursement possible. Especially throughout the idea-generation process, I encour- aged people to take risks in their problem-solving approach—no idea would be discarded without careful consideration.

4: Result

With key input from every representative of the emergency department team, I spearheaded the design of a facility and policies that everyone could embrace. Six months post- implementation, patient survey responses were at an all-time high (4.75 average), reimbursement rates climbed to their high- est levels ever (in excess of 80 percent, when rates for the previous five years varied between 57 and 68 percent), staff morale has turned around 180 degrees (absenteeism is well within normal limits, staff is happier, and people are not "post- ing" to leave the department), and service utilization has nearly doubled (for the FY just ended, average monthly patient visits grew from 1,250 one year earlier to nearly 2,500).

Sample STAR Statement for Resume

- Improved department utilization 100% while simultaneously increasing levels of patient satisfaction (boosted from an average 1.83 to 4.75 out of 5) over a 1-year timeframe through implementation of standards of care, improved com- munity outreach, and consistent focus on staff performance and development.

CASE 3: RON LEE

Background: Ron is the new 50-year-old GM of a small ($25 million) aerospace manufacturing company. Brocker Aerospace had been in existence for more than 40 years and was facing an industry-wide erosion in its customer base (it had shrunk by more than 20 percent over the past three to four years) and overall profitability (steady declines were posted over the preceding five years). Ron was recruited for his 20+ years of successful background turning around other small manufacturers in the aerospace sector, and for his vision for Brocker.

1: Situation

From as early as the first interview to the point of my first few weeks on the job, I quickly realized that although Brocker had been able to stay slightly ahead of the curve and generate a consistent profit to its owners (privately held), it was in danger of rapidly losing ground in this competitive industry. My diagnosis? A failure to stay ahead of the game, an absence of lean manufacturing methods, and no plan for implementing same.

2: Tactic

I was fortunate to have a willing team ready to jump on the bandwagon of the magnitude of change I was proposing. I initially identified strategic targets for immediate attention: reduce outsourcing of tooling (instead, optimize existing resources), improve quality assurance (to save on extensive backend costs and ongoing customer service issues), implement MRP, and aggressively attack the longstanding backlog.

3: Action

I worked with engineers, QA folks, procurement staff, and expediters to develop pinpoint plans to address each area of deficit. I simultaneously put in place an acquisition process for capital equipment necessary to optimize internal processes. I also held weekly strategy planning and checkpoint meetings (amazingly, the staff had never met regularly before except when there was a major problem). This served the dual purpose of ensuring that benchmarks were attained and keeping morale high. I instituted measures on the shop floor to provide a visual checkpoint on progress. With engineering's help, we reorganized the production-control group and put in place a build-to-stock plan.

4: Result

In the first few months, remarkable gains were achieved across nearly every measure. By the end of eight months, the outstanding backlog had been reduced by 70 percent, tooling costs were shaved more than 50 percent, and measurable gains in quality were realized, leading to an overall 50 percent cost reduction. Newly acquired equipment and MRP set the stage for future gains, and I began phase 2 of my master plan—working directly with the Sales VP to penetrate new markets for Brocker.

Sample STAR Statement for Resume

- Reduced overdue backlog by 70% in 8 months through multiple initiatives: Restructured production-control organization, deployed build-to-stock plans, used visual metrics on shop floor, and conducted daily management walkarounds.

CASE 4: JOSEPH ESPINOZA

Background: Joseph is a 58-year-old senior investment manager recently promoted within a premier Wall Street brokerage. In addition to ensuring SEC compliance, Joseph has been challenged to take over custody operations and put in place systems and architecture to efficiently handle transfers and reorganization.

1: Situation

Although it was not out of compliance, I could see that ABC Mutual Funds would be facing many risks for lack of enforced policies. Systems were not clearly in place for the movement of securities or the accounting thereof. Staff had not been cross-trained. There appeared to be little focus on professional development and virtually no written development plans or performance evaluations.

2: Tactic

I initially assessed that there was a "people problem" to fix first—I wanted to understand my staff's core competencies, goals, and unfulfilled needs. At almost the same time, I could see a need for getting a real handle on the workflows of the operation.

3: Action

Working with my most senior associate (Susan), I mapped out a strategy for Susan to develop optimal workflows that adhered to all regulatory requirements and ensured the proper handling of securities. I then tackled the inventorying of all staff—assessing skill level, completed training, licenses held, etc.—and determining through one-on-one meetings the best alignment of talent with task. Melding the necessary workflows with staffing capabilities, Susan and I created a master plan that could be implemented immediately. Ongoing performance checks with collaborative written performance assessments every six months would help keep everyone on the same page. At the same point, regulatory compliance would be verified on a biweekly basis to ensure that there were no unanticipated outages.

4: Result

In less than six months following my promotion to the head of custody operations, ABC Mutual Funds had in place a sustainable game plan that ensures compliance, productivity, and staffing levels. With newfound gains in productivity and a systematized workflow, the organization is poised to efficiently address significant growth and expansion of operations.

Sample STAR Statement for Resume

- Led design and launch of new staffing structure featuring enhanced service interactions, cross-training, and alignment of competencies with business needs. **Result:** Greater job satisfaction (75% reduction in staff turnover) and improved operational efficiencies (cut cycle times in half) in a high-volume environment.

CASE 5: DEVIN-LEIGH BEAUMIER

Background: Devin-Leigh is the new 39-year-old Director of Marketing with a major consumer goods manufacturer, Durrow + Howe. Specifically handling personal care products, she has inherited marketing ownership of a heritage line of products that has begun to falter over the past few years for the first time in the company's 75-year history (revenues were down more than $20M and market share had slipped by enough points to put the company in the #3 spot after years of being #1).

1: Situation

With constant competitive influx and new distribution channels continually eroding at Durrow + Howe's product base, I knew my greatest challenge would be to direct all resources toward innovating not only D+H's heritage products, but to ensure that new product launches would be on target, capture the desired audiences, and put this division of the company back on a trend-setting track.

2: Tactic

I was fortunate to have cultivated a background rich in creative, hands-on brand leadership and product development. I could bring to this role experience with a variety of boutique advertising agencies. I also had a solid internal creative team at my disposal. My first plan was to develop a twofold approach designed to (a) overhaul and rejuvenate the heritage line to capitalize on key brand attributes while addressing new market opportunities (new formularies plus new packaging will be inherent to success) and (b) institute demographically dictated lifestyle product tiers linked to progressive stages of life to solidify long-time customer loyalty in new products.

3: Action

I have always been considered to be a high-energy performer. Taking a cue from past successes, I established near-daily product innovation mini-conferences with my design team, brand managers, promotions assistants, and product engineers to mastermind brand-rejuvenation strategies. I brought in not only focus-group feedback, but in-the-field research culled from hands-on participation and analysis and that of key company staff nationwide. Top boutique talent acting in a consultative manner joined my team for creative sessions to spin new thought-leader campaigns. I divided groups into teams—my brand-overhaul "a" team and the new lifestyle product development "b" team. Creative incentives were put into place in a spirit of collaborative-yet-focused competition.

4: Result

Durrow + Howe's heritage brand returned to #1 in its category with a 62 percent increase in revenues over 18 months. Brand penetration was increased significantly. Further, I can take credit for leading D+H's most successful launch ever with an innovative product introduction featuring tiered lifestyle skin-care products; the campaign produced $125M in new revenues in just over one year.

Sample STAR Statement for Resume

- Quarterbacked execution of company's most successful product-line launch in 75 years with revenues of $125M in year 1 and projections in excess of $400M by year 3.

PUTTING IT ALL TOGETHER TO CREATE YOUR OWN ROI RESUME

Congratulations! You have just finished creating the cornerstones of your resume and your entire career marketing strategy. Your target, signature strengths, and STAR stories are the most important strands of a tightly woven, compelling, branded resume. Chapter 3 will give you step-by-step strategies to weave all of the strands together to create a value proposition that will uniquely position you for the targets you have established.

Executive Resume Writing Challenges

*"The secret of joy in work is contained in one word—
excellence. To know how to do something well is to enjoy it."*

—Pearl S. Buck

With your STAR stories carefully developed and a game plan created for your search that includes a precisely defined target, you are now ready to craft your resume. This chapter will help you select the correct resume format and categorize your information under the correct section headings.

REVERSE-CHRONOLOGICAL VS. FUNCTIONAL RESUMES: WHICH FORMAT IS BEST?

For nearly every case, we highly recommend a reverse-chronological format for executive resumes. Recruiters and hiring authorities alike almost universally prefer to see your most recent/current experience listed *first*, and older experience later.

Your resume should begin with a well-written executive summary that presents clearly transferable skills, key examples of success, and all-critical core leadership competencies; this should take up roughly one-third to one-half of page 1. The balance of page 1 should immediately begin to present actual employment data—your professional experience—so that a reader quickly glancing at your resume jumps right into the "meat of the matter." Industry surveys have shown repeatedly that recruiters and hiring authorities do *not* want to have to flip to page 2 to *begin* to see company/title/accomplishments.

So how did functional resumes gain favor? Probably most prevalent in the 1980s (when many people made rapid job changes), this style has been around for a very long time. On the surface, it would appear to be an effective way to group similar experiences under topical headings (for instance, leadership, sales, P&L, and so forth). However, this format almost always leads to questions such as, "Well, *where* did these superb accomplishments take place? *When* did she effect those results? *For what company* did he drive that type of perform-ance?" You don't want to put the hiring authority or recruiter in a position of having to flip back and forth between the pages of your resume trying to guess how recent an accomplishment might be or when you last had P&L responsibility.

The functional format became very popular for hiding gaps in experience, a widely disparate background, and frequent job jumps. Precisely *because* of that fact, recruiters and hiring authorities quickly judge a functional resume as being used by a prospective candidate to disguise something—the last impres-sion you want to give.

The bottom line on formatting? For nearly all executives, we recommend reverse-chronological resumes (most current info first) with amplified presenta-tion of accomplishments and future predictors of success in well-written quali-fications summaries.

STAR Strategy: Write from the Bottom Up

Nearly every professional resume writer develops the content of the resume starting at the bottom. You should, too. First enter your contact information at the top of page 1 and insert header information for subse-quent pages.

Then go to the bottom of page 3 and roughly outline your civic and community experience; fill in military experience, if applicable; add affil-iations and professional memberships; and enter degree information and significant continuing professional education. Next create an outline of employer/city-state/approximate (or actual) dates and title(s), working from the oldest to the newest.

Don't worry (yet) about paring out the oldest material—or cutting course-work, organizational involvement, and the like. This material can and will be honed down later. You'll also consider resume style and final formatting later. Once the preliminary sections are complete, you will be ready to focus on the two most critical sections of your resume: your Professional Experience and Executive Summary.

★ : ★ : ★ : ★ : ★ : ★ : ★ : ★ : ★ : ★ : ★ : ★ : ★ : ★ : ★ : ★ : ★ : ★ : ★ : ★

THE PRIMARY ELEMENTS OF YOUR RESUME

Following are the key elements of an executive resume. Keep in mind that you might not have information in every category (for instance, military):

1. Contact Information
2. Executive Profile/Summary
3. Professional Experience
4. Education and Professional Development
5. Affiliations and Professional Memberships
6. Military Experience
7. Civic and Community Background

The following sections give tips for creating each of these resume sections. These sections are presented in the order we recommend you write your resume: Following the creation of the blank resume document with your contact information at the top, we suggest writing "from the bottom up."

Contact Information

This section is very straightforward—but you'd be surprised at the questions that can and do crop up. Provide your name, home address, home telephone number, home fax number, mobile number, e-mail address, and Web address (for your portfolio, Web site, and/or blog).

Do not include your business phone number on your resume unless it is a direct line that you alone can access, or in the rare cases when your situation is widely known by others in the office—for instance, your company or division is closing and you (along with other staffers) are overtly in job search mode.

Provide a mobile number only if it is your personal cell; do not list a company-paid cell phone for contact.

NOTE: See the "Special Situations" section at the end of this chapter for recommendations on addressing androgynous names and other moniker questions.

Civic and Community Background

It can be important for executives to convey community involvement. This section of your resume allows you to highlight extra information that can set you apart from others. Here are some key questions to jog your memory:

- On what boards, commissions, or organizations do you sit?
- What positions of leadership do you hold?
- Were you elected or appointed?
- Did you lead any significant initiatives during your tenure?

> **NOTE:** See the "Special Situations" section (problem 13) at the end of this chapter for tips on addressing religious and political affiliations.

STAR Strategy: Handling Dates

If you were extremely active in a particular organization but ceased membership more than a few years ago, instead of showing the actual timeline (1979–1988), indicate the number of years:

Elected Selectman, Town of East Windsor, CT (9 years)

If you are interspersing more dated, but significant activities with more current ones, list the oldest involvements last.

Civic and Community Involvement

Federal Bureau of Investigation

- **Board Member, Community Partnership Program;** Atlanta, GA (2001–Present)

City of Decatur, GA

- **Member, Traffic Safety Advisory Committee** (2002–Present)
- **Member, Town Meeting;** Burrough 4 (2004–Present)

Appointments

City of Decatur, GA

- **Special Police Officer** (1998–2002)
- **Town Constable** (1996–1999)

Although it is usually adequate to name just the organization, location, position(s) held, and timeframe, there may be instances in which you provided above-and-beyond leadership or managed a particularly significant project. In these cases, you can include more detail.

Philadelphia Society for Multiple Sclerosis

- **Committee Chairperson** (2003, 2004); **Co-Chair** (2000–2003). Directed highly successful annual black-tie event attended by 900 people that raised more than $85,000 each year.

Military Experience

This section is straightforward. Include branch/field of service, highest rank achieved, significant honors or recognition earned, and honorable discharge status. If your experience directly links to your current goal, a brief highlight or two is fine. Otherwise, nothing further is needed, unless, of course, your military background comprises the bulk of your career. If that is the case, rather than include it in a separate "military" section, list it under Professional Experience and include all of your relevant accomplishments.

DYESS AIR FORCE BASE ● Abilene, TX (1981–1986)

Master Sergeant, Grade E-7 *(honorable discharge)*

- Managed maintenance production team of 15 on $280 million B-1B aircraft.

Affiliations and Professional Memberships

Separate from community involvement, these relate to your industry and field. It is optional whether you include the number of years you have been affiliated or the timeframe of your affiliation; you may choose to omit year/date information altogether. The important thing is to be consistent. You may opt to include positions held (elected/appointed) as well.

Affiliations

- Global Security Advisory Council
- National Society for Industrial Security
- American Health Care Anti-Fraud Association
- International Security Management Association
- Atlanta Community Partnership Foundation

Professional Memberships

New Haven Chamber of Commerce—President, Entrepreneurial Division
(3 years); Member (7 years)

Quinnipiac Bureau of New Business Owners—Founder/Co-President (4 years)

Association of Manufacturing Excellence—Member (2 years)

Professional Affiliations

- **National Science Teachers Association (NSTA)** • Member (1999–Present)
- **Minnesota Science Teachers Association (MSTA)** • Chairman, Membership Committee (2002–Present); Co-chair, New Curriculum Committee (2004–Present); Member (1999–Present)
- **National Education Association** • Member (2001–Present)
- **Minnesota Education Association** • Member (2000–Present)

Education and Professional Development

For the Education section of your resume, remember to include "just the facts." Include degree earned, institution, and city/state. There are many schools of thought on whether to include years. Here's the bottom line: Be consistent. Don't show the date of a recently minted MBA (say, 2002) but skip the year of your undergraduate degree (1978). Show both or neither.

If the potential for age discrimination is not a concern (and, frankly, for a senior-level executive, it is *expected* that you have years of experience in many instances), by all means show years. If, on the other hand, you are concerned about age perceptions, eliminate the dates of your degrees and be sure to truncate your work history as well. It does no good to eliminate the years in which you earned your degrees, but show employment beginning in 1965!

An exception: For a candidate who earned a baccalaureate degree more than 25 years ago, but completed an MBA from a top-notch school in the past few years, consider a bullet in the Executive Summary that reflects "MBA, Kellogg School of Management, 2004," but stick with the earlier advice: omit all years in the Education section.

Although you might be proud of your academic honors, we don't recommend detailing these on your resume unless they were truly stellar (for example, Rhodes or Fulbright scholar). Your achievements in your career are of greater value today. You might, however mention that you graduated with honors (*cum laude, magna cum laude, summa cum laude,* or another designation that appears on your diploma).

Do not mention any collegiate extracurricular activities (okay, if you were the star running back for three years, lettered all four, and earned the Heisman trophy, you can be permitted that indulgence).

Do not mention high school; one exception would be if you plan to network with alumni of an elite secondary school. For instance, if you are a graduate of Connecticut's Choate Rosemary Hall and you're using the alumni office to assist you, by all means include this information on those resumes only.

NOTE: See the "Special Situations" section at the end of this chapter for recommendations on addressing no formal education (problem 3), incomplete degree (problem 2), and other education-related concerns.

For Professional Development, highlight two or three significant programs or seminars that add value to your portfolio of skills and abilities. Timeliness is important—you don't want to show programs completed more than 10 years ago.

We recommend that you maintain a separate, comprehensive record (multi-page document, if necessary) listing *all* continuing professional education. Important details to include are program name, presenter, sponsoring organization, city/state, month/year of training, and duration of program (week-long, three-day, and so forth). From this listing, you can pick and choose particularly salient courses that complement your search efforts and include those few on your targeted resume.

Education

M.S., Business Administration—Boston University ● Boston, MA (1993)

B.S., Engineering—United States Military Academy ● West Point, NY (1990)

United States Military Personnel Management School ● Ft. Harrison, IN (1991)

Continuing Professional Education includes the following certifications:

- Executive Lean Manufacturing (2003)
- Certified Zenger Miller Leadership Trainer (2004)

Professional Experience

We recommend you stay away from using "Work History" as a heading, a rather dated caption that we believe connotes other-than-executive experience. See the sidebar on the next page for ideas for other titles to use for this critically important component of your resume. Ultimately, the decision regarding caption is yours; select the one you feel most comfortable with.

★ ：★ ：★ ：★ ：★ ：★ ：★ ：★ ：★ ：★ ：★ ：★ ：★ ：★ ：★ ：★ ：★ ：★ ：★

Other Possible Titles for Your Professional Experience Section

Executive Performance Overview

Experience and Accomplishments

Career Overview

Senior Management Experience

Professional Management Experience

★ ：★ ：★ ：★ ：★ ：★ ：★ ：★ ：★ ：★ ：★ ：★ ：★ ：★ ：★ ：★ ：★ ：★ ：★

In this section, it's essential to focus on those pieces of your background that indicate your value and predict your future success.

The best way to begin this section is by creating a chronology starting with your first position following graduation from college or discharge from the military. Initially, don't worry about "how far back" you are going to go along the timeline. Get the rudimentary outline on the computer screen first. Concentrate on having correct names of companies, headquarters location (city/state), years of employment, and your title. For organizations in which you were promoted, break out the specific titles (for now) and years of each. The following example shows a first draft of this chronological section.

Professional Experience

ALPHA CORPORATION ● Denver, CO   2003–Present

Vice President of Field Operations *(2005–Present)*

Director, Northeast Area *(2003–2005)*

CARDINAL HEALTH SYSTEM ● Boston, MA   1999–2003

Director, Network Planning and Integration

AC NIELSEN COMPANY ● New York, NY   1987–1999

Regional Operations Manager *(1995–1999)*

Senior Field Operations Manager *(1987–1995)*

DIGITAL EQUIPMENT CORPORATION • Waltham, MA   1979–1987

Field Service Branch Manager *(1981–1987)*

Field Service Unit Manager *(1979–1981)*

WANG LABORATORIES • Burlington, MA   1972–1979

Senior Project Engineer *(1975–1979)*

Project Engineer *(1972–1975)*

Again, professional resume writers find it works best (and is fastest) to start with the bottom of this section and move forward, leaving your current or most recent position for last.

At this point, you can begin to consider just how far back in time to go when culling material for your resume. As a sliding general rule, you probably won't want to include much detail for anything beyond 20 years out; you don't want to overwhelm the reader with dated, detailed material, particularly at the expense of more recent and more relevant positions.

BACKGROUND INFORMATION: SUMMARIZING OLDER EXPERIENCE

In the preceding chronological draft example, let's assume Steve, our hypothetical job seeker, graduated with his bachelor's degree in 1972 and went to work immediately at Wang (since defunct). We'll also assume, for this exercise, that it is now 2007. Using the yardstick of 20 years, we would initially suggest that detail is not necessary for any of his positions prior to 1987. (This is convenient; 1987 is when he began his career at Nielsen.) Therefore, the timeframe from 1972 to 1987 could be addressed with the following brief paragraph at the end of the Professional Experience section:

Additional Professional Background includes previous management and engineering positions in the high-technology manufacturing field (mainframes and PCs) working for Digital Equipment Corporation (subsequently Compaq, now Hewlett-Packard) and Wang Laboratories (has since ceased operations).

BACKGROUND INFORMATION: USING EDUCATION DATES STRATEGICALLY

Using this same strategy, let's assume that we'll also not reflect the year of Steve's B.S. (1972) or his MBA (2003) in the Education section. We will, however, ensure that his MBA and year are prominently noted in the Executive Summary. For purposes of strategic age reduction, if Steve follows this format, he has taken his actual age of 55 and recrafted himself as about 46. How? By counting back from 1987, the reader will perhaps think "six years for those management and engineering positions in high-tech…. He probably earned his B.S. in 1981; therefore, he's about 46."

NOTE: Our goal is not to have you focus undue energy on age—just to provide real-life scenarios to help you not reveal your entire work history and dates when you believe it might be strategically advantageous in your search. For some executives, younger perceived age might be an important competitive edge in some industries—at least for the first-impression resume screening. In actual fact, when interviewing begins, age takes a back seat to experience, accomplishments, and fit.

Moving into the remaining professional experience, we'll start again with the oldest—Steve's work at AC Nielsen.

AC NIELSEN COMPANY ● New York, NY   1987–1999

Regional Operations Manager *(1995–1999)*

Senior Field Operations Manager *(1987–1995)*

BACKGROUND INFORMATION: CAPTURING ACCOMPLISHMENTS FROM OLDER EXPERIENCE

Our goal was to capture the three or four most significant accomplishments in each of his two roles with Nielsen, as well as overview the breadth and scope of his leadership responsibility. Here is the same example text, with added information and STAR stories.

AC NIELSEN COMPANY ● New York, NY   1987–1999

Regional Operations Manager *(1995–1999)*

Promoted to direct regional operations comprising 20 managers, 4 engineers, 135 employees, and $15 million budget for Nielsen's household television meter service. Scope of service operation included 7,000 households across 12 markets. Management oversight for human resources, project management, and financial forecasting.

● Reduced operating expenses by $3.2 million annually through project innovations (developed, manufactured, tested, and implemented cutting-edge data-collection technology).

- Preserved strategic account relationship valued at $2.5 million through effective leadership of customer service focus team.
- Led engineering team that developed operational plans for deployment of Nielsen's personal passive meter.
- Played leadership or key roles on teams charged with design/implementation of WAN, PC/mainframe software design, development, and testing as well as developing hardware specifications.

Senior Field Operations Manager *(1987–1995)*

Managed team of 5 managers and 40 employees, $950K budget, and all field activities (installation, maintenance, and service support) in Dallas, Philadelphia, San Francisco, and Boston branch offices. Challenged to turn around faltering Chicago branch.

- Implemented comprehensive HR program that transformed Chicago branch office from one of the worst performance records into top-performing field office.
- Recognized as Manager of the Year with President's Award.
- Following 7.1 California earthquake (1989), restored San Francisco branch to above-goal performance within 2 weeks.

✳ ✳

STAR Strategy: Apply Your Earlier "Homework" to Good Advantage in Your Resume

Use the STAR stories you developed in chapter 2 to add salient, quantifiable information (the key bullet points) for each of the recent positions on your resume. If you have developed three or four top STAR stories for each of the positions you'll be profiling on your resume, you're in excellent shape. As a rule of thumb, devote the most space to your current (or most recent) position and decrease the amount of space allotted as you go backward in time.

✳ ✳

BACKGROUND INFORMATION: CONVEYING MANAGEMENT MASTERY

Moving on to Steve's next position in building his resume, we'll take a look at Cardinal Health, the timeline covering 1999–2003. Steve used the bullet points to convey his mastery of managing within the telecomm discipline, tackling multiple challenges.

CARDINAL HEALTH SYSTEM • Boston, MA   1999–2003

Director, Network Planning and Integration

Here is the same example text with added information and STAR stories:

CARDINAL HEALTH SYSTEM • Boston, MA   1999–2003

Director, Network Planning and Integration

Brought on board to spearhead complex integration initiative for emerging leader in healthcare products, services, and technology. Challenged to direct successful development and rollout of voice and data network in 6,000+ node multi-protocol data environment and 13,000+ voice environment.

- Key projects managed included NetWare upgrade, WAN resiliency addition, Ethernet switching, FDDI backbone, and voice/data convergence across ATM WAN links.

- Increased network performance through enterprise-wide design and implementation of TCP/IP routing (RIP and OSPF) as well as link-state routing of IPX/SPX (NLSP).

- Ensured greater than 99% uptime through management of design/installation project providing redundant routers and communication links.

- Expertly managed project that stabilized NetWare environment by upgrading nine NetWare 3.12 and 4.02 servers to NetWare 4.1 and three NetWare SAA gateways to version 2.0.

BACKGROUND INFORMATION: SHOWING SPECIFIC SUCCESSES

Steve's experience at Cardinal proved pivotal to his being aggressively recruited to take over as Director of Alpha's Northeast Area operations. He has integrated key data into the content of both the director and VP positions to reflect specific successes and outcomes and show his progression to an accomplished, results-oriented, senior-level manager.

ALPHA CORPORATION • Denver, CO   2003–Present

Vice President of Field Operations *(2005–Present)*

Director, Northeast Area *(2003–2005)*

Here is the same text from the example with added information and STAR stories.

ALPHA CORPORATION ● Denver, CO   2003–Present

Vice President of Field Operations *(2005–Present)*

Director, Northeast Area *(2003–2005)*

Alpha is a $750 million leader in converged voice and data networking solutions providing optimal choice and value at favorable price point. With VoIP technology a particular strength, Alpha serves a diverse customer base spanning both enterprise/private-sector organizations of all sizes as well as municipalities, government, education, and other not-for-profit entities worldwide.

Vice President of Field Operations *(2005–Present)*

Promoted to stabilize field operations and manage a team of 10–12 in the eastern continental U.S. Oversee multiple virtual teams, 25–30 members each, handling installation, network, and analysis services. Direct key post-sales activities throughout operational span with complete P&L responsibility (on track to expand from $23 million to $40 million).

● In 12 months, grew services revenue from $1.8 million to $5.5 million per quarter through enhanced focus on service sales (installations, implementations, and professional services).

● Executed successful revitalization plan capitalizing on staff's unique strengths; reversed 30%–40% turnover trend to zero, retained key talent, and instilled solid leadership as well as clear, measurable objectives.

● During 12–18 month period of limited resources, established strategic alliances with third parties to augment implementation capability, increasing capacity by 20% and enhancing customer service.

● Revamped business model to focus on implementation services, streamline maintenance agreements, and eliminate lower-end services with small profit margin yield.

Director, Northeast Area *(2003–2005)*

Stabilized organization experiencing widespread change; managed effectively during technology sector volatility while staff increased from 14 to 21 direct reports.

● Drove active and effective recruitment strategies to service a business increasing at 16% annually.

● Assumed additional responsibility for managing both pre- and post-sales engineering for the Northeastern Area.

● As Alpha transitioned out of large enterprise business, successfully retained key talent in organization through multipronged plan providing training opportunities (Cisco Certified Network Administration [CCNA®] program) and stay-on bonuses to ensure completion of all project requirements.

STAR Strategy: Use Context to Make a Powerful Impression

For greatest impact, frame your career history and accomplishments within the context of specific challenges, market conditions, or other circumstances that existed when you took each job or during your tenure. In the preceding examples, note how the introductory paragraph includes language that "puts the reader in the picture" as to what Steve was expected to do or what challenges he faced; then the accomplishments indicate what he did in those circumstances. This structure and context make it easier for readers to understand your career activities and achievements.

Another powerful strategy for conveying your value is to lead off each position with a concise summary of your overall achievement during that time, followed by a more low-key position description and then the bullet points that detail specific accomplishments.

In the following example, you can see how the brief introductory paragraph frames this individual's entire tenure, and the details that follow more explicitly communicate what he did and how he achieved results.

McGOWAN GROUP CONSULTING SERVICES, San Francisco, CA
(2005–Present)

Managing Director, IT Division

Drove a performance turnaround: restructured operations, restored relationships, invigorated growth, and repositioned firm for critical market differentiation. Stock price doubled in last 2 years.

Recruited to McGowan Group to engineer post-recession turnaround. With the executive team, redefined the value proposition around best practices, benchmarking, and the firm's intellectual capital. Addressed operational, marketing, and customer challenges, developing and executing strategies to return the company to aggressive growth mode.

Member of company Leadership Team and Managing Director for a $15M P&L— the newly combined IT Division, combining high-level IT consulting, information delivery systems, and data warehousing. Manage 80+ consultants and the company's most strategic and highest-revenue alliances.

Performance Highlights

- Achieved successful turnaround and steady upward growth of the combined P&L:

    Increased revenues to $15M, +20% in FY06.

    Personally delivered more than $8M in sales.

    Landed key anchor accounts including SBC, Teatro, JD Donlan, Xcaliber, and others.

- Built the critical alliances that create market credibility and generate major portions of company revenue:

    Restructured the IBM alliance and earned IBM's prestigious "Regional Systems Integrator of the Year" award for driving more than $80M in influenced sales.

    Led Accenture relationship from inception to lucrative partnership—currently delivering more than 15% of McGowan Group's total revenue.

STAR Strategy: Control Length to Captivate Readers

To keep your resume readable and your readers interested, keep your paragraphs short—preferably no more than four or five lines—and limit your lists of bullet points to no more than five or six. If you have too many items or too much information, consider ways to break up the text:

- **Use second-level bullets.** See the preceding example, where a major bullet point is supported by sub-bullets.

- **Add subheadings.** Again in the preceding example, the subheading "Performance Highlights" is used. If the list of bullet points gets too long, group the bullet points according to common themes and add a second or third subheading as needed.

- **Create a Critical Leadership Initiatives addendum.** Described in chapter 4, this document allows you to expand on the most significant accomplishments of your career without bogging down your resume.

Executive Profile/Summary

In a well-developed business plan, the Executive Summary appears first; however, it is always written last, after all components of the plan have been developed. Your resume will come together the same way. The title of this section is up to you; recommendations follow in the sidebar.

✳ ✳

Other Titles (Exchange "Profile" and "Summary" at Will)

Professional Profile

Executive Management Profile

Executive Profile

Executive Summary

Senior Management Summary

Key Accomplishments

Career Profile

Or you can include no title at all, employing a "headline format" to immediately communicate who you are (see the examples later in this chapter).

✳ ✳

The information to be presented in the Executive Summary, as with a business plan, should summarize the key value proposition you offer. To begin the process of writing your profile, give careful consideration to each of the following questions.

- In what areas do you have special expertise?
- What are your core competencies?
- What areas of performance have distinguished your career?
- What are your most significant achievements?
- What specific technical proficiencies (if relevant) do you possess?
- What other defining information about you could be important to impart in the quick 10-second read your Executive Summary might get?
- What additional distinguishing characteristics do you possess (for example, multiple language proficiencies, key industry credentials, prestigious board of directors roles, or a name-brand MBA)?

You might find it helpful to begin to group areas of strength under specific sub-headings (these subheadings might or might not become a part of the final Executive Summary). We also highly recommend that you refer to the exercises in chapter 2, particularly your responses in the Signature Strengths section of that chapter.

✶ ✶

STAR Strategy: Be Crystal-Clear Right from the Top

It is absolutely essential that in your Executive Summary you immediately communicate your career focus. In those first 10 seconds, readers must be able to tell who you are. It's not necessary to limit yourself to one job title or industry, but do be sure that readers can instantly glean this critical "who are you" information so that they can place you in context and have the right expectation for what you will present in the rest of the resume.

✶ ✶

Executive Profile

Highly accomplished executive qualified for President/CEO/COO with company demanding expertise in all aspects of management, from energizing sales and tar-geting new markets to effectively managing crises and successfully turning around declining operations.

- Catalyst for strategic change: Able to anticipate and plan for changing business needs and demands; a visionary with keen business savvy and strong strategic planning abilities.
- Dynamic leader and dedicated team player with reputation for leveraging highly effective analytical and problem-solving skills.
- Solid business builder; proven performance reflects consistent increases in sales revenues across multiple industries.
- Demonstrated track record of leveraging maximum value and results from organizations.

Some individuals prefer to use keywords in lieu of a caption for this section. In other words, instead of leading off with the caption "Executive Summary" just below their name and contact information, they might opt to place critical key-words in that same location followed by a subset of specific expertise and then a breakout of core competencies.

We like this approach because it positions key distinguishing information front and center and helps readers immediately perceive "who you are." All of the following examples employ this "headline" approach.

CEO / DIVISION PRESIDENT / MANAGING DIRECTOR: TECHNOLOGY SERVICES

High-Growth • Turnaround • Fortune 1000 Customers • Fortune 100 Alliances

Accomplished senior executive, expert in business-building strategies for technology services organizations:

- Key contributor to explosive growth of McGowan Group to nearly $1B market capitalization and recent turnaround to aggressive growth (+20% in 2006).
- Marketing strategist and revenue driver, positioning Chronis and Abalone Technology for rapid market penetration and acquisition by industry leaders.

Visionary strategist with equal strengths in tactical execution. Compelling speaker, able to convey business and product messages with passion and purpose to influence sales, investor support, and positive press and analyst reaction. Early consulting and corporate background with Deloitte and IBM. Wharton MBA.

Proven Executive Competencies

- Business Strategy/Solutions to Complex Challenges
- Positioning/Messaging/Market Differentiation
- Investor, Analyst, & Customer Presentations Relationships
- Acquisition Positioning/Integration
- Executive Team Collaboration
- Board, Investor, & Alliance

Senior Sales Executive: Technology & Telecommunications

Expert in igniting revenue to achieve dynamic growth in highly competitive markets: revenue, customer, and team focused. Skilled in all facets of sales/business leadership, from defining the strategy through building the team and managing P&L for the operation. Widely experienced in multichannel U.S. and international sales.

▶ **Drive rapid revenue growth in sales of complex services.**
Over $800M revenue over 5 years with Transcom; $380M new revenue in one year for MCI; $100M in contract agreements for start-up XComm in 6 months.

▶ **Build top-performing sales/account management teams.**
Transformed underperformers to top 25% nationwide for MCI; led Transcom team to 131% of goal; consistently beat quotas in all sales leadership roles.

▶ **Successfully launch new technology products in new sales channels and new (global) markets.**
Quickly generated $200M in new channel revenue for Transcom; led IP sales channel that delivered rapid revenue growth to MCI; led global expansion for both Transcom and XComm.

Construction Industry Operations Management Executive

- Consistently delivered exceptional quality and profitability in managing complex, logistically challenging construction projects globally. Broad experience in telecommunications, chemical, bulk paper, and pharmaceutical industries.
- Led startup and turnaround organizations to successful, stable, profitable operations.
- Implemented organization-wide standards and practices to improve project performance in quality and profitably. Set industry standards for consistency and reliability.
- Structured and negotiated innovative alliances and complex project contracts that delivered win-win outcomes; successfully communicated value and benefit to clients and partners.

Key Areas of Expertise

- Project Management & Execution
- Process Planning & Implementation
- Contract Negotiations & Administration
- Administrative Management
- Strategic Business Alliances
- Global Business Ventures

Safety and Environmental Manager Risk Management • Industrial Safety • Emergency Planning Fire • Nuclear • Chemical	
Key Accomplishments	
Leadership ...	Led multiple integrated readiness assessment and safety analysis teams for nuclear process startups at complex commercial and government nuclear facilities. Spearheaded work control process reengineering effort at a national laboratory.
Technology ...	<u>Safety</u>: Department of Energy nuclear safety regulations and guidelines, NCR licensing and safety analysis, OSHA regulations, NIOSH recommendations, Enhanced Work Planning, ALARA principles, Integrated Safety Analysis, process hazard evaluations, radiological hazards evaluations.
	<u>Computer</u>: PC and Mac platforms, Microsoft Word, Excel, PowerPoint, Access, Outlook, and Project; ACT.

NOTE: There could conceivably be as many as four or five subsections in this portion of your resume.

SPECIAL SITUATIONS

There are probably as many special problems that can occur in resume writing as there are innovative strategies for addressing them. We'll walk through some of the more typical cases we face as resume writers and provide some suggested solutions for your consideration.

PROBLEM #1: AGE

I'm concerned about my age. What's the best way to handle that on my resume?

Solution: Earlier in this chapter we mentioned that age might not necessarily be a bad thing. In fact, we daresay that *most* savvy, accomplished senior-level executives are not 26 years old. However, from our work with candidates, we do know there are concerns among some about their age—or, more specifically, that they will appear to be "too old."

We see this most often in executives who have established decades-long careers within one industry (and sometimes one company) who find themselves unexpectedly unemployed in their late 40s, 50s, or even 60s. Financial implications aside, the vast majority of candidates in this situation have tremendous expertise and experience to offer. Yet, for some, their job searches become mired in self-doubt for a variety of reasons.

The primary root cause can often be attributed to a lack of experience *conducting an executive job search* and perhaps expecting too much too soon. (If this describes you, refer to chapter 1 for proven strategies and a quick-start action plan.)

Although each situation is unique, a widely used benchmark is that for every $10K–$15K in desired compensation, you should allocate one month to the search process. (In other words, if you are seeking a position in the $150K range, you might need to invest 15 months in searching, networking, and negotiating to ultimately land your next position.) Of course, this is just a guideline. We have seen $500K executives land a new position in two or three months, whereas others in the low-six-figure range search hard for a year or more. Still, keeping this as your guideline will help you from becoming too impatient after just a few weeks or months of searching!

Dealing with Age on Your Resume

However, let's assume that your expectations are realistic but that for any number of reasons you want to disguise your age on your resume. Here is a recap and further explication of the strategies we recommended under the Education and Professional Experience sections earlier in this chapter:

- It is okay to omit years of graduation from your degrees—provided you do so consistently.
- It is permissible to not tell the *whole* story; your resume is not your professional autobiography. You do not need to go "all the way back."

CAVEAT: You might be asked to complete an employment application/form that does require virtually all employment; so you need to have this information available. However, at the point in the process that this may become necessary, you are usually through all of the gates.

Dealing with Age in Interviews

In terms of concerns about age, personal appearance is another topic worthy of mention. This is true whether an individual is concerned about age or simply seeking to optimize all factors for informational and interview meetings.

Men. If you haven't outfitted yourself with several new suits, shirts, and ties in the past 18 months, now is the time to upgrade your wardrobe. You can't go wrong with a dark suit (navy, gray, charcoal, or black); quality is what is key. A neatly pressed (light starch is good) shirt—white is still the best option—is your best bet. Be sure your tie is up-to-date. Consult a high-quality executive men's clothier for up-to-the-minute advice.

Wear dark, over-the-calf socks that match your suit. Your shoes should be black and polished (wing tips or the style you prefer) and in perfect condition (soles, too). Any jewelry should be conservative—at most, a wedding ring or school ring and watch; should an earring be part of your look, you should leave it off during your search.

Your briefcase should look professional and be in impeccable condition. Your pen and portfolio (letter-writing case) should be high-quality. This is not the time to grab a Bic pen quickly from the car.

For gentlemen, fortunately, hairstyles that continue to be very popular include close-shorn hair and the look of complete baldness. If that's not a look for you and if hair loss is a problem, consult a good hair salon (you might have to part company with your long-time barber) for advice. No matter the direction you go, try to stay clear of the combover. Be sure whatever style you choose is neatly trimmed with a very recent haircut. Hair color is also a viable consideration for men today, regardless of age. Whether it's highlights or full color, don't hesitate to enhance this aspect of your appearance, particularly in the job search stage. Clean-shaven remains most appropriate for most senior-executive positions. If you do wear facial hair, ensure very careful, neat trimming. Omit cologne altogether. A delicate breath mint is fine (avoid Altoids—you don't want an interviewer distracted with concern of what you are covering up). Finally, if you wear glasses, be sure your frames are up-to-date.

Women. Depending on your industry, select a well-cut skirted suit or pants suit, preferably dark. Avoid bright colors and patterns (unless you are in advertising, public relations, media, or fashion). Wear nude, tan, or sheer black hose—avoid the bare-leg look that was so popular a few years ago. Ensure that your shoes are high quality and in perfect condition; wear stilettos or high heels only if you are absolutely perfectly balanced. A mid-height heel or lower is recommended. Be conservative in jewelry and accessories (interview dress is not the best time for a large, dominating scarf). Avoid dangly earrings and any jewelry (necklace, chains, or bracelets) that jingles and makes sound when you move.

Just as for men, you should carry a professional-looking briefcase in impeccable condition containing a high-quality pen and portfolio.

If you prefer to carry a purse separate from a small one that tucks into your briefcase, we recommend one with a long strap so that you can wear it over a shoulder, carry your briefcase in your left hand, and reserve your right for shaking hands. As with your briefcase, ensure that your purse is of superior quality and condition.

Conservative and attractive are the guiding words for hair and makeup, selecting what is appropriate for your field. As with accent colors/blouse for suits, brighter colors/heavier makeup are more appropriate to specific industries (media, PR, advertising, and so forth). More conservative is better in finance, for instance. Err on the side of natural. Hair should be worn in a style attractive to your facial shape and one that does not require constant "playing with" in a meeting. As with men, omit perfume altogether; use a delicate breath mint if you wish; and be certain your glasses, if you wear them, are an updated style.

PROBLEM #2: NO DEGREE

I never earned my degree. I stopped just a few credits shy of a bachelor's. How do you recommend handling this on the resume?

Solution: Our number-one solution is never to lie on your resume; don't give in to the temptation to turn your college studies into a college degree! In the first place, it's unethical; in the second place, it can be cause for immediate dismissal if it is ever found out (and it's extremely easy for employers to check); and finally, have the confidence that your expertise, experience, and proven accomplishments are of most interest to employers.

CAVEAT: If you do not have a degree, you will probably find that executive recruiters are not a viable channel for your career marketing activities. Because they are programmed to fill "specs" that almost universally include a bachelor's degree or, in many cases, an MBA, recruiters will not be inclined to bend the rules for you when they (typically) have so many other candidates. This will not be a problem, of course, if you follow our ROI strategies and action plan in chapter 1!

Here are several different approaches for downplaying lack of a degree on your resume. Consider the following:

University of Massachusetts ● Amherst, MA

Pursued Bachelor of Science, Business Management (1989–92)

Connecticut College—New London, Connecticut

- Matriculated in B.S., Accounting.
- Successfully completed all but 9 credits toward degree.

University of California at Berkeley

- Completed coursework toward a degree in Sociology.
- Transferred undergraduate credits from Pomona College.

PROBLEM #3: NO POSTSECONDARY EDUCATION

I have never attended college. What's the best way to address "Education" on my resume?

Solution: The best recommendation is to omit this section altogether—and be prepared to address it in the interview (providing examples of continuing professional education that you have completed over the years as well as a very brief indication of why you did not go to college conventionally at age 18—perhaps a tremendous work opportunity was offered to you, or perhaps financial circumstances did not permit). The key is to make no apology and, instead, demonstrate through wealth of accomplishments and success how this has not impeded your progress while still demonstrating great respect for the institution of advanced education.

PROBLEM #4: VOLUNTEER EXPERIENCE REVEALS RELIGIOUS AFFILIATION

What's the best way to talk about my work in the community with my temple? I've heard it's not always a good idea to reveal religious background.

Solution: Although there are exceptions to every rule, it is probably wise for most candidates not to mention specific religious affiliation. Instead, you can simply speak about leadership experience in a general context within the civic section of your resume (for example, "Quarterbacked fund-raising project that raised more than $300,000 for a religious organization in Dayton.").

> **CAVEAT:** If your faith is an extremely important part of your life—playing a role that helps to define your professional work—it is appropriate to specifically list actual religious affiliations. Likewise, if you make your living in a field of work that has a religious connection (for instance, a director of development for a large, faith-based organization), it is again appropriate to be specific.

PROBLEM #5: LEADERSHIP EXPERIENCE REVEALS POLITICAL AFFILIATION

I've been very active in town government for many years. How do I show this on my resume without offending someone?

Solution: Similar to Problem #4, political ties are potentially problematic. We generally advise using the generic approach: "Elected Chairman of Town Committee, Town of Binghamton, NY—4 years" (omitting whether you are a Republican or a Democrat).

> **NOTE:** The same advice as provided for problems #4 and #5 (religious and political affiliations) holds true for any memberships in what might potentially be construed as controversial organizations (for example, the NRA, Planned Parenthood, Gay & Lesbian Alliance Against Defamation, and so forth). In fact, omission of such memberships altogether is almost always recommended. In general, although it might be an important cause or group to which you belong or support, such affiliation is generally not germane to your job search and you don't want readers becoming overly hung up on such details.

PROBLEM #6: PERCEIVED JOB-HOPPING

I've moved around quite a bit. How do I deal with this on my resume so that I don't look like a job-hopper?

Solution: For the most part, your resume will show years only (and not months); therefore, if you held a position for part of a year only, it is acceptable to omit it altogether on your resume. For example:

XYGen Systems • San Diego, CA	2004–Present
Senior Vice President, Sales	
Abacus Office Products • San Diego, CA	2003–2004
Executive Vice President	
International Paper Products, Inc. • San Diego, CA	2000–2002
Vice President, Sales	

In this example, we omitted a position as Director of Sales between June 2002 and March 2003, but because months are not shown, the gap is not apparent.

PROBLEM #7: RETURNED TO PRIOR EMPLOYER

I made a career change several years ago, but ended up being recruited back to my original company. How do I show this on my resume?

Solution: If any of your jumps has been back to a prior employer, you can combine years of experience. The emphasis of the content would be on the more recent accomplishments with perhaps a cursory bullet or two included at the end of that segment to address any noteworthy accomplishments. Here's an example using the earlier template:

XYGen Systems • San Diego, CA   2004–Present; 1998–2000

Senior Vice President, Sales; Senior Sales Manager

Recruited in 2004 to rejuvenate entire national sales division…

Abacus Office Products • San Diego, CA   2003–2004

Executive Vice President

International Paper Products, Inc. • San Diego, CA   2000–2002

Vice President, Sales

PROBLEM #8: UNDEREMPLOYMENT

Following a stellar 20-year career with a Fortune 100 company, I was terminated following a takeover. Despite serious attempts to secure a similar position with another top company, I was unsuccessful after 18 months—and now am the manager of an office-supply store. How do I handle this?

Solution: Our recommendation is to be open and candid, citing every accomplishment and how you've leveraged your experience in this new opportunity. Take nothing for granted. If you put in place a new staffing model, reduced absenteeism, or boosted productivity, be sure to highlight it. There's no shame in honest, gainful employment and, following the dot-com bust, many senior-level executives were forced to take positions in commissioned sales (see problem #9) and many other fields offering significantly less compensation (essentially to cover health benefits and basic expenses—from mortgage to college tuitions for their kids) while continuing to build skills, make contacts, and find the right executive opportunity. Your cover letter will help you to address this situation effectively (cover letter development is discussed in chapter 4, "Additional ROI Documents," and augmented by more samples in chapter 6, "Gallery of Executive Career Documents").

Another approach might be to omit this position altogether, provided that does not leave too much of a gap. If you are currently a clerk at Home Depot, for example, it could be more detrimental to add this to your resume than to show a year or so of unemployment. Or, if you want to list the employment to cover all gaps, be as brief as possible instead of trying to make a truly stop-gap job into a significant career experience.

PROBLEM #9: FORCED CAREER CHANGE

I was caught in industry-wide cutbacks nearly two years ago. I was unsuccessful finding anything remotely appropriate. So I've gone into commissioned sales. This is not what I want to be doing. How do I reflect this on my resume?

Solution: As with problem #8, lead with your strengths in this role. A strategically written cover letter will best address the timeline and decisions you've made. And as much as possible, emphasize any strategic activities and company-wide contributions during this sales role.

PROBLEM #10: LONG UNEMPLOYMENT

I've been out of work for more than a year and a half. I know that putting the title 'consultant' on a resume is a quick giveaway to unemployment, but I have been doing some consulting for pay, although not full-time. What do you recommend?

Solution: Provided that it is accurate and that you have been working in some capacity as a consultant (whether for pay or not), it is fine to reflect this on your resume. It shows initiative that, while seeking a permanent post, you sought to apply significant skill and knowledge to helping other organizations build, turn around faltering performance, and so forth. Be sure to highlight key accomplishments and success stories and do mention types of industries and problem scenarios faced. The fact that this work has been part-time or unpaid is not relevant, so don't mention it.

PROBLEM #11: MAINTAINING CONFIDENTIALITY

How should I handle confidentiality when it comes to presenting proprietary numbers?

Solution: This is actually a common scenario. You might have an incredible success story to tell about turning around a division or a company, but you need numbers for credibility. The problem? The company is privately held and this information is proprietary; you can't reveal the numbers.

Consider creating a small graph to include on your resume depicting the positive direction, using actual numbers in the Excel formula (but without printing the numbers on the graph itself). You can label the graph appropriately to show several years of tracking data (presumably one year before you were in the position to change things positively) and several years of consistently increased performance since.

Here's an example:

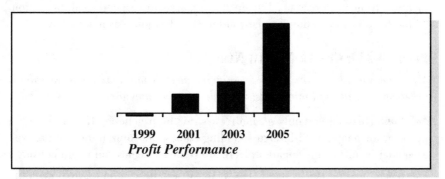

Another solution is, of course, to use percentages to reflect change and your success. Consider these examples:

- Generated 10% annual revenue growth while industry as a whole declined at least 5% per year.
- Grew market share 50%, boosting customer base through innovative product development, a pioneering customer-care hot line, and new customer support centers.

PROBLEM #12: EMPLOYMENT GAP FOR PERSONAL REASONS

The sudden death of my spouse required me to re-prioritize, resigning to handle the estate and care for our young children. Frankly, I needed some time, too, to get things clear in my head. Now, eight months later, I am ready to go back to work on a full-time basis for a new company. How do I address this?

Solution: This is best addressed in a conversation; however, for the gap on the resume, it is appropriate to address the timeline openly and honestly. It is also important to convey—especially to a recruiter—that you have worked through the grieving process (difficult, we know) and are fully ready to bring your talents and broad expertise to bear for the right organization. A very positive outlook and approach is required; despite the tragedy you've experienced, you want to demonstrate strength and not appear to be desirous of any sympathies outwardly expressed (give a simple "thank you" and move on).

For your resume, consider the following:

Short-term Full-time Parent (following death of spouse)   3/2005–11/2005

- Since 11/2005, have been actively seeking appropriate executive opportunities.
- From 3/2005–11/2005, handled family matters.

Of course, if the gap is barely noticeable, you might prefer simply to omit any mention from your resume. But do be prepared to respond to the question, "What have you been doing since you left your last job?" as noted above.

PROBLEM #13: GENDER-NEUTRAL NAME

My name is gender-neutral. This sometimes leads to confusion and awkwardness in telephone calls and interviews. What do you recommend?

Solution: This can certainly go both ways, for both genders. It can also be a problem for people with foreign-sounding names whose pronunciation as well as gender is not readily apparent. Here are some strategies you might consider:

- For names such as Tracy, Dana, and Sandy that could be used for both men and women, a common strategy is to spell out your middle name in the contact line (for example, "Dana Joseph Bisceglia").

- For names that do clearly denote gender but are sometimes confused (for instance, Frances for the female gender and Francis for the male gender), the same approach can be considered (Frances Anne Capella). If Francis prefers to be addressed as Frank, the resume contact line can read Francis "Frank" E. Donovan.

- For foreign-sounding or unusually spelled names, consider adding a nickname if appropriate (Nadezhda "Nadia" Gurov) or a phonetic equivalent (Thanh (Tom) Nguyen). If you are most comfortable with your nickname, feel free to use it in place of your given name (Tom Nguyen).

PROBLEM #14: GO BY A NICKNAME

For several decades I have used as my first name a nickname by which everyone in business knows me. There is no connection whatsoever to my given name. What's the best strategy for ensuring clarity?

Solution: For those who use a nickname in virtually all business dealings completely unrelated to their given name (for instance, Julian Hummell Knox is widely known as Bill), the contact information on the resume can read Julian "Bill" H. Knox. For the signatory line on a letter, the typed name can appear the same, Julian "Bill" H. Knox, with the penned-in signature simply saying Bill Knox.

PROBLEM #15: DEFUNCT EMPLOYER

A major company I worked with for a number of years (and produced well for) is no longer in existence. How do I handle this on my resume?

Solution: If the company was well-known, as "major" would suggest, it is not necessary to indicate that the company no longer conducts business. If responsibilities ultimately included disposing of assets, you can reflect this in a bullet point (usually one of the last points in the section on this position, possibly ending with "Company ceased operations in 2001").

PROBLEM #16: EMPLOYER HAS CHANGED NAME

A company I worked for in the past has changed its name. How should I address this?

Solution: Using the example of Steve in the chronological draft resume, he worked at Digital Equipment from the late 1970s through the mid-80s. After he had moved on in his career, Digital was acquired by Compaq—and subsequently acquired by Hewlett-Packard. With mergers and acquisitions as commonplace as they've been over the past 15 or so years, this is quite typical. Using the Digital example, but presuming it reflects more current history that will be detailed, we suggest the following:

DIGITAL EQUIPMENT CORPORATION (subsequently Compaq, now Hewlett-Packard)

Waltham, MA   1979–1987

Field Service Branch Manager *(1981–87)*

Field Service Unit Manager *(1979–81)*

In actuality, because this does reflect dated work history, this section of Steve's resume will ultimately be abbreviated to a summary paragraph, and this multi-company-name history is briefly explained:

- **Additional Professional Background** includes previous management and engineering positions in the high-technology manufacturing field (mainframes and PCs) working for Digital Equipment Corporation (subsequently Compaq, now Hewlett-Packard) and Wang Laboratories (has since ceased operations).

FINAL THOUGHTS ON YOUR RESUME CONTENT: BIG-PICTURE STRATEGIES

No matter what your specific circumstances or unique challenges, when preparing your resume, keep in mind these critical points; they will help you to make good decisions about how (or whether) to position specific items within your document.

- Your resume is a marketing piece, *not* an autobiography. Your objective is to entice the reader into calling you for more information (an interview), not to share every detail about your career.

- Your resume must clearly communicate your career focus and paint a strong, compelling picture of a top-flight executive. Omit or downplay information that does not support current objectives or might create a negative first impression.

- Your resume must convey your value in the career marketplace—the ROI you have delivered to past employers and the value you promise to your future employer. When deciding what information to include, always choose value-packed statements and quantified results over less-relevant details or generic "job duties" that could be written by anyone else who has held similar jobs.

- Your resume must resonate with your executive brand and your "authentic self." All of the material in the resume must be congruent, and you must be able to support the resume with relevant stories, examples, and amplifications at every stage of your job search.

POLISHING YOUR DRAFT

Now that you've drafted the content of your resume, it's time to review, edit, proofread, and polish it into a top-quality document.

Proofread for Accuracy

Resumes have certainly evolved from the dry CV format of several decades ago, but one thing that hasn't changed is the need for your resume to be error-free. Repeated proofreading and fact-checking is the only way to ensure that your resume contains no mistakes. Have a trusted friend or two read it critically and "red-pen" any questions or errors they see. As you review your bullet points, think about how you would expand on each briefly stated accomplishment. Are all the numbers and results accurate and consistent with the stories you'll tell?

Check for Readability

Next, assess your resume for readability. Consider font size (neither too large nor too small), white space, and overall appearance of each page. The resume should look professional and be appropriately formatted for an executive appearance. There are no hard-and-fast rules about format, but the examples in chapter 6 will give you some good ideas. (Keep in mind, these have been reduced in size to fit the format of this book.) Most executive resumes will fit nicely on two or three pages.

Unless you are a word-processing whiz, we don't recommend that you get too fancy with your document. Use a clean format, readable font, adequate spacing, and appropriate highlights (bold, italic, underlines, and so forth) so that your resume is attractive, presents key facts in a quick skim, and is inviting to read.

Distribute Your Resume Effectively

In most cases, you will be e-mailing your resume to network contacts and in response to ads. For these purposes you will need a Microsoft Word document, which will be the most useful format throughout your search. You should also print your resume (as needed) on high-quality paper in an "executive" color (white, off-white, ivory, or gray). Use the same paper for your cover letters and all of your career marketing documents. We love Crane's stationery (www.crane.com), but there are many excellent papers that will create the right appearance for your documents. Visit the stationery/resume paper section of your local office-supply store and choose the one that you like best.

The final format that you will possibly need is a text-only file that might be required for online recruiter databases. Use the "save-as" editing feature in Word to create a "plain text" document (.txt file extension); you'll find that this strips out all formatting and creates an unattractive but highly machine-readable document.

YOUR RESUME IS JUST THE BEGINNING

So, you've completed your resume—the traditional document for career transition. Following our guidelines, you've created a value-packed, fairly concise summary of your career experiences and achievements. You'll find this to be a truly essential document for many of your activities during the weeks and months of your job search.

In the next chapter, we share strategies and examples of additional career documents that, combined with your resume, will give you a true competitive edge in your executive search.

Chapter 4

Additional ROI Documents

"Don't be afraid to take a big step if one is indicated. You can't cross a chasm in two small jumps."

–David Lloyd George

There's no question that the executive resume is the foundation of your career-search plan. However, you'll want to give careful consideration to some additional tools. Several may prove to be absolutely necessary. Others, although optional, are capable of providing significant leverage in your search.

Here are the recommended add-on tools senior-level executives find most useful:

- Cover letters (traditional and abbreviated)
- E-mail messages and transmittal covers
- "Elevator" speeches
- Networking scripts
- Critical Leadership Initiatives documents
- One-page networking/abbreviated resumes
- Targeted search summaries
- Business cards
- Professional biographies

We explore each of these in detail, provide examples, and project the ROI you can expect from the use of each in your search.

COVER LETTERS

Almost no search can be conducted effectively without a cover
letter. Quite simply, you need to

ROI value: ✶✶✶✶
Recommended for: All executives

send a letter or note that explains why you are sending a resume. Thus, every
executive will use a variety of cover letters, depending on the circumstances:
who you're writing to and why you're writing.

Optimally, a cover letter is uniquely created for each opportunity. Practically
speaking, provided that your search is for similar positions in the same industry, a well-developed cover letter should serve you well for most communications, with just minor revisions to customize it for each position. We recommend
that you write one, two, or a handful of cover letters to meet a variety of needs
(discussed later in this section) and then use those as templates for each subsequent letter you write.

Cover letters should also be written specifically to their intended audience. Typical examples include the following:

- To a hiring authority with a particular opportunity in mind
- To a hiring authority where availability of an opening is not known
- To a recruiter for a specific opportunity
- To a recruiter to establish contact
- To a networking contact

Traditional Cover Letters

Generally speaking, a cover letter should be one page in length. Exceptions
include the following:

- **Letters being sent only via e-mail where length is not apparent.** Although
  we recommend your e-mail letters be especially crisp and immediately
  attention-getting, at times a lengthier letter is more beneficial. In these
  instances, we recommend that you keep your letter to no more than
  two printed pages.
- **Cover letters that serve as proposals.** In these cases, you will be
  spelling out salient details of your specific recommendations and their
  ROI. A two-page proposal letter—or even longer—is perfectly acceptable.

At a minimum, a cover letter should include the following components:

1. **Opening paragraph:** Your reason for writing, referral or source, and a
   clear link to the opportunity.

2. **Middle paragraph(s):** The strongest section of your letter, clearly demonstrating fit to the opportunity at hand and including a solid presentation of attributes that match the desired traits and key distinguishing characteristics.

3. **A compelling closing paragraph:** Including the classic "call to action," spelling out steps you'll take next, and providing important contact instructions.

Beyond the essentials, consider these additional features and strategies that can add impact, depth, and meaning to your cover letters:

- **Performance highlights:** Usually in bullet-point format, presenting three to five concise achievements, areas of core competency, and key strengths, all corresponding with identified needs of the position and company.

- **Third-party endorsements, literal quotes from exemplary letters, reviews, media articles, and so forth,** that bolster your executive image. You might include one or more quotes at the top of the letter, as a footer, or offset and indented within the body of your letter.

- **A T-format:** An overt alignment of hiring needs/challenges on one side compared to candidate strengths and experiences directly opposite. Although this is not our preferred format (it tends to invite apples-to-apples comparisons, and you must be an "11" on a 10-point scale to stand out), it does invite easy skimming, and it is fairly easy to construct this type of letter quickly.

STAR Strategy: Don't Give Up the Advantage by Sharing Compensation Information

Although it is acceptable to provide a target range to recruiters to place you in the ballpark of appropriate opportunities, we recommend that you not mention salary at all in cover letters to hiring authorities, even if your salary history is requested in an online or classified advertisement. Reserve discussion until you've created desire, demonstrated your value proposition, and can negotiate from a position of strength—face-to-face.

Our many years of research and experience tell us that, almost universally, hiring authorities read your resume anyway and will call you for an interview if your qualifications are a match, even if you haven't provided the salary data they requested.

Other cover letter suggestions:

- For both recruiters and hiring authorities, it does make sense to mention your situation with regard to relocation. If you are able to relocate without hindrance, say so.

- If you are targeting specific geographic regions—nationally or abroad—indicate this as well, particularly when contacting recruiters.

The primary purpose of the cover letter is to create interest and excitement about your candidacy. It is designed to elicit sufficient interest in the potential value you bring to motivate the reader to move on to your resume. The ultimate goal? You want the reader to initiate contact by e-mail or telephone so that the real discussions can begin.

STAR Strategy: Get to the Point

In the following examples of cover letters and additional career documents, you will see language and strategies that worked for specific individuals given their unique circumstances. Some letters are long; some are very short indeed; and others fall somewhere in the middle. The key factor is not the length of the document, but the content and overall presentation.

When crafting your own documents, think first, "What information can I share that will make the reader want to talk to me?" Don't burden readers with your entire life story (they really don't care). Give them compelling information that supports your executive brand and your current career targets. In these documents, just as in your executive resume, it's all about demonstrated expertise, proven capabilities, and results.

Figures 4.1 through 4.4 are examples of executive cover letters written for a variety of situations.

Dear Mr. Martinez:

I am very interested in being considered as a candidate for the position of Chief Financial Officer for which you are currently recruiting, as sourced through ExecuNet. I am a well-qualified senior business manager with background as a CFO for a plastics manufacturer. My track record of performance is characterized by successful turnarounds, development of strong organizations in a number of fields, effective management of capital projects, and well-diversified financial planning and administrative management experience. I believe my background provides a unique match with the qualifications your client is seeking in the selected candidate.

Throughout my career in finance, I have effectively managed all aspects of finance, from capital projects, audit, and treasury to forecasting, analysis, budgeting, cost accounting, and restructuring debt. In addition, in several of my positions at IBM as well as with U.S. Datacorps, I had oversight responsibility for facilities planning, acquisition, construction, retrofit, and compliance. I have extensive experience handling and managing all accounting functions, from general ledger, A/P, and A/R to financial forecasting, reporting, audit, inventory control, and complete financial sales support as well as union experience. I have successfully planned and managed several financial system conversions throughout my career.

With more than 20 years of successful, senior-level finance and administration management background as well as direct, hands-on experience, I have established and significantly achieved key growth and operational control measures for every organization with which I've been associated. My managerial style is effective and I empower those reporting to me by example. I utilize strong business principles and ethics in establishing clear objectives for my areas of organizational responsibility; I hold everyone's performance, including my own, to the highest levels of accountability. I believe in a business philosophy that embraces an emphasis on doing all of the basics expertly. I have always aspired to exceed the expectations of "the customers" as well as the stakeholders. My professional experience is complemented by both a Bachelor's degree in Accounting and an MBA.

I would value the opportunity to speak with you after you have had an opportunity to review my background and qualifications. I am confident of my ability to make a significant contribution as a member of your client's senior management team, and I look forward to speaking with you. Thank you for your consideration.

Sincerely,

Robert DeStefano

Figure 4.1: Cover letter to a recruiter for a specific opportunity.

Dear Mr. Howard:

Transforming "good" to "great" operations is my passion, and my career record provides evidence of my ability to cut costs, improve customer satisfaction, and increase productivity—all while boosting staff morale and building a dedicated, high-performance workforce.

If your company has a need for a senior operations executive, I can deliver results like these for you:

- Challenged to build a new national service organization for GE Capital, I quickly identified a more cost-effective and more efficient operating structure. I then led a virtually flawless effort that delivered superior service to our most important customers.

- As Zone Operations Manager for an 8-state region, I led my team to best-in-the-nation performance in expense control and customer satisfaction.

- Twice assigned to lead underperforming service regions, I achieved rapid turnaround and was recognized among the top 10% of GE employees worldwide.

In brief, I am an accomplished operations executive with a drive for *continuous* improvement. I quickly assess the current state of the organization and put in place the programs and initiatives that deliver measurable improvements, even within mature industries and organizations.

My methodologies are based on world-class GE management training (I was selected for the company's prestigious Manager Development course and also completed its core Six Sigma training), U.S. Army leadership experience, and a solid foundation in business/financial analysis that enables me to drill down to root causes and carefully measure performance in all areas.

The enclosed resume provides additional details of my qualifications and evidence of my success in diverse assignments. I am eager for new professional challenges and would like to discuss your current needs and the value that I offer to your organization. Thank you for your consideration.

Sincerely,

Leslie P. Simpson

Figure 4.2: Cover letter to a hiring authority without knowledge of a specific opening.

Dear Ms. Allen:

With regard to your current need for a VP—Sales and Marketing, I have the industry expertise and proven track record you are looking for.

During my 13-year career in sales and marketing of new residential construction, I have consistently exceeded goals and delivered results in the most challenging circumstances:

- Turned around a sales team 60% below goal to 200% above goal in less than 2 years.
- Redesigned and repositioned home communities that were lagging behind the competition—creating top sellers at price points 30% or more above comparable homes.
- In less than a year, rose to the #1 sales producer for a thriving builder/developer of single-family homes.

In short, I know how to design, brand, position, and sell residential communities; lead a sales team to top performance; and improve sales processes to achieve operational efficiencies that not only help the bottom line but enable us to complete more transactions than ever before.

My enclosed resume provides additional details of my experience, qualifications, and track record. I would like to speak with you about your current sales and marketing challenges and how I can help you meet and exceed aggressive goals for growth of the business.

Sincerely,

Joan K. Chow

Figure 4.3: Cover letter to a hiring authority for a specific opening.

Dear Jill:

I seek your advice and assistance.

As you know, for the last three years I have led Jupiter Networks to unprecedented success, with record growth in revenues, earnings, new accounts, and membership. Much of this success is due to my deep knowledge of national accounts—how to win the business and manage key relationships to ensure customer satisfaction and retention.

Although my time at Jupiter has been professionally satisfying, a new leadership team means changes that might impact our growth in both the short and long term. I see enormous potential for our industry and am eager to continue building revenues, relationships, and success stories like these:

- Achieving 2005 revenue 106% to plan, net income 210% to plan, and—for the first time—membership above one million.

- Capturing key business from Agate. I persistently pursued the 30,000-member Nutek account, structuring a proposal that positively leveraged existing providers and growth guarantees.

- Closing 400 new small-group accounts in California, after taking ownership for a project that "couldn't be done" for the last seven years.

Jill, I know you are aware of my deep expertise in the health insurance industry with market leaders Acme, United, and Jupiter. My greatest strength is leading sales for national accounts—I know the markets and have the relationships with key players. I am a visible leader (recently elected to the Board of Directors of NAHI) and have a career-long record of achievements and contributions in our industry. In short, I am a "proven product" who can hit the ground running in a new assignment.

Knowing of your deep contacts in insurance, healthcare, and the Greater Atlanta market in general, I would appreciate your insights; and I will call you in a few days to see if we can get together for a cup of coffee. Thanks!

Best regards,

Steve Saxon

Figure 4.4: Networking cover letter.

Abbreviated Cover Letters

A short version of your cover letter is useful when networking with colleagues or when contacting recruiters or hiring authorities with whom you have already had a conversation. Because of a past conversation or relationship, you don't need to provide as much background information, and often you will want to use a more informal tone.

Frequently, you will fax or e-mail the abbreviated cover letter, but you can also print it on executive-sized stationery (also known as "Monarch," sized 7.25 inches by 10.5 inches) or on traditional 8.5 × 11 paper.

The purpose of the abbreviated letter is to reiterate key points shared in the earlier conversation, bolster points you feel you did not sufficiently emphasize, and introduce any important information you inadvertently omitted in discussion.

Figures 4.5 through 4.8 are examples of abbreviated cover letters for a variety of situations.

Jeff, I want to thank you for taking the time to meet with me next week. I appreciate your willingness to share your perspectives and insights. Let me emphasize that my purpose in asking to see you isn't to request employment. Nor do I expect you to know of an opening for me. At this point, I just need information to help me focus my job search efforts and broaden my visibility in the job market.

Please let me know what day next week would be best for you; I can meet for coffee any morning.

Figure 4.5: Abbreviated cover letter to a networking contact.

Sally, thanks so much for speaking with me today; I'm so glad Jane put us in touch! As promised, I am attaching my resume.

I understand you may not be hiring now. However, both Jane and I felt your perspective would be extremely valuable, and I'm interested in picking your brain: how you got into this line of work, what you like best, your ideas for someone with my background and skills, and what trends you see.

Would you be available for a lunch meeting next week?

Figure 4.6: Abbreviated cover letter to a networking contact.

Diane, several people have mentioned that the startup of your new division might create a need for someone who can manage a full set of financial and accounting controls. If that's true, I'd like to express my interest. If my friends are mistaken and there's no prospect for employment here, then perhaps we could go to Plan B: That is, I'd welcome the opportunity to informally network about the market for controllers and CFOs in high-tech manufacturing in this region.

My resume is attached, and I'll follow up with a phone call by Friday. Thank you.

Figure 4.7: Abbreviated cover letter to a networking contact.

Mr. Andrews, thanks for speaking with me this morning. It seems that your area of specialization is a good match with my background and expertise, and thus I value the opportunity to connect with you and submit my resume for your review and database.

The position at Worldwide seems promising, and I am eager to learn more about it. In any event, I will value your feedback and your consideration for future opportunities.

Figure 4.8: Abbreviated cover letter to a recruiter.

E-MAIL MESSAGES

Your e-mail message can, of course, be your actual cover letter or abbreviated cover letter, as dis-

ROI value: ✶✶✶✶
Recommended for: All executives

cussed in the preceding section. It might seem obvious what to say in an e-mail that accompanies your resume. However, our experience has shown that many executives, while extremely adept in their verbal transactions and highly competent in communicating electronically about business matters, tend to freeze when sending an e-mail with their all-important resume. So we'll present, for your consideration, several flavors of e-mail communications from which you may select to tailor your own electronic correspondence (see figures 4.9 through 4.11).

Subject: CEO / Carnegie Mellon

I am very interested in being considered as a candidate for the Chief Executive Officer's post with the Carnegie Mellon Institute.

I believe you will find I am uniquely qualified for this position, based on my leadership background spanning 23 years in senior-management capacities with highly respected organizations and a track record reflecting significant achievements in development and capital project management. In addition, my pursuit of global humanitarian efforts in conjunction with managing development operations; cultivating donors; and garnering community, corporate, and foundation support aligns perfectly with attributes you are seeking in the selected candidate.

You will find my cover letter and resume/addendum directly below (in plain-text format); I have additionally attached both files as Microsoft Word documents for your convenience. I would value the opportunity to speak with you about this exciting opportunity and can make myself available to be in Philadelphia or New York as appropriate. Your confidential consideration is appreciated.

Sincerely,

Samantha L. Sutton

Figure 4.9: An e-mail message for transmitting a resume to a recruiter.

Dear Ms. Owens:

As a senior-level merchandising executive in the retail industry, I have a consistent history of successful performance in category management and product marketing. My responsibilities have increased with each of the companies with which I have been associated.

The skills that have been instrumental in my success include

-- LEADERSHIP - Strong ability to communicate strategic goals to teams. I motivate teams to achieve their professional goals through training and coaching and build trust and confidence using a partnership approach.

-- CREATIVITY - Sourced product focused to customer needs. Developed successful advertising strategies. Talent in overall merchandising and presentation of product at store level.

-- FINANCIAL MANAGEMENT - Proven track record of positive financial results. Highly developed financial skills include all aspects of financial planning, OTB management, and positive gross margin results.

-- DECISION-MAKING - Gather and review all available data to make timely, proactive decisions.

-- NEGOTIATIONS - Focus on building beneficial vendor relationships. Maintain a high level of integrity and use a win/win approach to negotiation.

My background is diverse, encompassing many product categories. I have achieved success within each product group. Financial results achieved for 2005 included sales of +15.90% and gross margin dollars of +16.65%.

I would value the opportunity to discuss the position of Senior Vice President of Merchandising with you.

Sincerely,
Dominic L. Sabatino

Figure 4.10: An e-mail cover letter transmitting a resume to a hiring authority.

Dear Jim,

After more than 20 years of running operations as President at The Diamond Company, I have decided to actively (and confidentially) pursue a change in direction. I am seeking opportunities where I can turn around a faltering operation or contribute to continued growth of an existing well-run company—in the capacity of President, General Manager, or even VP/Director of Operations of a large division. As you know, manufacturing is my forte and optimizing operations utilizing lean, best-practice principles, is my approach.

I'd be interested in hearing any ideas, leads, or referrals you might have for me. I'll call you next week to see what comes to mind. I appreciate any assistance you can offer me.

Best regards,
Tim Chamberlain

Figure 4.11: An e-mail cover letter for transmitting a resume to a colleague.

"ELEVATOR" SPEECHES

Called "elevator speeches" for their ability to be delivered in the 30-second span of an elevator's

> ROI value: ★★★★
> Recommended for: All executives

ascent to a destination, these are useful introductory summaries for a number of situations:

- Business association meetings (Chamber of Commerce and the like)
- Networking events
- Exploratory "cold" phone calls
- Holiday and other social events (weddings, block parties, graduations, retirement dinners, and so forth)
- Referral and follow-up phone calls
- Impromptu "meetings" of colleagues/vendors/neighbors at community functions; kids' sporting/scouting events; at the theatre, mall, golf club, or restaurant; and other unanticipated opportunities

For the executive job seeker, the elevator speech must memorably convey with clarity, "sizzle," and speed four key elements:

- Who you are
- What you do
- What you are seeking
- Other key information that can be imparted in a few seconds

Following are some examples of elevator pitches:

"Hello. I'm John Esposito, a senior finance professional with 20 years of experience leading finance organizations of Fortune 500 companies. My specialties are in the aerospace and high-tech industries. I've earned a reputation for optimizing operations, introducing highly effective controls, and identifying and bringing to fruition complementary M&A pursuits. I'm targeting CFO opportunities presenting challenges related to growth, where my background and experience will add value and help the company achieve its goals."

"Hi, Mr. Delaney. I am a human resource vice president with expertise in leadership development, training, and team-building. My background is in product development, sales, and marketing, working with a broad range of industries. My greatest strength is my ability to establish rapport quickly with people from a wide range of backgrounds and identify talent. I am looking for VP/director opportunities working with middle-tier to large firms in human resources."

"My expertise is turning around manufacturing operations to world-class standards. Three times in the last 10 years with Columbia Manufacturing, I've taken over plants that were in danger of being closed due to low productivity, substandard quality, and high costs. In each case, in less than a year we led the company in all three areas: productivity, quality, and expense control. I'm looking for an opportunity in manufacturing to apply Lean Six Sigma methods, combined with true team-building and morale-boosting, to turn poor performers into stars. I can operate either as an employee or a hands-on consultant/interim manager."

NETWORKING SCRIPTS

For many executives, it helps to craft a networking script prior to beginning the process. Although

ROI value: ★★★★
Recommended for: All executives

these scripts are highly individual, here are some ideas to get you started.

Example networking script for a warm lead (someone you know):

"Hi, George, this is Bob Donaldson [then insert something that connects, such as "My wife and I really enjoyed spending time at the golf tournament with you and Joan," "I want to tell you again how pleased I was to read of your promotion in the XYZ Journal," ... or "Wasn't that a great game the kids played over the weekend?"].

"Listen, have I caught you at a good time? The reason for my call is that I'm beginning to explore, confidentially, senior-level operations and general management opportunities in the high-tech manufacturing sector. As I know you're aware, I've been the VP of operations for Arizona Components Company for the past 14 years ... I know, it doesn't seem possible, does it?! [pause] My strengths are building and leading lean, optimally performing manufacturing organizations; driving productivity; and positioning a company for rapid, sustained growth and market leadership. With your connections—and your sphere of influence—I knew you'd be an excellent person to share my plans with. I'm very interested in picking your brain—who you know, what contacts you have, where you think my skills might best be utilized."

Example networking script for a referral lead (someone you haven't met yet):

"Hello, Mr. Thomson [usually use full salutation]. This is Bob Donaldson. I was referred to you by Stephen Pitkin. I'm a senior-level operations manager in the manufacturing sector. I've been the vice president of a large aerospace manufacturing company in Arizona for the past 14 years. My strengths are building and leading lean, optimally performing manufacturing organizations; driving productivity; and positioning a company for rapid, sustained growth and market leadership. I am confidentially exploring senior-level operations and general management opportunities in the manufacturing sector. I understand from Stephen that you might be interested in someone with my background there at Anodized Products and that you are in a position to have other key contacts you could put me in contact with. Would you have a few minutes to meet with me?"

Continue to read, edit, and rehearse your script until it is completely natural. Be sure not to say it too fast! Just because you know it well (and you will know it very well!), remember that the listener is hearing it for the first time. Develop a nice and comfortable cadence and delivery—don't rush.

Other add-on questions and points to consider in crafting your message include the following:

- "What ideas, leads, or referrals might you have for me?"
- "Who, among your network, might be interested in someone with my leadership experience and background?"
- "What related industries can you think of, and contacts do you know, where these skills might prove valuable?"
- "I have a short list of companies I'm trying to crack. Who do you know at [name any specific target companies you've identified]?"
- "I've also been thinking about some other manufacturing areas. Who do you know in pharmaceuticals? Any key contacts at Merck? How about Lee Manufacturing? [etc.]"
- "What about people you might know outside of business? Who in your church (temple/mosque) might be able to refer me to someone in these areas? Who do you know from your health club who might know someone in these companies or industries?"

Here are two sample scripts for closing the conversation:

"You've been a great help, Tom. These leads sound very promising. I'll let you know if anything comes out of this. Listen, I'd like you to keep your eyes and ears open for me. Are you going to be in town next week? Great. I'll call you on Friday to see if you've heard anything new or thought of anything else. I really appreciate this and if I can return the favor, you can be sure I will."

"Tom, you just know so many people in this business. Would you mind if I call you once every week or two until I land the right position? You're bound to hear something on the grapevine sooner or later. If you don't have any new leads, you don't even need to take the call. I'll just leave a message and if you don't ring back, I'll know it's because you haven't heard anything. I don't want to inconvenience you."

Keep in mind that the more purposeful networking you do, the more skilled you will become. It's like anything else—with practice, you will perfect a totally natural delivery.

CRITICAL LEADERSHIP INITIATIVES DOCUMENTS

A relatively new tool in the cadre of professional search materials for executives, the Critical Leadership Initiatives document is typically one page but could be up to two pages. Most often, three to five STAR stories (see chapter 2 for in-depth assistance in creating your own) are expanded to provide a very clear indication of what results an executive is able to deliver.

ROI value: ✷✷✷
Recommended for: Executives with a vast background and an abundance of STAR stories; executives who prefer a crisp two-page resume; executives who are pursuing multiple targets (for example, both General Manager and VP Marketing) and will create an addendum of powerful stories for each target; and executives who will gain value simply from the process of formally detailing their STAR stories in ROI format

Remember, the STAR approach (Situation-Tactic-Action-Result) that you developed as part of the exercises in chapter 2 should focus on those key accomplishments in your background that are most significant, most relevant to your current goals, and ideally represent what you are most capable of achieving. Further, these should be highly indicative of what you will be able to accomplish in your next position.

You can effectively use the Critical Leadership Initiatives piece as a companion document as well as a standalone tool. The most useful ways to employ it are the following:

- As a leave-behind document following a discussion with a recruiter or meeting with a board or decision-maker. ("You might find these additional details regarding several specific accomplishments relevant in assessing my ability to make a difference in your organization.")
- As a follow-up piece to a resume already provided to a recruiter, board, or decision-maker. Use a similar transmittal message: "In addition to the information already conveyed in my resume, you may find the enclosed document that highlights several specific accomplishments relevant in assessing my candidacy."
- As a component in your complete resume/cover letter package.

In chapter 5 you will read the stories of several executives and how they used the various pieces of their career marketing package (including Critical Leadership Initiatives) during a successful search.

Figure 4.12 is an example of an effective Critical Leadership Initiatives document.

CRITICAL LEADERSHIP INITIATIVES

Change agent for corporate social responsibility within Freshfruit. As a corporate executive with extensive on-the-ground experience in global agriculture, advocated that the company adopt environmental awareness as an explicit and clear strategic objective. Tasked with leading the charge, developed a comprehensive and specific action plan putting the strategy into action. The plan was quickly accelerated as environmental awareness became a "hot button" in Central and South America.
Outcomes:
- Formal alliance with the Ecology Partners and highly successful Eco-Fruit program positioned Freshfruit as an environmentally friendly company.
- Freshfruit's corporate responsibility initiatives have become models for its industry and others.

Transitioned Wacom Wireless to customer-centric strategy. Brought on board to stem loss of business customers to aggressive competitors, built a team and led a strategic initiative to understand the competitive landscape, clearly define service value, and better track customer-related activities via a pioneering online CRM system.
Outcomes:
- "Recapture" program recaptured $1M+ annual recurring revenue and was recognized as a model program and duplicated on the residential customer side.
- Competitive assessment/reporting format became widely used throughout the company, providing the business intelligence for more preemptive and proactive strategies. Most competitors have since exited the market.

Drove innovative sourcing for Abacom in Europe. Faced with plummeting market share due to EU import restrictions, assembled cross-functional source-to-market teams to establish high-quality/low-cost product sourcing in countries with preferential access to the EU.
Outcomes:
- Achieved immediate and consistent increase in products to high-value customers from nontraditional sources.
- Strengthened local and trans-Atlantic partnerships, resulting in greater supply flexibility for business in the U.S. as well as in Europe.
- Cut distribution costs by 5%, delivering $4M straight to the bottom line.

Figure 4.12: An example of a Critical Leadership Initiatives document.

One-Page Networking/Abbreviated Resumes

An abbreviated form of your resume can serve a variety of purposes. Used during informal networking, the one-page resume presents a succinct summary of your chronological work history, educational background, and

ROI value: ✶✶
Recommended for: Executives with a three-page or longer resume; executives who will be attending frequent networking meetings or reaching out to a large number of new contacts

strongest accomplishments, usually preceded by a shortened version of the full executive profile that appears on your resume.

This tool provides a nonthreatening "read" for first-time networked contacts when a full executive resume (often three pages in length) might appear intimidating or "over the top." Of course, the one-page networking/abbreviated resume is always presented as just that—with the promise of a full resume as desired or requested.

A one-page abbreviated resume can also be an effective companion to the Critical Leadership Initiatives document, offering the reader adequate information on which to base a decision to proceed to the next phase in the candidate preselection process.

Figure 4.13 is an example of a networking resume.

Targeted Search Summaries

As discussed in chapter 1, a key component of a targeted search strategy is identifying companies that are potentially a good fit for your expertise and interests. In a Targeted Search Summary, you present these companies—by name—along with a brief summation of your qualifications.

ROI value: ✶✶
Recommended for: Executives who will be attending frequent networking events; executives who will benefit from a readily available visual reminder of their target companies

In formal networking meetings, where the entire purpose is to exchange leads and ideas, your Targeted Search Summary is a valuable tool that makes it easy for colleagues to help you. After all, it tells them who you are, what you do, and what companies you are interested in.

You will need to update your Targeted Search Summary repeatedly throughout your search as you refine your list of companies. The summary is also a useful tool to help you define and focus on those targets.

Figure 4.14 is an example of a Targeted Search Summary.

TRENT M. LOCKHART

163 Canyon Boulevard East • Oakland, CA 94601
(510) 241-8143 • cell (510) 391-4810 • trent.lockhart@tmmc.com

---

PROJECT MANAGEMENT • DATA ANALYSIS • SYSTEM INTEGRATION • HEALTHCARE MANAGEMENT

LEADERSHIP • EXPERT COMMUNICATIONS • ORGANIZATIONAL SKILLS

Highly accomplished VP/Operations Professional with a background reflecting consistent progression and achievement of objectives. Demonstrated expertise in leading effective research and analytical teams as well as project management groups complemented by strong interpersonal abilities; experience includes **insurance, healthcare/medical billing,** and **systems/IT** disciplines.

PROFESSIONAL EXPERIENCE

TRI-STATE MEDICAL MANAGEMENT COMPANY • San Francisco, CA   1992–Present
Vice President (Promotion, 2004–Present); **Director** (2002–2004)
Actuarial / Underwriting Reporting & Analysis

Promoted to serve as Vice President and manage significant projects entailing analytical expertise, new system integrations, and data integrity. Considered Subject Matter Expert in development of corporate rating codes (essential link to benefits and subscriber identification).

- Manage department comprising 1 Director, 20 Senior Analysts, and 45 Data Analysts. Provided cross-training opportunities and ensured effective overall operations of department.

- Played lead role on Tri-State's MME project, consolidating enrollment and billing systems for Washington and Oregon into California's system; identified opportunities for improved efficiencies and streamlined processing. Added value to project team for systems expertise and quality control throughout project management process.

- Quarterbacked coordination and implementation of rate adjustments for Tri-State's West Region on consistent quarterly basis; timely implementations resulted in continuity of business, policy coverage, and revenue flow.

Lead Analyst II (Promotion, 1995–2002)
Decision Support Services

Expertly maintained Northwest Regional Small Group Quoting System—taking project from concept to completion while assimilating new data.

Senior Data Analyst II/III (Promotion, 1992–1995)
Institutional Contracts & Reimbursement

Earlier Professional Background with Tri-State Medical Management includes positions as **Medicare Secondary Payor Data Analyst** (1991–1992) and as **Customer Service Representative** (1990–1991).

EDUCATION

UNIVERSITY OF CALIFORNIA AT BERKELEY
Bachelor of Science, Public Health Administration (1990)
Major: Health Systems Management

Figure 4.13: An example of a one-page networking resume.

Raymond J. Clark

rjclark@gmail.com • 617-249-3490

Background

11 years of marketing experience with technology products; 5 years in Product Management, focusing technical resources of organizations on

- creating and executing marketing plans
- driving sales channels with training and support
- addressing target markets by setting development priorities

Professional strengths:

- Open and precise communication – clearly defining expectations and then meeting or surpassing them
- Profit focus – creating marketing strategies that meet a variety of business objectives but never overlooking profitable revenue

Search Objective

Direct the development, marketing, and sales of products from initial definition through design to finished products. A perfect fit will exploit my technical background, excellent communication skills, and drive for successful commercialization of technology products and systems.

Targeted Companies

Boston / Eastern Massachusetts / Southern New Hampshire / Rhode Island

- Boston Scientific
- Boston Bioscience
- Advanta Medical Products
- Haley Microsystems
- Cranston Cryogenics
- Alliance Health Systems
- Technology startups (at least second-round funding)

Figure 4.14: An example of a Targeted Search Summary.

BUSINESS CARDS

Your business card is an essential tool for the wide variety of business meetings you'll have during

ROI value: ✶✶✶✶
Recommended for: All executives

your job search. If you are still employed, you can use your existing business card; but if you are not currently employed or expect to be leaving your job at some point during the transition, it is best to produce a card just for this purpose.

You can design and print your own business cards, if you want, using templates readily available in Microsoft Word. However, fitting a lot of information on a small card can present a design challenge, so don't hesitate to work with a designer if you are having difficulty creating a good-looking card. Also, be certain you are happy with the weight, look, and feel of the card stock you purchase to run through your printer; some brands are flimsy, others have rough edges, and some can smudge after printing.

You can avoid all of these problems by having your cards professionally printed; you'll find the cost is low (less than $50) and the design and color options are limitless. Any local print shop should be able to produce these for you. You might also check out the services available through online print sites such as Vistaprint (www.vistaprint.com). Strive for a professional, executive appearance, preferably matching the type and style to your resume and other career marketing documents.

Although small in size, the business card provides ample space to communicate more than just your name, address, and contact data. You can print on both the front and back if you like. Adding information that communicates your executive brand will make your card (and yourself) more memorable and serve almost as a mini-resume and powerful networking tool.

The card samples in figures 4.15 through 4.18 showcase a variety of styles and information, from plain-and-simple contact data to a much more marketing-oriented presentation.

THOMAS R. KNIGHT

**CHIEF EXECUTIVE OFFICER /
CHIEF OPERATIONS OFFICER**

813-338-1987
tomknight@email.com
1400 Heron Way • Tampa • FL • 33602

Figure 4.15: A basic sample business card.

Christopher D. Rawling

**SENIOR MANUFACTURING MANAGEMENT
EXECUTIVE:
OPERATIONS MANAGER / GENERAL MANAGER**

**Building and Leading Lean Manufacturing
Organizations;
Driving Productivity and Positioning for Rapid,
Sustained Growth and Market Leadership**

83 Siesta Key Boulevard • Tampa, FL 33602
(813) 315-3840 (res.) • (813) 315-9842 (fax)
(813) 842-9536 (cell) rawlingcd@comcast.net

Figure 4.16: A business card with added information.

Jorge L. Stevenson

3966 Cape Hope Road ■ Dallas, TX 75201
214.270.3870 ■ mobile: 214.399.6604 ■ stevensonjl@aol.com

**SENIOR-LEVEL HR MANAGEMENT
PROFESSIONAL**

**EXPERTISE: BENEFITS ■ OUTSOURCING ■ M&A ■
PROJECT MANAGEMENT ■ SERVICE DELIVERY**

Figure 4.17: Another business card with additional information.

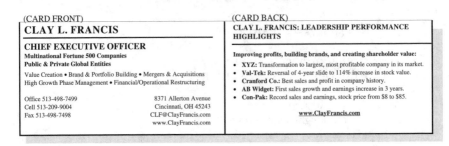

Figure 4.18: A two-sided business card.

PROFESSIONAL BIOGRAPHIES

A professional biography is a distinguishing document that can augment an executive's job search portfolio.

> ROI value: ✷✷✷
> Recommended for: All executives, particularly C-level professionals and those who aspire to board-level status

Initially, a bio can be used by a recruiter in advancing a potential candidate to a client company. The bio provides crisp narrative that will help the recruiter make an appropriate introduction or deliver a candidate description without any additional work on the recruiter's part.

As a candidate moves further into the process, the bio can work once again in candidate introductions to other decision-makers within the organization and to members of the board of directors.

Finally, at the conclusion of the hiring process, the bio can be used to develop the new executive's press release and internal communications/announcements. It is the highly professional executive who provides this document immediately prior to the start of new employment.

Separate from job search, a professional biography also serves the executive well for public-speaking opportunities, professional appearances and appointments, press releases, and so forth. Figures 4.19 through 4.21 are examples of professional bios.

An essential business partner to the Sonar Development Corporation team is its Chief Financial Officer, **Jane Allyn.** With more than 30 years of professional experience as a CPA, Jane specializes in accounting and auditing. Key disciplines of interest include tourism and retail, for which she has a wealth of background and expertise. She brings this breadth of knowledge to Sonar, advising in a number of capacities while maintaining responsibility for the company's financial information and ensuring compliance with all state and federal regulations regarding timely filings and taxation.

Jane is a Managing Partner with Allyn, Thompson, and McNamara, LLP, in Boston, a practice she co-founded in 1983. Through Jane's growth-oriented direction, Allyn, Thompson, and McNamara has expanded its scope of operations significantly, growing from two CPAs to a professional staff comprising three partners, seven CPAs, six paraprofessionals, and three administrative staff. Complementing a strong general practice is a specialty niche in tourism and mall development. Additionally, the firm operates as an instruction-oriented practice. Of note, Allyn, Thompson, and McNamara has consistently earned a "clean opinion" (highest possible ranking) in triennial peer reviews.

Prior to starting her firm, Jane gained extensive experience working for more than 10 years as a CPA with a large international accounting firm. In that capacity, she specialized in working with large hoteliers and developers throughout the Gulf Coast. Her expertise was in conducting comprehensive property evaluations and formulating recommendations regarding those properties and projects most viable from a financial standpoint. She earned her Bachelor of Science degree in Accounting from Bowdoin College and her MBA from Boston University.

Jane augments her professional work with a variety of volunteer pursuits. She serves on the Board of Directors as Treasurer of the Wellfleet Visitors' Society, is a Board member for Big Brothers/Big Sisters, and serves as a sponsor for the Young Entrepreneurs Organization.

Serving in an advisory capacity as an integral member of Sonar Development's leadership team, Jane's dual focus is ensuring that projects complement the organization's mission to produce benefits through key alliances, but also make financial sense for all participants. With a keen eye for assessing realistic value and projecting future performance results, Jane offers an insightful and pragmatic approach as the financial partner in Sonar Development Corporation's projects. Her goal is to help bring to fruition every project so that all goals are met and a maximum return is achieved for each property for the benefit of all collaborators in these strategic partnerships.

Figure 4.19: A sample biography for a Chief Financial Officer.

Stephen LaFountain is an accomplished finance management professional with more than 20 years of senior-level management experience in both municipal and corporate environments. He is currently the Assistant Superintendent of Weston Public Schools. Prior to that post, he was the Director of Finance and Information Technology for the Hartford Housing Authority.

His corporate background includes positions as Chief Financial Officer and General Manager with such companies as New Abacus Technologies, IBM, and General Electric. His responsibility has included broad financial management and operations with organizations producing annual revenues totaling more than $250 million. His expertise ranges from oversight of Finance, Human Resources, and capital budgets to effectively managing operations, developing municipal budgets, directing organizational growth, and facilitating complex negotiations (managing in both union and non-union environments). A proactive, senior-level manager, he has been recognized throughout his career for a keen business acumen, strong strategic planning and project management skills, and excellent negotiation and communication abilities.

Stephen earned his undergraduate degree in accounting from Northeastern University and his Master's degree in Business Administration from Rensselaer Polytechnic Institute. He is the President of the Greenwich Falcons Football Gridiron Club and has been an active booster member of the club for three years. He coached recreational basketball for middle school boys for seven years and was a recreational soccer coach for two years. He has served as a Project Graduation volunteer for more than 10 years.

Figure 4.20: A sample biography for a public-/private-sector manager.

Roberta Diaz has spent her career instilling best-in-class human resources practices at Fortune 500 corporations in diverse industries. As an HR executive, she partners with the executive management team to develop and implement programs that are aligned with business objectives, support the organizational mission and goals, and deliver long-term results.

Currently Diaz directs human resources for the North American division of Cray, Inc. In addition to this HR generalist role, in which she addresses key challenges of recruitment, retention, compensation, and performance measurement and improvement, Diaz also works with Cray executives and organizations on diverse initiatives that affect the global organization. Her expertise has been instrumental in establishing a performance-based culture throughout the enterprise.

At Cray, Diaz has spearheaded numerous programs related to her passion for leadership development, talent management, and executive coaching. She has been a key player in identifying high-potential employees and putting in place the programs and processes to nurture, develop, and support them. She has introduced 360 feedback and coaching, balanced-scorecard methodology, assessment tools, and a global leadership curriculum. The result at Cray has been greater bench strength as well as significant cost reduction.

Previously, Diaz advanced through three vice president positions at Mar-Cal, culminating as VP of Organization and Leadership Development for the global enterprise. Previously, she managed all HR functions for a new department providing consolidated services to discontinued and divested businesses. In that role she centralized human resources for three corporate centers and realized more than a million dollars in annual cost savings. In her first role with Mar-Cal, as VP of Human Resources for Mar-Cal Investments, she redesigned the HR function into a partnership/internal consultant model with executive management and launched a process for talent development and succession planning.

Diaz's early career was with GE, where she advanced through four human resources management roles in four years. She then served as VP of Organization Development with Toll Brothers, a leading U.S. builder with 3,500 employees.

Diaz has a BS in Business Administration and an MBA, both from the University of Michigan. She has multiple certifications related to organizational development, change management, personality type, career planning, creative leadership, and performance assessment for both individuals and organizations.

Figure 4.21: A sample biography for a human resources/development professional.

PUTTING YOUR DOCUMENTS TO USE

Throughout your search, you'll need a variety of documents to communicate with others, showcase your capabilities, and document your past successes. In preparing and sending each communication, think about the needs and interests of your audience and what will stimulate their interest in you and your professional capabilities. Be careful not to overload your readers with too much information too early in the process; instead, carefully select and present the documents that will position you appropriately at each step of the process from first contact through final job offer and acceptance. In the next chapter, you'll see how other executives have done just that.

Chapter 5

Successful Transition Stories

"Example is more forcible than precept."

–Robert Cecil

Now that we've given you the strategies, structures, and tools you'll need for your successful transition, we want to show you—in a few vivid examples—how other executives have put these ideas to work. In the following pages you'll meet five individuals who invested in the process of career development. Each spent a great deal of time in preparation and purposeful activity. In addition, each worked with a career professional to craft a resume and related documents and, in some cases, to gain ongoing guidance throughout their search.

Our vignettes will take you through the process each executive followed. You'll see that there are many similarities, yet some significant differences, in how each executive approached the process, how long it took, and where each ended up. Of course, every individual has a unique story to tell and specific challenges or circumstances that presented potential difficulties. Their stories and examples will give you ideas as you tackle the specific challenges of your own search.

Case Study #1: Thomas R. Knight (Resume Writer: Cindy Kraft)

Documents Included

- Three-page executive resume
- Two-page Critical Leadership Initiatives document
- One-page cover letter

Unique Challenges

- Supply-chain background (and strong successes) could overshadow significant experience and tilt the perception away from the CEO/COO role he was targeting.
- Target industry was very specific (large retail).

Case Study

Tom Knight left his position with ABC Retailer after 10 years, having had a major influence on the company's "5-year unprecedented growth" (as stated in his resume). He had joined the company as Senior VP of Distribution and Transportation, and then moved rapidly through a variety of supply-chain, transportation, and logistics leadership roles until he was named COO in 2000 and President/CEO in 2003.

Much of his work at ABC had involved straightening out the supply chain. He introduced major improvements and technologies to build a truly world-class supply and distribution system that led directly to significant financial improvements.

Tom was seeking a similar CEO/COO/President role with another major retailer, and he wanted to be sure his supply-chain background did not pigeon-hole him or overshadow his other successes. Thus, he peppered his resume with a variety of strong results, leading with per-store sales improvement and new store openings rather than distribution-related accomplishments.

Similarly, on his critical leadership initiatives addendum, he led with a broad growth story rather than specific supply-chain successes, although these were included later in the two-page document.

Tom's transition to a new position was spectacularly swift. The primary reason? He had high visibility in his prior role and had strategically positioned himself with the media. (Notice how he used media quotes to create strong impact in his resume and cover letter.) Thus, he was on the radar screen of other retailers and executive recruiters while he was still employed with ABC. When news of his departure became known, he was immediately contacted by several recruiters who were confident they could place him in a new position.

Tom aligned himself with recruiters who specialized in the retail industry. This was a critical strategy, in that these individuals had connections within the nation's major retailers. In addition, Tom worked his extensive network to gain behind-the-scenes knowledge of when a company might be making a change. As a result of his active networking and small cadre of specialized recruiters, Tom learned about three or four excellent opportunities and got on the early interview track.

One of these opportunities, related to him through a network contact, was as CEO of a nationwide retail portrait studio, one of the largest photography providers in North America. Tom first met with a board member about a month before the announced departure of the CEO. Tom never even gave his resume to this individual, but he did share his Critical Leadership Initiatives addendum during the meeting and left it with the board member. The storytelling format gave great insight into how Tom had handled a variety of challenges in his prior positions, and because the new company faced similar challenges, it was clearly evident that Tom's background was an excellent fit for their needs.

By the time the CEO resigned and other candidates emerged, Tom was already a prime favorite of the board, company president, and rest of the executive team. Four weeks later, after the board had interviewed several other potential CEOs, Tom was offered and accepted the position.

Time from first contact with company to offer: Two months

Total transition time: Three months

THOMAS R. KNIGHT

813-338-1987
tomknight@email.com
1400 Heron Way ▪ Tampa, FL ▪ 33602

CHIEF EXECUTIVE OFFICER / CHIEF OPERATIONS OFFICER

High-performance C-level executive with Fortune 500 experience and effectiveness in high-profile roles. Documented record of maximizing corporate performance to drive growth, generate revenues, capture market share, improve profits, and enhance value. Exceptional talent scout and mentor with the ability to create an environment of integrity in all areas of leadership.

"Loss of an Important and Highly Respected Manager: President and COO Thomas R. Knight. The resignation of Tom Knight is a meaningful loss for ABC Retailer, in our view, in light of his significant leadership role." Deborah Weinswig, Citigroup

Provided the visionary leadership that captured 33 consecutive quarters of increased earnings and over a 5-year period doubled sales from $2.75 billion to $5.28 billion, increased net income by $123 million, and opened 2,141 new stores.

PROFESSIONAL EXPERIENCE

ABC RETAILER, INC., Tampa, Florida
(Fortune 500 "extreme value retail" operating 5,900 stores with 35,000+ employees, generating annual sales of $6 billion)

Identified for leadership ability to turn around failing distribution and logistics operations suffering from distribution gridlock, lack of space, excessive delivery time frames, inventory shortages, escalating employee turnover rates, and a threat of unionization.

President and Chief Operating Officer – 2003 to 2006
Contributed to enterprise-level vision, strategy, problem-solving, and leadership with 3 executive direct reports and more than 34,000 indirect reports. Full P&L responsibility for all aspects of internal operations. *Directly involved in company's 5-year unprecedented growth, pioneered the best-in-class supply chain organization, introduced a culture of process and standardization to store organization, and led the real estate team that opened more than 2,000 new stores.*

Executive Vice President and Chief Operating Officer – 2000 to 2003
Executive Vice President Supply Chain and Real Estate – 1999 to 2000
Senior Vice President Distribution and Logistics – 1997 to 1999
Senior Vice President Distribution and Transportation – 1995 to 1997

Performance-based promotions into increasingly responsible senior-level positions. Elected to the Board of Directors in 2000. Functional areas of accountability spanned store operations, real estate, distribution, merchandise logistics, and supply chain. Drove higher in-stocks, improved store layout, enhanced merchandise mix, managed shrink, reduced delivery times, oversaw construction, and ensured compliance with company standards.

Bottom-Line Results

➤ **Drove per-store sales increases of $117,000 through improvement of store standards and processes.**

➤ **Increased annual store openings from 350 to 500 and improved first-year sales productivity from 81% chain average to 96%.**

Figure 5.1: Thomas Knight's executive resume.

➢ Reduced distribution construction time from 14 months to 8 and increased the number of facilities from 2 to 8.

➢ Raised distribution-center service levels from an average 65% to 95%.

➢ Deployed cross-dock distribution, achieving more than 40% flow-through.

➢ Negotiated $150+ million in state and local incentives across a 7-state area.

➢ Completely eliminated the union attempt.

➢ Introduced warehouse management systems and processes that boosted productivity by nearly 200%.

DISCOUNT CAR PARTS, INC., Springfield, West Virginia
(More than 1,100 retail auto parts stores in 19 states operating under the brand names of Checker Auto Parts, Schuck's Auto Supply, and Kragen Auto Parts, with $1.6 billion in annual revenue)

Senior Vice President Distribution and Logistics – 1993 to 1995
Selected to manage 3 full-line distribution centers, 4 regional cross-dock centers, domestic and international transportation functions, and product quality testing and certification. Oversaw 4 executive direct reports and 500–1,000 indirect reports. One of 4 executives reporting directly to the CEO. Held full P&L responsibility.

Bottom-Line Results

➢ Championed the creation of custom distribution software and initiated a highly automated, mechanized, paperless flow-through and batch-pick system that reduced transportation / distribution expenses from 4.2% to 3.4% of sales.

➢ Launched four regional cross-dock facilities for the top 200 SKUs, translating to 80% of the weight shipped to stores.

NATIONAL PRODUCTS COMPANY, INC., Tempe, Arizona
(National retailer generating average annual revenues of $2.3 billion)

Recruited into the company at the director level; identified for visionary leadership ability and promoted into increasingly responsible positions. **Youngest named Director, Officer, and Senior Officer in the entire company.**

Senior Vice President Distribution and Transportation – 1992 to 1993
Senior executive with P&L responsibility for 7 hard-line distribution centers, 3 defect processing centers, 3 private trucking fleets, 1 jewelry distribution center, 11 jewelry repair centers, import purchasing, outlet stores, and a $25 million mail-order division. Managed 5 direct and 1,000 indirect reports.

Vice President Transportation & Distribution – 1989 to 1992
Assistant Vice President Transportation & Distribution – 1988
Director of Transportation / Distribution Group – 1986 to 1987
Director of Logistics – 1985
Promoted 3 times in 4 years. Directed planning, warehousing, logistics, distribution, and quality control functions. Key member of executive task force redefining company's strategic approach to demand forecasting, inventory control, and cross-dock distribution. Established the company's first-ever Merchandising Logistics Department to evaluate freight terms and allowances and improve purchase-order routing.

(continued)

(continued)

THOMAS R. KNIGHT ▪ 813-338-1987 ▪ Page 3

Bottom-Line Results

➢ Captured a $1.4 million annual cost savings by closing a hard-lines distribution center in response to reduced storage needs and expanding automation processes in other centers.

➢ Pioneered cross-dock distribution methods, saving more than $1 million in costs annually.

➢ Reduced on-hand inventory by $150 million.

➢ Expanded and realigned hard-lines distribution network providing full-scale distribution for 72 stores post-acquisition, saving $6 million in freight expense.

PRIOR PROFESSIONAL EXPERIENCE

SERVICE MERCHANDISE COMPANY, INC., Nashville, Tennessee
(Fortune 500 national retail chain)

Hired as a part-time Sales Associate during college. Brought in full-time upon graduation, earning 6 promotions within 5 years.

Assistant Director of Transportation ▪ **Manager of Domestic, International, & Catalog Transportation** ▪ **Transportation Coordinator** ▪ **Fleet Equipment & Safety Manager** ▪ **Dispatcher** ▪ **Sales Associate**

EDUCATION & TRAINING

Bachelor of Business Administration
Florida State University, Tallahassee, Florida

Annual attendance at leading retail industry seminars and conferences
Numerous seminars annually, including presentations by Michael Hammer ▪ Tom Peters ▪ Steven Covey

THOMAS R. KNIGHT

813-338-1987
tomknight@email.com
1400 Heron Way ▪ Tampa, FL ▪ 33602

CRITICAL LEADERSHIP INITIATIVES

▪ **Drove unprecedented growth from 1999 to 2005, displacing Wal-Mart as Discount Retailer of the Year in 2003; cementing status of ABC Retailer as a Fortune 500 and S&P 500 company; earning recognition as one of the "Top 20 High-Performance Retailers" by** *Chain Store Age;* **and a #1 ranking on Cap Gemini's Consumer Awards.**

Approach … Expanded into the urban market; reengineered store processes; created and executed new store organizational structure; championed the use of exception-based reporting tools for loss prevention; deployed new warehouse management systems; introduced flow-through (cross-dock) distribution; pioneered Retek replenishment systems; and established Merchandise Planning, Allocation, and Replenishment departments.

Bottom Line
➢ Provided the visionary leadership that saw 33 consecutive quarters of increased earnings.
➢ Almost doubled annual sales from $2.75 billion in 1999 to $5.28 billion in 2004 with simultaneous net income increases from $140 million to $263 million.
➢ Drove the number of stores from 3,324 to 5,466 in five years, with average store sales increases from $849,000 to $966,000.

▪ **Transformed ABC Retailer's struggling distribution and transportation division.** Recruited as Senior Vice President Distribution and Transportation in August of 1995 to turn around a distribution network in shambles. Distribution centers were gridlocked and out of space; vendor deliveries were running eight weeks; fill rates were around 68%, resulting in excessive out-of-stock items in stores; employee turnover at the new Arkansas Distribution Center topped 200% annually, affecting inventory integrity; and the Teamsters were knocking on the door.

Solution … Within six weeks, leased additional warehouse space and created a second distribution network for promotional products.

Bottom Line
Within first six months,
➢ Closed down the revolving door of employee turnover.
➢ Increased fill rates from 68% to low 80s and ensured ad goods were in stock.
➢ Transformed customers' shopping experience.
➢ Spearheaded redesign of a new prototype distribution center.
➢ Began construction on a 300,000-square-foot expansion of the Arkansas distribution center.
➢ Halted the union attempt.

▪ **Reengineered antiquated distribution network and warehouse management systems into a Supply Chain organization reputed to be "best in niche" and one of the "best in retail."**

Solution … During first 18 months in office, analyzed size, shape, and velocity of all products. Selected six different methods of distribution that would provide optimal results for each type of product and developed a supporting distribution center design. Researched, selected, modified, and installed a new WMS system (Catalyst). Determined the level and types of mechanization to be used in the distribution center prototype (high-speed sorting, cross-dock systems, pick-to-light, radio-frequency scanning, aerosol and flammables processing, etc.). Finally, introduced additional technology, engineered and documented every process, and created engineered standards and rewards systems for performance against standards.

(continued)

Figure 5.2: Thomas Knight's Critical Leadership Initiatives.

(continued)

Bottom Line
➢ More than doubled productivity from 48 cartons of merchandise for each paid hour of payroll to more than 125 cartons per paid hour and improved accuracy rates from 95% to 99.85%.

▪ **Consolidated and unified processes across 5,000 individual stores to drive payroll sales productivity improvements.** Individual store operations functioned like 200 little chains, with each District Manager setting individual priorities.

Solution ... Created an engineering team to prioritize tasks based on impact to sales and payroll, reengineer each task to best methods, and roll out the new processes company-wide. Assembled focus groups of store and district managers to identify 5–10 of the most critical success factors, a precursor to the "Anytime 5" concept evangelized throughout the organization. Developed a weekly snapshot report of execution at the store, district, regional, division, and market-type level to drive store improvement efforts.

Bottom Line
➢ Drove annual payroll productivity improvements of store operations for five consecutive years.

▪ **Championed the development and implementation of new tools for recruiting, hiring, and screening and initiated company-wide management training.** Challenged to address a serious chain-wide shortage of applicants, lack of management training, excessive turnover, and poor interviewing skills by field personnel.

Solution ... Created a website with online application capability; posted openings on major job boards; included recruiter email addresses on all store material; and deployed Unicru, a comprehensive online application system. Replaced the existing policy manual with a four-course training program. Created management skills assessments to evaluate potential management candidates and establish succession planning. Initiated background checks and conducted 90-day anniversary retention interviews to halt turnover.

Bottom Line
➢ Drove applicant flow from 50 monthly electronic applications to 20,000+, populating the candidate pool with qualified candidates.
➢ Significantly reduced turnover, holding at 10% below ABC's direct competitor.

▪ **Key contributor to the executive team redefining National Products' future growth strategy.** Tasked with addressing shrink, supply chain, and distribution challenges to foster company growth.

Solution ... Collaborated with the 7-person executive team representing all functional areas of the company. Over a 6-month period, created the company's strategic approach to demand forecasting, inventory control, cross-dock distribution, and shrink. Improved fulfillment, order entry, and computer systems. Redesigned and automated the jewelry distribution center.

Bottom Line
➢ Generated an inventory reduction of $150 million.
➢ Doubled productivity in jewelry distribution, reduced turnaround time from 10 days to 48 hours, and increased accuracy to 99.9%.

THOMAS R. KNIGHT

813-338-1987
tomknight@email.com
1400 Heron Way ▪ Tampa, FL ▪ 33602

April 30, 2007

Steven L. Whitman
Whitman Partners, LLC
309 Peachtree Plaza West, Suite 447
Atlanta, GA 30316

Dear Mr. Whitman:

After a long and successful career with ABC Retailer, Inc., *where I spearheaded the 5-year growth that nearly doubled sales and net income and more than doubled shareholder equity,* I am now ready to seek new opportunities and challenges.

Perhaps you currently have a client who is in need of a **C-Level Executive** with a documented track record of dynamic and visionary leadership. My commitment to integrity, combined with excellent communication, process thinking, and problem-solving skills, translates to a documented record of creating a shared vision, building effective teams, and motivating people to go the extra mile to exceed corporate objectives.

My attached résumé and addendum detail critical leadership initiatives throughout my distinguished career. Additionally, I have…

- Leveraged the higher sales and ROI of urban stores to develop a profitable initiative being rolled out to a total of 1,200 stores by the end of September. We created a new urban organizational structure; redefined and increased support from HR, LP, and logistics; invested in payroll; focused on presentation and restocking; and implemented leading-edge technologies. *The result has been increased sales and merchandise margins and reduced shrink and turnover at the 800+ stores already converted.*

- Transformed an antiquated "storage and retrieval" approach to distribution through implementation of cross-dock technologies. *Reduced labor costs and increased yearly inventory turns from 11 to 19, saving more than $230 million in inventory investments.*

- Reengineered the real estate department and pioneered the use of statistical and computer models to accurately project new-store sales, *translating to first-year sales productivity increases from 81% to 96%.*

If you do have a client who is looking for a results-driven **Chief Operating Officer or Chief Executive Officer** to join its **Senior Management Team,** perhaps we should talk.

Thank you for your consideration. I look forward to speaking with you.

Sincerely,

Thomas R. Knight

Enclosure

Published Investment Firm reaction to my departure:

"The departure of Tom Knight is clearly a major disappointment to many investors. Mr. Knight was well-known to the Street and had been instrumental in efforts such as "anytime 5" store operating initiatives." Michael Exstein, Credit Suisse First Boston

"We are downgrading ABC to neutral from overweight given the recent management shakeup and departure of President and COO Tom Knight, which we believe will delay the company's turnaround, making it hard for the stock to outperform in the near future." Shari Swartsman Eberts, JP Morgan

"ABC also unexpectedly announced the resignation of its President and COO Tom Knight. This is a major loss in our opinion. The stock is down over 6% today and hasn't been this low since 2001." Patrick McKeever, SunTrust Robinson Humphrey

Figure 5.3: Thomas Knight's cover letter.

CASE STUDY #2: DIANA BRAYSON (RESUME WRITER: JACQUI BARRETT)

Documents Included

- Two-page resume
- Two-page Critical Leadership Initiatives
- One-page customized cover letter
- One-page executive summary
- Elevator pitch

Unique Challenges

- Delivering the right message to explain recent downsizing after just over a year on the job.
- Commensurate need for a fairly rapid transition to avoid financial hardship.
- Need for truly compelling documents to give Diana the edge for appropriate opportunities that would not require her to relocate.

Case Study

Diana was seeking a sales and marketing leadership role at midsized companies in diverse industries. Although she would relocate if no other options arose, her strong preference was to remain in the Greater Los Angeles area.

The first step was to create a powerful executive resume and a one-page "executive summary" that she could use when the resume would be too much.

Diana then collaborated with her resume writer on a four-paragraph elevator pitch that launched with this: "I help midsized companies struggling to meet their revenue and profit potential to become high-performance, high-profit, and globally competitive forces." Diana used this pitch and her executive summary during local executive networking meetings, capitalizing on one of her strengths—reaching out and interacting with others both locally and abroad. She was also good at follow-up and extremely adept at tailoring her value proposition to the identified needs of specific companies.

Moreover, Diana selectively handed out her one-page executive summary to networking associates when the opportunity arose.

Diana posted her resume to the top $100K job sites as her primary "passive" strategy, and invested most of her time on targeted search and active networking.

Within a week and a half of posting to the job banks, Diana cinched an interview for a sales management position at a midsized manufacturing organization in Seattle. With the interview at hand, she worked with her resume writer to develop a critical leadership addendum to use as a "leave-behind." The addendum incorporated a blend of sales, sales-management, and marketing-focused achievements.

An interview with a second company materialized about two weeks later, garnered through a networking contact. The position was as vice president of sales at a medical equipment manufacturer. Following a positive interview and a prompt thank-you follow-up letter, Diana quickly switched gears and prepared for yet a third company's interview, this time at a Germany-based manufacturing company.

The plot thickened as opportunity number two (with a medical equipment manufacturer) converted into a job offer. Not only were opportunities number one and three still warm, but she had two other interviews scheduled at companies number four and five. Diana used business savvy and etiquette in expressing enthusiasm for the job offer coupled with a desire to review the proposal and get back with the company at a later date, buying time to complete interview processes with the other, "live" opportunities. In the end, she declined the medical equipment manufacturer opportunity.

Fast-forward to two months later, when Diana earned an offer for a position as national sales manager for a custom bag manufacturer—compensation: $175K; location: Orange County, California. If she accepted this position, her future potential was a role as vice president, sales and marketing, as the incumbent was scheduled to retire in two years. Concurrent with this offer, Diana was offered a vice president of sales position at a $45M, very profitable manufacturer in the pharmaceutical industry—compensation: $200K; location: Los Angeles.

Diana carefully examined the pros and cons of both opportunities, determining which job most aligned with her passion, skills, long-term goals, and work-life balance and decided on the VP of sales position. She negotiated final terms of the offer and began work just three months after initiating her job search.

Time from first contact with company to offer: Two months

Total transition time: Three months

DIANA BRAYSON
Web Portfolio: www.powertalent.net/dianabrayson

12345 East Way, Los Angeles, California 91205
Home: 310.407.1111 ▪ Office: 310.407.2222
E-mail: dianabrayson@comcast.net

SENIOR-LEVEL SALES & MARKETING EXECUTIVE

Expert in leading businesses to profitable growth/diversification:

85% of business from 12 markets vs. 40% from one market .... Global Products, Inc.

38% growth (Pneumatic); 25% growth (Filter) .... DEF Corporation

25% sales jump; 27% distributor sales growth in 2 years .... Abco Technologies

118% sales boost in 2 years .... Molded Products, Inc.

High-performance leader with 15+ years of professional experience creating and executing value-based sales and marketing propositions that propel revenue/profit growth. Visionary and strategist with extreme savvy in establishing strong negotiating positions, communicating competitive value, and exploiting new business opportunities. Proven sales performer skilled at leading and motivating sales teams to success in highly competitive, global markets. An effective change agent with a high level of integrity.

Empowering people to take initiative ... Requiring personal/team accountability ... Inspiring success.

Areas of Expertise

- Strategic Business Planning/Execution
- Multichannel Marketing & Distribution
- New Business Development/Growth
- Direct/Indirect Sales Organizations
- Pricing Strategies & Structures

- Competitive Market Intelligence
- Recruiting Superior Talent
- Turnaround Reorganization
- Distribution Management
- Performance Metrics

- Financial/P&L Management
- New Product Development
- Diverse OEM Experience
- Employee Development
- Performance Improvement

EXECUTIVE PERFORMANCE OVERVIEW

GLOBAL PRODUCTS, INC., Los Angeles, California (www.gciproducts.com)   2004 to Present
$400M diversified industrial manufacturer and subsidiary of Global Corp., Inc.; NYSE: GCI.

VICE PRESIDENT OF SALES & MARKETING – MEDICAL PRODUCTS DIVISION

Commenced role in VP position, circumventing a 6-month Director position based on compelling leadership strengths outweighing those of then-VP. Immediately challenged to turn around a marginally performing sales organization charged with negotiating large, multiyear, multimillion-dollar contracts and champion a "customer first" cultural change. Oversee all marketing initiatives: product requirements, position, segmentation, pricing, and communications. Optimize current products and launch new ones.

Sales Organization Reengineering/New Business Development & Profit Growth

- **Imposed accountability** on field sales representatives, spurring a more-proactive, performance-driven organization, aligning **value proposition**/solutions-selling methodology with manufacturing/customer support.
- **Captured more than $10M** in new, annualized **business opportunity.**
- **Generated $3.6M in new business** revenues in 3 months, offsetting loss of single, $2.5M customer.
- **Landed $3M in new medical sales** revenues via European sales agent sign-on after rolling out international market strategy.
- **Boosted profit 15%,** orchestrating domestic competitive sales advantage by developing comprehensive global supply chain.

REVCOR PRODUCTS, Campbell, California (www.revcorproducts.com)   1999 to 2004
Custom manufacturer of pneumatic actuators for automation applications to diverse industrial markets.

NATIONAL SALES MANAGER/MARKETING MANAGER – NORTH AMERICA

Reporting directly to General Manager, led cross-functional team: Regional Sales Manager; 50-distributor network; and a combined total of 10+ Application Engineers, Customer Service Representatives, and Marketing Coordinators. Met challenge to retool an unskilled, unpolished, and deficiently trained sales force. Instrumental member of new product development team performing market analysis and originating marketing materials/forecasts/promotions.

Sales Channel Transformation/Revenue & Profit Growth

- **Effected a dramatic reallocation** of distributor channels that had been drawing 40% of revenue from a single market. After reallocation, generated 85% of total business from 12 unique markets.
- **Selected/recruited the best talent,** developed skills via joint sales calls/training, and clarified vision and priorities.
- **Generated $1.2M in sales in 6 months** and captured 69 new OEM customers in 11 industries by improving sales strategies and developing and instituting technical sales and product training programs for domestic and international distributors.
- **Drove $2.9M in 2 years;** vaulted gross margin 18.2% in last 2 years; cut SG&A expenses by 9.7%.

Figure 5.4: Diana Brayson's executive resume.

Diana Brayson   Home: 301.407.1111 Office: 301.407.2222   Page Two

- **Influenced 22.6% in new customer bookings,** meeting corporate growth objectives by redefining "quality" new business targets and then charging Regional Sales Managers to jointly create sales development/penetration strategies. Instituted performance tracking/accountability measures. Projected long-term impact: **30% to 35% incremental increases** in bookings.

DEF CORPORATION, Phoenix, Arizona (www.def.com)   1995 to 1999
World's leading diversified manufacturer of motion and control technologies and systems.
BUSINESS DEVELOPMENT MANAGER, Automation Group – Pneumatic Division (1996 to 1999)
Promoted to direct a 6-person sales team and their distribution network (total field sales organization equaled 65+). Inherited and then successfully influenced tenured group of Territory Managers in a paradigm shift to stimulate business growth. Contributed to 4-person team driving major new product developments/introductions.

Double-Digit Business Growth/New Product Introductions
- **Hoisted business 38%** (from $8.3M to $11.5M) and yielded **20% profit increase.**
- **Keys to business growth:** Overhauled dated strategic/tactical selling practices via 5-point program: 1. Sales Management Initiatives; 2. Tactical Execution Strategies; 3. Quarterly Distributor Performance Reviews; 4. Target Account Program Management; and 5. Analyzing Industrial Distribution Model for Channel Development/Distribution Management.
- **Increased distributor sales $842K** across all product lines by launching new target account program.
- **Drove sales of $1.5M in 3 years** via 4 new product-line recommendations, 3 of which garnered new OEM clients.
- **Acquired $440K** in less than 1 year by recruiting/training 2 new distributors. Generated $200K via 2 private-label accounts.

REGIONAL SALES MANAGER, Filtration Group – Finite Filter Division (1995 to 1996)
Managed distribution network and select OEM accounts for $8M division across 13 states. Provided technical product and field sales training for instrumentation and fluid power distributor sales staff.
- **Ignited sales 25% in 12 months (103% to plan vs. 71% prior year)** in largest region in the division.
- **Keys to sales growth:** Formed/instituted strategic plan, pinpointed business opportunities, and prioritized/managed results-focused time line. Inspired distributor sales teams through management, team building, and training, **boosting sales 20%.**
- **Spurred sales from $1.6M to $2M** with 45% profit margin by landing new OEM business.

ABCO TECHNOLOGIES, Louisville, Kentucky (www.abcotechnologies.com)   1993 to 1995
One of the world's leaders in supply of motion and fluid control technologies for diverse industry sectors.
DISTRICT MANAGER
- **Grew regional sales 12%+** (from $7.5M to $8.4M+) and distributor sales 27% in 2 years.
- **Landed $180K in new** actuator **business** by converting major private-label customer. Managed 2 $1M+ private-label accounts.

MOLDED PRODUCTS, INC., Louisville, Kentucky   1991 to 1993
Leading producer of engineered seals and molded products.
AREA MANAGER
- **Doubled sales** from $1.1M to $2.4M in 2 years.
- **Awarded $248K** governmental sole-source supplier contract after building cost-containment solution.
- **Ranked #1** of 20 area managers.

MAJOR TIRES, Boise, Idaho (www.majortires.com)   1987 to 1991
Manufacturer of tires, engineered rubber products, and chemicals in 80+ facilities across 28 countries.
REGIONAL ACCOUNT EXECUTIVE, Engineered Products Division
- **Catapulted region** from #7 to #2 Ranking in 18 months.
- **Grew sales 79%** (from $3.9M to $7M) in 3 years by cementing relationships/negotiating long-term contracts.
- **Boosted** existing OEM **sales volume $1M** and generated $590K in new sales.

EDUCATION AND DEVELOPMENT

BS, Marketing Management, Purdue University, West Lafayette, Indiana
Management Development Course (MBA Equivalent), Fortune 500 Corporate Management Programs & American Management Association

DIANA BRAYSON

Web Portfolio: www.powertalent.net/dianabrayson

12345 East Way, Los Angeles, California 91205
Home: 310.407.1111 ▪ Office: 310.407.2222
E-mail: dianabrayson@comcast.net

RESUME ADDENDUM ▪ CRITICAL LEADERSHIP INITIATIVES

Widened sales reach domestically and globally to secure multimillion-dollar revenue results.

As Vice President of Sales and Marketing, Global Products, challenged to exploit domestic medical industry sales opportunities and forge a European medical market presence. Orchestrated new product line roll-out (fine wire products), engaged in targeted trade shows, produced sales materials and technical / white paper presentations, and mentored product manager on sales, product training, sales representative development, and contract negotiations. Executed international market strategy.

Results   Captured $1.2M domestic revenues from 14 new customers in 8 months, representing a broad product portfolio (biopsy forceps, guide wires, catheters, surgical staples, dental instruments, and inoculation needles). Secured $3M globally in new medical sales via European sales agent sign-on.

Strengths   *Possessing a global / strategic mind-set, I clearly comprehend how to create, communicate, and capture value in varying customer requirements and have the ability to pass these skills on to sales team members.*

Kindled sales group to drive $10M+ new opportunity and surmount key customer loss with 144% of prior revenues.

As Vice President of Sales and Marketing, Global Products, recruited to rejuvenate an unfocused national sales organization to generate both climbing sales and profitability. Ignited and diversified a well-balanced sales organization via reorganization and leadership initiatives – training and institution of a relentless "customer first" culture as keystone to business success.

Results   Cultivated a focused sales team (Regional Sales Managers and Manufacturers Representatives) that consummated $10M+ in new, annualized business opportunity. Generated $3.6M in new business revenues in 3 months that offset loss of single $2.5M customer.

Strengths   *I am a sales hit man. I can be dropped into situations and add instant credibility through my professionalism and command of the market, products, and technologies.*

Dissected broad promotional directive and created manageable action steps that spurred double-digit profits.

As National Sales Manager / Marketing Manager, Revcor Products, challenged to ramp up sales promotion materials within 300-person distributor field sales organization to bolster sales-call effectiveness. Collaborated with corporate marketing department to devise illustrative materials communicating client challenges and victories related to custom actuator products.

Results   Developed cost-effective promotional method (using easily distributable PDF file) that described product / prototype development and testing efforts, for allocation to design engineers at the customer level. Exemplified Revcor's niche position and custom service and realized abilities to generate 30%+ margins.

Strengths   *My ability to think outside the box and tap into creative juices and my skill at communicating our value propositions into very specific applications are appreciated by the sales team and clients.*

Broke through perceived economic barriers by innovating offerings, promoting value-add, and garnering sales.

As National Sales Manager / Marketing Manager, Revcor Products, challenged to liberate custom-engineered product (metal-fabrication) sales despite a declining manufacturing economy. Originated and launched nationwide direct-mail campaign targeting design / development engineers within wide distributor network client base.

Results   Transcended multiple industries and markets by stimulating multiple new / current clients, vaulting potential targeted business opportunities to $5.2M.

Strengths   *I drive an organization forward through action, creating new products and services, building skills, generating momentum, and selling value-add that increases perceived value of products and services.*

-CONTINUED-

Figure 5.5: Diana Brayson's Critical Leadership Initiatives.

Diana Brayson	Home: 310.407.1111	Office: 310.407.2222	Page Two

Refocused marketplace penetration across a broader, more diversified audience.

As National Sales Manager / Marketing Manager, Revcor Products, challenged to stabilize business structure that saw 40% of overall revenues emanate from a single industry. Revolutionized the business model—dramatic reallocation of distributor sales channel focus, accountability / strategic directional requirements, and training for distributor sales managers—to stimulate customer-base growth, market penetration, and profitability.

Results   Snagged $2.9M new business in 2 years, boosted gross margin 18.2% in last 2 years, and curbed SG&A expenses 9.7% after reallocation that bred 85% of total business from 12 markets. Further influenced 22% in new customer bookings with projected long-term impact of 30% to 35% incremental booking increases.

Strengths   *I see where the true opportunities lie, both at present and in the future. With this information, I make subtle course selections that have a great impact on the bottom line.*

Outperformed competition by executing competitive market intelligence and driving new-product development.

As National Sales Manager / Marketing Manager, Revcor Products, challenged to pinpoint and develop customizable products for niche markets that were adaptable to diverse automation applications. Spearheaded national Distributor Representative Council to amass competitive market intelligence from which to determine potential product developments.

Results   Originated twin-bore actuator that fulfilled both standard automation and custom modification requirements and outperformed largest offshore competitor. Projected revenues of $8M to $10M over next 3 years.

Strengths   *Because of my innovation and foresight, I am compelled to mine the wealth of market intelligence from within any organization for which I work, allowing even very lean marketing staffs to function as larger entities.*

Influenced turnaround of underperforming group of territory managers, stimulating sales among business partners.

As Business Development Manager, Pneumatic Division, DEF Corporation, challenged with change effort involving paradigm shift across long-term, complacent territory sales managers to fuel business expansion among distributor business partners. Key initiatives included revamp of dated, strategic / tactical selling practices involving sales management, tactical execution, performance reviews, account management programs, and industrial distribution model analysis.

Results   Revenues climbed $1.3M and product sales increased $1.5M (Northeast Region) after buy-in by distributors and sales teams.

Strengths   *I possess strong credentials in engineered / custom product sales to OEM and end-user customers, both direct and through distribution. I am quick to meet the demands of change, open to new ideas, and constantly seeking ways to speed the process of completing a job.*

Captured double-digit sales increase in company's largest region, nationwide.

As Regional Sales Manager, Filtration Group, DEF Corporation, charged with spurring sales and managing distribution network / select OEM customers. Fortified customer relationships (current and new) among engineering and procurement and pioneered workshop methodology to exploit distributor field sales knowledge for product presentations.

Results   Vaulted sales 25% in 12 months in nation's largest region and inspired distributor sales teams—via management, team building, and training—to drive a 20% sales increase.

Strengths   *My influence skills, inducing customer behavior change, are well tuned, as are my abilities in reengineering a marginally performing sales organization—veterans and rookies. My frankness and integrity are much appreciated and facilitate the development of trust.*

Reversed sales slump and boosted market share, hammering out long-term, multimillion-dollar contracts.

As Regional Account Executive, Major Tires, Engineered Products Division, charged with halting 3-year run of flat sales by expanding customer base and hoisting sales in the Northeast Region. Deepened relationships in major accounts and with potential clients; orchestrated solutions to customer needs (fitting technical / design capabilities with application needs); squarely faced competitor presence; and ultimately secured long-term contracts.

Results   Consummated multiyear, multimillion-dollar contracts, growing sales 79% in 3 years. Spawned $590K in new OEM sales and boosted sales volume $1M via existing OEM customers.

Strengths   *I create competitive value, identify and exploit business opportunities, and build market share by leveraging my proven technical sales abilities.*

DIANA BRAYSON
Web Portfolio: www.powertalent.net/dianabrayson

12345 East Way, Los Angeles, California 91205
Home: 310.407.1111 ■ Office: 310.407.2222
E-mail: dianabrayson@comcast.net

April 30, 2007

Elaine P. Rhodes
Executive Vice President
Olympia Products, Inc.
Seattle, WA 98130

Dear Ms. Rhodes:

Are you looking for a profit-oriented sales and marketing executive dedicated to market dominance and who demonstrates this commitment through aggressive strategic planning, dynamic leadership that transforms underperformers into overachievers, and high-impact communication skills that articulate a company's competitive value? If so, we have good reason to meet, as I can make a significant contribution to Olympia Products.

When Global Products—currently on the auction block and fraught with challenges—wanted to lead a revenue performance turnaround, paradigm shift to a performance-driven mind-set at the field sales level, and develop a comprehensive global supply chain, they came to me. Squarely facing those challenges, I captured over $10M in new, annualized business opportunity, underscoring my abilities in aggressive strategic sales planning.

Let me highlight some of the achievements that reflect the quality and caliber of my professional career, as well as bottom-line contributions I have made:

- *Sales and Profit Performance:* Spurred double-digit sales and profit growth year upon year, including the gripping turnaround of a distributor channel network that stabilized marketplace opportunities across 12 unique markets (Revcor Products) and the radical business growth (38%) at DEF Corporation resulting from the overhaul of a 5-point sales strategy.
- *Talent Recruitment, Motivation, and Mentoring:* Harnessed latent talent to reignite sales productivity and recruited, trained, and motivated new sales professionals, cementing sales skills via joint sales calls and clarification of vision and priorities.
- *OEM and Distributor Sales:* Boosted OEM sales via new product-line recommendations (DEF Corporation) and expanded OEM customer base by 69 new customers (Revcor Products). Rocketed distributor sales over $800K (DEF Corporation) and 27% (Abco Technologies).
- *Cross-Functional Leadership:* Reporting to top management, led cross-functional teams (regional sales management, distributor networks, application engineers, customer service professionals and marketing staff) and worked collaboratively across key departmental management to fulfill customer requirements and manage market trend fluctuations.

I am confident that I can make an immediate impact on your bottom line based on my extremely successful record of profitable business development, and I look forward to discussing my capabilities in more detail. I will call within a few days to schedule a meeting at your convenience. Thank you for your time and consideration. I look forward to speaking with you soon.

Sincerely,

Diana Brayson

Enclosure

Figure 5.6: Diana Brayson's cover letter.

DIANA BRAYSON

Web Portfolio: www.powertalent.net/dianabrayson

12345 East Way, Los Angeles, California 91205
Home: 310.407.1111 ▪ Office: 310.407.2222
E-mail: dianabrayson@comcast.net

SENIOR-LEVEL SALES & MARKETING EXECUTIVE

Expert in leading businesses to profitable growth/diversification:

85% of business from 12 markets vs. 40% from one market...Global Products, Inc.

38% growth (Pneumatic); 25% growth (Filter) .... DEF Corporation

25% sales jump; 27% distributor sales growth in 2 years ....Abco Technologies

118% sales boost in 2 years ....Molded Products, Inc.

High-performance leader with 15+ years of professional experience creating and executing value-based sales and marketing propositions that propel revenue/profit growth. Visionary and strategist with extreme savvy in establishing strong negotiating positions, communicating competitive value, and exploiting new business opportunities. Proven sales performer skilled at leading and motivating sales teams to success in highly competitive, global markets. An effective change agent with a high level of integrity.

- Strategic Business Planning / Execution
- Multichannel Marketing & Distribution
- New Business Development / Growth
- Direct / Indirect Sales Organizations
- Pricing Strategies & Structures

- Competitive Market Intelligence
- Recruiting Superior Talent
- Turnaround Reorganization
- Distribution Management
- Performance Metrics

- Financial / P&L Management
- New Product Development
- Diverse OEM Experience
- Employee Development
- Performance Improvement

EXECUTIVE PERFORMANCE OVERVIEW

■ GLOBAL PRODUCTS, INC., Los Angeles, California (www.gciproducts.com) — 2004 to Present
VICE PRESIDENT OF SALES & MARKETING – MEDICAL PRODUCTS DIVISION
Challenged to turn around marginally performing sales organization charged with negotiating large, multiyear, multimillion-dollar contracts and champion a "customer first" cultural change. Oversee marketing efforts: product requirements, position, segmentation, pricing, and communications. Captured $10M+ in annualized business opportunity.

■ REVCOR PRODUCTS, Campbell, California (www.revcorproducts.com) — 1999 to 2004
NATIONAL SALES MANAGER / MARKETING MANAGER – NORTH AMERICA
Direct report to General Manager. Led sales, marketing, and 50-distributor network team. Retooled an unpolished and undertrained sales force and performed product development efforts: analyzed markets and built marketing materials / forecasts / promotions. Realigned distributor channels; attained multimillion-dollar sales / double-digit gross margin increase.

■ DEF CORPORATION, Phoenix, Arizona (www.def.com) — 1995 to 1999
BUSINESS DEVELOPMENT MANAGER, Automation Group – Pneumatic Division (1996 to 1999)
Promoted to direct a 6-person sales team and their distribution network (total field sales organization equaled 65+). Inherited and then successfully influenced tenured group of Territory Managers in a paradigm shift to stimulate double-digit business growth and profit increase (via 5-point program). Part of team driving major new product developments.

REGIONAL SALES MANAGER, Filtration Group – Finite Filter Division (1995 to 1996)
Managed distribution network and select OEM accounts for $8M division across 13 states. Provided technical product and field sales training for instrumentation and fluid power distributor sales staff. 103% to plan vs. 71% prior year.

■ ABCO TECHNOLOGIES, Louisville, Kentucky (www.abcotechnologies.com) — 1993 to 1995
DISTRICT MANAGER
Oversaw 10-state region, spearheading distributor, major OEM, and national account management initiatives. Drove double-digit regional and distributor sales results. Managed 4 major product groups.

■ MOLDED PRODUCTS, Louisville, Kentucky — 1991 to 1993
AREA MANAGER
Managed and developed OEM accounts and directed distributor sales. Secured over $1M sales increase (from $1.1M to $2.4M) and ranked #1 of 20 area managers. Awarded $248K governmental sole-source supplier contract.

■ MAJOR TIRES, Boise, Idaho (www.majortires.com) — 1987 to 1991
REGIONAL ACCOUNT EXECUTIVE, Engineered Products Division
Led sales / marketing initiatives across multiple product groups. Leveraged marketing / technical support resources from 4 production facilities in U.S. and Canada. Catapulted region to #2 ranking (from #7) and grew sales nearly 80%.

Figure 5.7: Diana Brayson's executive summary.

DIANA BRAYSON

ELEVATOR SPEECH

I help midsized companies struggling to meet their revenue and profit potential become high-performance, high-profit, and globally competitive forces. For example, I diversified one company's business from 40% drawn from a single market to 85% of business derived from 12 unique markets.

With more than 15 years of top-flight sales leadership experience, I advocate value-based sales and marketing propositions. Applying strong influence skills, I compel change in sales teams and customer behavior, and employing a strategic marketing mind-set, I am able to articulate value to diverse customers.

Further, my financial business expertise balances profitable growth with capital, and my strength in solid systems thinking applies processes, procedures, and performance metrics to achieve broad goals.

During my most recent challenge as Vice President of Sales & Marketing at Global Products, I turned around a marginally performing sales organization and generated more than $10M in new, annualized business opportunity. I did this by championing a "customer first" cultural change and igniting a more proactive, performance-driven organization.

I'm looking for an equally stimulating challenge with another midsized organization that seeks sales growth.

Figure 5.8: Diana Brayson's elevator pitch.

Case Study #3: William H. Brandiff (Resume Writer: Deborah Wile Dib)

Documents Included

- Three-page executive resume
- One-page executive summary
- Two-page summary of key initiatives and successes
- One-page cover letter

Unique Challenges

- Six-month unsuccessful search before connecting with his resume writer, during which he relied on his network contacts but approached them ineffectively and damaged some relationships.
- Two-year non-compete agreement with his former employer, requiring that he transition to a different aspect of the financial industry (or a different industry altogether).
- Need to land a job *fast*—due to lengthy time out of work and a large family to support.
- Inability to relocate.

Case Study

In his mid-50s, Bill had an exceptional career that culminated in managing a trading desk for a high-profile New York investment firm. When Bill recognized some questionable practices and reported them (internally), instead of being thanked, he was shown the door. Thus, he was out on the street with literally no notice, a small severance, and a very large family (seven children) to feed.

Bill had a good network, but before reaching out he did not carefully prepare his introduction and explanation for why he left his company. He left some negative impressions by "bad-mouthing" the company, and some of his anger and bitterness showed through. His resume was lengthy but focused primarily on activities rather than the considerable value he had delivered. As a result, six months later, Bill was still unemployed, was receiving limited help from his network, and was quite discouraged.

Not only that, but his former company had recently been charged for improprieties and featured noticeably on the front page of the *Wall Street Journal*. Although Bill felt vindicated, in fact his former alliance with that company did not do much to boost his search.

When he paired up with his resume writer, Bill engaged in an in-depth process of discovering his "executive brand" and translating that brand and his substantial successes to his career marketing documents. Together they created a three-page resume that clearly communicated his value. Supplementary documents included a two-page expanded version of his most notable successes, to be used as a leave-behind; a one-page executive summary, to serve primarily as a networking tool; and several cover letters, one of which is included here.

Bill had a great response to his new documents. In addition to circulating it to his network contacts (who became enthusiastic again about helping him with his search), he posted it to a Web site for Wharton MBAs, and almost immediately it was downloaded by an investment firm that invited him to interview for a position as a senior analyst. Because he would not be actively involved in trading, the role did not conflict with his non-compete agreement, so Bill eagerly pursued the opportunity.

A planned two-hour interview turned into a seven-hour "marathon," during which he met with most of the senior leadership team of the firm. He left with each of them his key initiatives addendum and followed up appropriately with letters, e-mails, and phone calls over the ensuing weeks.

As this opportunity developed, Bill also earned an interview for the top finance role for a large group of auto dealers, and he met with several of his network contacts and their referrals to explore business challenges where his expertise would be a good fit.

Just a few weeks later, Bill received an offer for the senior analyst job. Although the salary was considerably below what he had made in his heyday as a bond trader, he considered it carefully and decided to accept. He liked the firm, liked the people, and felt confident he could soon move up. The job did not require him to move, and he felt extremely relieved to be providing for his family without continuing to draw down his retirement savings.

Four months into his new position, Bill is performing well, building a new network of contacts, and updating his resume so that he can pursue new opportunities that may arise. He intends never to be caught flat-footed again!

Time from first contact with company to offer: One month

Total transition time: Eight months (two months after working with resume writer)

WILLIAM H. BRANDIFF
SENIOR-LEVEL FINANCIAL SERVICES EXECUTIVE

233 Linden Street, West Orange, NJ 07052
Home: 973-292-4371 Mobile: 973-300-3333
whbrandiff@yahoo.com

EXPERTISE

> Capital Markets Management
> Trading Strategies & Execution
> Debt & Equity Research
> Modeling & Analytics
> Risk Analysis & Risk Management
> Institutional, Advisor, & Retail Channels
> Channel, Product, & Category Management
> High Yield, MBS, & GSE Debt Specialist

LEADERSHIP

> Driven to succeed and excel
> Motivated by challenge with a purpose
> Skilled in building organizations
> Innovative in thought and solutions
> Quick to foster confidence and trust
> Committed to value for all stakeholders
> Seasoned and effective public speaker
> Trusted, well liked, with spotless integrity

KNOWLEDGE

> Startup & Growth Management
> Turnaround & Change Management
> Strategy, Planning, & Execution
> Business Development & Marketing
> Sales & Sales Management
> Consultative & Relationship Sales
> Branding & Awareness Building
> Channel & Category Management
> Regulatory Reporting & Compliance
> Relationship & Account Management
> Training, Mentoring, & Team Building

BRAND

A visionary and ethical rainmaker, **I propel triple-digit advances in growth and revenue** through the conception and building of new businesses and products. When I build a business, I do what I say, and I do it the right way—without micromanaging—to deliver **spectacular results and winning teams.**

Most effective in a **core leadership role** (VP or above) in a **growing, forward-thinking financial services firm.** I am focused on creating or revitalizing internal groups, building and managing client relationships, and training/mentoring teams to outperform the competition.

ROI

Rainmaker & Business Builder
Created high-yield trading desk, **increasing first-year profits 230%**... Revitalized MBS trading desk, delivering **3X increase in institutional account base and 53% boost in profits** in year one... Grew GSE trading profits to **$5+ million from $750,000, with 430% boost in distribution in one year,** creating most profitable trading desk in fixed-income division.

VALUE

Financial Services & Management Professional
20+-year career highlighted by recruitment, promotion, and retention by leading firms, including Reliance Investing and Wesley Johnston. Wharton MBA. Early career training at Redmond & Smith. International experience with a focus on Japan.

Growth & Turnaround Architect
Identify strategic opportunities in all market cycles. Create organizations and enable mission-critical business initiatives—international expansions, start-ups, distribution channels, sales strategies, performance improvements, culture shifts, and change management.

Ethical Leader & Corporate Citizen
Produce exceptional results with vigor, tenacity, self-confidence, and an ethical, compliance-based stance that nurtures respect and supports healthy growth and profit. Identify and develop high-potential candidates. Use internal promotion to build a staff with invaluable, brand-building, success-driving "institutional memory."

PROFESSIONAL EXPERIENCE

RELIANCE INVESTING, Hampton, NJ   1993 to present

Vice President—Dealer Sales, GSE & Municipal Securities 2002 to present
Vice President—Senior Research Analyst 2000 to 2002
Vice President—High Yield Securities Trading 1996 to 2000
Vice President—Director, MBS Trading 1994 to 1996
Vice President—GSE Head Trader 1993

Ten-year tenure with global financial services firm distinguished by: Triple-digit revenue enhancements... Performance-based promotion, excelling in every position... Recruitment from outside and inside to plan and execute mission-critical business initiatives... Formal recognition for personal contributions to driving corporate growth, improving operational performance, and enhancing profitability... Clear talent for positively influencing knowledge, competency, productivity, and ultimate career paths of others.

(continued)

Figure 5.9: William Brandiff's executive resume.

(continued)

WILLIAM H. BRANDIFF   Home: 973-292-4371 ∣ Mobile: 973-300-3333 ∣ whbrandiff@yahoo.com ∣ page 2 of 3

RELIANCE INVESTING: ACCOUNTABILITY & ACHIEVEMENT HIGHLIGHTS

As **VICE PRESIDENT—DEALER SALES, GSE & MUNICIPAL SECURITIES,** recruited internally to start up, grow, and manage dealer sales program for GSE and Municipal Securities business.

➤ Facilitated **15% increase in retained earnings**—reduction in hard-dollar commissions—and 200% boost in trading volume by successfully creating Dealer Sales channel for GSE and Municipal Securities products.

➤ **Expanded distribution more than 50%** by adding nearly 300 accounts to the client list.

➤ Excelled in managing a mission-critical business initiative that showed **immediate and significant improvements in revenue, profitability, and internal operations**—client services/value, trader communications, and sales support.

As **VICE PRESIDENT—SENIOR RESEARCH ANALYST,** published both equity and fixed income research. Provided commentary for institutional accounts with focus on Enterprise Software sector. Utilized sophisticated models, hybrid valuation techniques, and advanced analytical methodologies.

➤ **First U.S. analyst to initiate equity coverage of SEMS and LDS Systems with "Sell" ratings.** Within months both fell 30% and 40%, respectively.

➤ One of first **municipal analysts to forecast/quantify scope of financial crisis in state and federal government sectors.** Published MBS Research, correctly predicting timing of interest rate cycle in spring/summer 2001.

➤ Improved quality of **proprietary research** by imposing low multiple threshold and modified GAAP on equity models.

As **VICE PRESIDENT—HIGH-YIELD SECURITIES TRADING,** promoted to establish, grow, and optimize Reliance Principal Markets' High Yield Securities business. Refocused selling/trading approach, identified/acquired new clients, led 20-city road show, established risk parameters, managed execution of trades, and orchestrated ongoing product education seminars and training programs.

➤ **Built, grew, and managed a new profit center.** Accelerated success of High Yield project by employing prior desk management experience and institutional memory, and by recruiting internal stakeholders to staff the new venture.

➤ Delivered **230% increase in High Yield profits in first year, 38% in 1997 and 25% in 1998.** Navigated growth during periods of market turbulence by employing variety of risk metrics and inventory controls.

➤ Designed a flow-trading model that **minimized risk while providing real-time pricing** to all client groups—institutional, advisor, and retail. Introduced an intranet trading platform in 1999.

As **VICE PRESIDENT—DIRECTOR, MBS TRADING,** managed all aspects of desk activities, including new-business development, sales stratagems, cross-selling, distribution, and client management. Leveraged retail corridor to take advantage of trending demand for spread products. Improved risk management by floating inventory parameters to mirror customer flows. Wrote weekly MBS commentary for Fixed Income Department.

➤ Increased **institutional account base threefold and produced 53% increase in retained earnings.** Instituted best-practices commission schedule to coordinate product distribution with customer risk profiles.

➤ Introduced **mentoring approach to promotions,** in conjunction with HR, to broaden pool of internal candidates. To date, two of these individuals continue to prosper at the firm.

➤ **Demystified MBS by initiating product education programs for all client segments,** as well as field training program for retail representatives in branch network and regional call centers.

As **VICE PRESIDENT—GSE HEAD TRADER,** charged with growing business and improving firm's market position and profitability in debt instruments. Established benchmark objectives compatible within larger framework of RPM's general strategy for growth.

➤ Soared over revenue/profitability goals—grew **net profits to $5+ million from $750,000 within one year.**

➤ Played **pivotal role in Reliance, being accepted as selling group member** for National Credit Bank.

➤ **Originated and directed initiative to provide intensive training**—on-site product education seminars, sales support/customer relations training, and weekly call-in conferences—to more than 1,500 telephone representatives at four U.S. mega-phone sites.

➤ Delivered dramatic **increase in distribution of GSE product (430% increase in number of GSE holders).**

WILLIAM H. BRANDIFF   Home: 973-292-4371 ǀ Mobile: 973-300-3333 ǀ whbrandiff@yahoo.com ǀ page 3 of 3

WESLEY JOHNSTON, Hartdale, MA   **1990 to 1993**
Cofounder of the GSE Desk for the Bond Brokerage Division of this multinational financial services firm.

VICE PRESIDENT—GSE BROKERAGE

Brought excellent reputation and solid book of business to a team of four brokers to form a new GSE desk. Developed and executed business plan, identified/generated new business, rolled out brand/products, negotiated pricing strategies, executed trades, and built/retained relationships. Participated in recruitment, training, mentoring, and leadership of eight additional brokers (recruited from competitors) as GSE desk grew over three years. Shared P&L accountability for desk performance and daily operations management (IT, telecom, administration, reporting, and regulatory compliance).

➢ **Cofounder of GSE desk** and **one of four high-performance brokers.** Team reversed firm's two-time failure at entering the GSE brokerage market. Personally recruited by firm's President.

➢ **Captured 35% market share**—more than twice management's 15% goal—in first year of operation.

➢ **Increased firm-wide account base 25% within 24 months** by establishing global buy-side client relationships—U.S., Japan, and Canada—and leveraging cross-selling opportunities with the Corporate Bond desk.

➢ Positioned the firm as **first to offer screen-based brokerage of GSE products** outside the Primary Dealer community by establishing relationships with 10 super-regional banks. Created first brokerage platform for floating-rate GSEs.

➢ Conceived and implemented **"vertical account coverage"** by realigning broker assignments based on product expertise—a highly successful program that created solid competitive differentiation.

THOMAS, WRIGHT & SMITH, Concord, MA & Tokyo, Japan   **1982 to 1990**
Recruited to lead high-level international business strategy and domestic growth initiative for this bond brokerage firm.

VICE PRESIDENT, BOND BROKERAGE—GSE SECURITIES

Provided strategic direction, growth management, operational oversight, and team leadership to bond brokerage business. Spent 12 months in Japan acquiring government/regulatory approval for establishing operations. Relocated to U.S. to spur growth at Concord home office. In both situations, implemented sales and marketing strategies—acquired, developed, and managed accounts—and recruited, trained, and motivated new brokers.

➢ Carved out **significant growth path** and **secured major competitive win** for TW&S through personal contributions—Japanese language skills, product knowledge, cross-cultural relationship building—to secure coveted Representative Office designation from Japanese Ministry of Finance.

➢ Distinguished as **first New York GSE broker to establish non-Primary Dealer relationships**—adding $110 million in monthly volume to the broker desk—with dealers in Boston (Massachusetts Bank) and Charlotte (First Banking).

➢ **Increased commissions 42% within one year** by reviving nonperforming account base at MA headquarters.

EARLY CAREER

REDMOND & SMITH, FRISK FINE WINES, SPARKLING COLA—Field Manager & Sales Representative

EDUCATION, CERTIFICATION, & DEVELOPMENT

MBA in Finance—THE WHARTON SCHOOL, Philadelphia, PA, 1995
Elected Vice President of the Graduate Business Association

BA in Political Science—PRESTON UNIVERSITY, Smithfield, NH, 1975
Intern to the United Nations. Selected to the American Semester Program.

Certificate in Advanced Risk Management and Credit Analysis—THE WHARTON SCHOOL, 2000

NASD—Series 7, 24, 55, 63

GUEST LECTURER—City College and Preston University Graduate Schools of Business

WILLIAM H. BRANDIFF
SENIOR-LEVEL FINANCIAL SERVICES EXECUTIVE

233 Linden Street, West Orange, NJ 07052
Home: 973-292-4371 Mobile: 973-300-3333
whbrandiff@yahoo.com

Financial Manager I Growth & Turnaround Architect I Rainmaker & Business Builder I Ethical Leader

20+-year career with leading firms, including Reliance Investing and Wesley Johnston. Wharton MBA. International experience with a focus on Japan. Propel triple-digit advances in growth and revenue through conception/building of new businesses and products, delivering spectacular results and winning teams. Most effective in a core leadership role (VP or above) in a growing, forward-thinking financial services firm.

Identify strategic opportunities in all market cycles. Create organizations and enable mission-critical business initiatives, including international expansions, start-ups, distribution channels, sales strategies, performance improvements, culture shifts, and change management. Focused on creating or revitalizing internal groups, building and managing client relationships, and training/mentoring teams to outperform the competition.

Produce ROI with vigor, tenacity, and an ethical, compliance-based stance that nurtures respect and supports growth and profit. Created high-yield trading desk, increasing first-year profits 230%. Revitalized MBS trading desk, delivering 3X increase in institutional account base and 53% boost in profits in year one. Grew GSE trading profits to $5+ million from $750,000, with 430% boost in distribution in one year, creating most profitable trading desk in fixed-income division.

FINANCE

- Capital Markets Management
- Trading Strategies & Execution
- Debt & Equity Research
- Modeling & Analytics
- Risk Analysis & Risk Management
- Institutional, Advisor, & Retail Channels
- Channel, Product, & Category Management
- High Yield, MBS, & GSE Debt Specialist

MANAGEMENT

- Start-up & Growth/Turnaround & Change
- Strategy, Planning, & Execution
- Business Development & Marketing
- Sales & Sales Management/Consultative & Relationship Sales
- Branding & Awareness Building
- Channel, Category, Relationship, & Account Management
- Regulatory Reporting & Compliance
- Training, Mentoring, & Team Building

CAREER HIGHLIGHTS

RELIANCE INVESTING, Hampton, NJ   **1995 to present**
Vice President — Dealer Sales, GSE, & Municipal Securities   Vice President — Director, MBS Trading
Vice President — Senior Research Analyst   Vice President — GSE Head Trader
Vice President — High-Yield Securities Trading

Planned and executed mission-critical business initiatives, driving corporate growth (with triple-digit revenue enhancements), improving operational performance, and enhancing profitability and team performance. Facilitated 15% increase in retained earnings (reduction in hard-dollar commissions) and 200% boost in trading volume by successfully creating Dealer Sales channel for GSE and Municipal Securities products. Delivered 230% increase in High Yield profits in first year, 38% in 2000, and 25% in 2001. Grew net profits to $5+ million from $750,000 within one year.

WESLEY JOHNSTON, Hartdale, MA   **1990 to 1993**
Vice President — GSE Brokerage

Cofounder of the GSE Desk for the Bond Brokerage Division of this multinational financial services firm. Captured 35% market share — more than twice management's 15% goal — in first year of operation. Increased firm-wide account base 25% within 24 months. **(Resigned to attend Wharton full-time, graduating with MBA in 1995.)**

THOMAS, WRIGHT & SMITH, Concord, MA & Tokyo, Japan   **1982 to 1990**
Vice President, Bond Brokerage — GSE Securities

Recruited to lead high-level international business strategy and domestic growth initiative. Spent 14 months in Japan, acquiring critical government/regulatory approval for establishing operations. Relocated to U.S. to spur growth at NYC home office. First New York GSE broker to establish non-Primary Dealer relationships, adding $110 million in monthly volume to broker desk. Grew commissions 42% in one year by reviving nonperforming account base at NY headquarters.

EDUCATION, CERTIFICATION, & DEVELOPMENT

THE WHARTON SCHOOL: MBA in Finance, 1995; Certificate: Advanced Risk Management & Credit Analysis, 2000
PRESTON UNIVERSITY: BA in Political Science, 1975 I NASD — Series 7, 24, 55, 63
NEW YORK UNIVERSITY & COLUMBIA BUSINESS SCHOOL: Guest Lecturer

Figure 5.10: William Brandiff's executive summary.

WILLIAM H. BRANDIFF
SENIOR-LEVEL FINANCIAL SERVICES EXECUTIVE

233 Linden Street, West Orange, NJ 07052
Home: 973-292-4371 Mobile: 973-300-3333
whbrandiff@yahoo.com

PERFORMANCE INDICATORS & DRIVERS

Bill Brandiff on Bill Brandiff...

> My prerequisites for **organizational culture**: it must **embrace progress and be fearless of innovation,** offer challenges, reward performance, and place high value on human capital.

> **I love to win—and win the right way.** In business, witnessing the success of someone I have mentored is akin to parenting; it gives me satisfaction to send a good corporate citizen into the business world.

> Sometimes the path less traveled provides **more rewards over the long term.** By drawing upon internal candidates for promotion, I reduce turnover ratio, retain people who are on the same ethical page, and **build brand-critical institutional memory.**

Corporate Leaders on Bill Brandiff...

> Bill's knowledge of High Yield and ability to connect with the team **allowed us to reach new heights this year.** He created **enthusiasm and interest in a product where none existed.** Bill has ethics... is a team player... understands the culture... and is **critical to running a business group.** —*Senior Vice President, Reliance Investing*

> Bill is the **smartest guy on the trading floor... and the most honest.** —*Manager, GSE, Treasury Trading, Reliance Investing*

> Over a six-year period, Bill **spearheaded the growth of U.S. agencies** (GSEs), mortgage-backed securities, and high-yield bonds at Reliance Investing, establishing risk parameters and trading metrics for each segment along the way. —*Reliance Investing Website Bio*

> Bill was assigned the task of building the Agency business at FCM, and the **success of his efforts was seen immediately,** with gross revenues growing to over $5,000,000 from $750,000. —*Director of Fixed Income Sales and Trading, Reliance Investing*

KEY INITIATIVES & SUCCESSES

START-UP & NEW-BUSINESS DEVELOPMENT   VP, High Yield Securities—Reliance Investing

Challenge Build, grow, and manage a High Yield trading desk in alignment with firm's investment strategy and risk guidelines. Strategic initiative was critical to advancing Reliance's growth and competitive position.

Action Planned and executed product rollout strategy and partnered launch with full-scale education program targeted to distribution groups—institutional sales, financial advisors, and retail branch network.

Result *230% first-year increase in profits from High Yield trading. Hired, mentored, and led a high-performance team of traders that continued to produce double-digit gains even after my transfer to Research.*

Analysis Recognized as an originator and driver of new initiatives, I was recruited internally to lead this important effort and was successful in building an innovative product group, creating a winning team, and establishing this first-ever function within Reliance, advancing the firm's growth, competitive position, and profitability.

MODELING, ANALYSIS, & REPORTING   VP, Senior Research Analyst—Reliance Investing

Challenge Create a new valuation model for the Enterprise Software Sector.

Action Meshed existing equity valuation methodologies with innovative "value" approach (acquired through 10+ years in fixed income) to produce comprehensive, meaningful equity reports for this dynamic industry sector.

Result *Published research reports for Enterprise Software sector, with price targets that proved to be the most accurate of the entire research group, and provided other analysts with an alternate template to employ in their own reports.*

Analysis Bottom line, I was the first U.S.-based analyst to initiate coverage of both PeopleSoft and BEA Systems with "Sell" ratings. (Note: Both stocks fell precipitously within a few months of published commentary, and a later report on PeopleSoft captured the bounce in that stock as well.) My ability to identify weak spots in a firm's financial reporting and assess the potential impact to that firm's securities restored a commonsense approach to research.

(continued)

Figure 5.11: William Brandiff's summary of key initiatives and successes.

(continued)

INTERNATIONAL BUSINESS DEVELOPMENT   VP, Bond Brokerage—Thomas, Wright & Smith (Tokyo)

Challenge   Relocate to Japan to facilitate attainment of Representative Office status from Japanese Ministry of Finance. Establish and build business relationships with securities firms in Japan.

Action   Presented TWS to Japanese securities firms to gain credibility, demonstrate long-term commitment to the Tokyo market, and establish relationships in Japan.

Result   *Gave TWS the competitive edge in acquiring Japanese-based accounts by playing a frontline role in establishing TWS as a stable part of the Japanese brokerage landscape. Enabled firm to gain regulatory approval as a Representative Office in Tokyo.*

Analysis   Effectively interacting in a new culture was critical to the success of our entry into the Japanese marketplace. I leveraged my proficiency in Japanese to demonstrate my willingness to embrace the local culture and adapt to Japanese business practices. The result was improved relationship building that outpaced our competitors.

TURNAROUND & GROWTH MANAGEMENT   VP, Mortgage-Backed Securities—Reliance Investing

Challenge   Revitalize an MBS trading desk that had stagnant growth and declining earnings.

Action   Relaunched MBS business line with aggressive yet meticulously ethical marketing program—exposing less-sophisticated investor classes only to more vanilla product offerings—supported by comprehensive MBS product / theory education program for sales force and traders.

Result   *Threefold increase in institutional account base and 53% boost in profits within one year. Established presence on trading floor as an "innovative desk" while avoiding potentially serious compliance issues inherently present in MBS. Highest profit per trader within Fixed Income during my tenure.*

Analysis   Timing and unique ability to breathe new life into a product and group helped me bring new traders up from the ranks, share my knowledge and experience, and set high standards for profit performance *and* business ethics.

TOP- & BOTTOM-LINE PERFORMANCE IMPROVEMENT   VP, Head Trader—Reliance Investing

Challenge   Maximize revenue and profit potential of GSE trading within Reliance Investing.

Action   Upgraded risk measurements to support increased inventory levels, tailored product offerings to diverse sales groups—institutional, correspondent, advisors, and retail representatives—and provided educational seminars to stakeholders explaining evolution of spread products.

Result   *Grew GSE profits to $5+ million—from $750,000—in first year alone. Distinguished GSE as the most profitable trading desk in Reliance's Taxable Fixed Income division. Positioned RI for invitation to membership in the Federal Farm Credit Bank selling group—a powerful marketing tool for the sales force.*

Analysis   Used product knowledge, sales skills, trading acumen, management talents, and tenacity to drive a mission-critical initiative from start to finish.

SALES MANAGEMENT & PRODUCT KNOWLEDGE   VP, MBS—Reliance Investing

Challenge   Empower, optimize sales force performance, and educate other stakeholders in Collateralized Mortgage Obligations (CMOs).

Action   Authored educational pieces "tiered" to sales groups and customer demographics. Created seminars for MBS borrowed from my presentations as an invited Guest Lecturer at both Boston College and the University of Massachusetts Graduate Schools of Business.

Result   *Armed sales professionals, traders, and other key individuals with a repository of information on these complex securities, encouraging a best-practices approach to marketing MBS.*

Analysis   Identified an opportunity to improve performance and took the initiative to create a road map for success. Although only a limited degree of simplification could be accomplished when describing complex financial instruments, investing the extra time to conduct presentations and seminars allowed participants to raise their comfort level with these investment vehicles.

WILLIAM H. BRANDIFF
SENIOR-LEVEL FINANCIAL SERVICES EXECUTIVE   **CAPITAL MARKETS RAINMAKER**

April 30, 2007

Steven P. McNerney
Executive Vice President
Fine & Fine Financials
40 Wall Street
New York, NY 10005

*A visionary and ethical rainmaker, I build
and energize businesses, propelling double- and
triple-digit advances in growth and revenue.*

Dear Mr. McNerney:

Price transparency, increased competition, a stricter regulatory environment, and rapidly changing distribution opportunities are all critical issues for today's financial services industry. As an experienced financial services professional I can help you meet these tough challenges, enabling you to…

- **Leverage distribution opportunities in the new world of transparent competition** by turning challenges to advantages, utilizing the firm's core capabilities as a launching spot.
- **Instill teams with "best practices" mindsets** that embrace the advantages of ethics and compliance.
- **Drive innovation and profit** by bringing new ideas to the table, targeting opportunities, flexing priorities, and recognizing customers' changing demands before the competition.

With more than 20 years of experience—the past **ten years in five VP positions with Reliance Investing**—in the management of profitable trading desks, brokerage operations, research sectors, and distribution channels for a number of world-class firms, I can provide Fine & Fine with the capability to WIN. Throughout my career I have delivered prime results by identifying opportunities where I…

- **Created a new business—a High Yield trading desk** for Reliance—with *profits that rose 230% in the first year* alone.
- **Reinvigorated Reliance's dormant Mortgage-Backed Securities Trading Desk**—delivering in only 18 months a unit with the *highest profit per trader* in all of the Capital Markets.
- **Secured coveted Representative Office designation** for a New York-based brokerage firm from the Japanese Ministry of Finance through *cross-cultural relationship building*.
- **Grew retained earnings five times over in the first year of operation** of Reliance's GSE Trading Desk, while working within the parent firm's strict compliance guidelines and creating intelligent risk management parameters. The *group continues to be among the firm's top performers.*
- **Became the first equity research analyst in the US to initiate coverage on both BEA Systems and PeopleSoft with SELL recommendations.** It was risky to be out front with SELL ratings before it became fashionable, but I was proven right as the *stock prices of both firms hit my targets within the quarter following my initiations.*

Mr. McNerney, the enclosed resume and leadership profile highlight many more results that reflect my ability to spearhead growth, overcome obstacles, and fulfill revenue and profitability goals in a variety of businesses. I will contact you early next week to determine your interest in an informal meeting to discuss the possibility of a position with Fine & Fine.

Sincerely,

William H. Brandiff

Enclosure: Resume and Leadership Profile

**233 Linden Street, West Orange, NJ 07052 • Home: 973-292-4371 • Mobile: 973-300-3333
whbrandiff@yahoo.com**

Figure 5.12: William Brandiff's cover letter.

CASE STUDY #4: DAVID RAMIREZ (RESUME WRITER: LOUISE KURSMARK)

Documents Included

- Three-page executive resume
- One-page Critical Leadership Initiatives
- One-page cover letter
- Elevator pitch

Unique Challenges

- Career comprised 19 years with the U.S. Army, followed by a one-year less-than-successful position with a large corporation; both needed to be presented and explained appropriately in his documents and messages.
- Target companies included only very large corporations.

Case Study

After nearly 20 years in the U.S. Army, David "retired" and took the first position that was offered to him. A major insurance firm, AXA Group, had heavily recruited him for its new executive development program. Not only was he flattered, he found it very easy to move directly from one role to the other without having to conduct a serious job search.

Unfortunately, the new job was not exactly what David had expected. Not only did it not lead to the general management role that he had been promised, he found that he had to travel and work overseas more than three weeks out of every four. Combined with an ailing parent and the normal demands of his family life, this schedule became too burdensome and he resigned about a year after starting the program.

Now David did the "homework" he should have done originally, giving deep thought to what he wanted to do for the rest of his career. As he examined his experience and activities, he came to realize that human resources, and specifically leadership development, was his passion and his true expertise. Thus, he decided to pursue an executive position in leadership development with a large organization.

In preparing his resume, he and his resume writer worked to evoke his relevant activities, skills, and accomplishments, making sure not to weigh down the document with too much "Army talk" or too many activities that were unrelated to his target. Thus, his resume clearly communicated that he had been heavily involved and very successful in leadership development within one of the largest and most complex organizations in the world.

David also prepared a separate one-page document that expanded on his most salient leadership initiatives. He planned to use this as a leave-behind following interviews.

Working with his coach, David prepared an elevator pitch that explained his short-term role with AXA Group while focusing primarily on his relevant experiences and his current targets.

Although David was not a "natural networker," he realized that to penetrate to the executive levels of large corporations he had to do more than send in a resume. He spent a great deal of time reading up on his target companies, identifying senior executives, and looking for opportunities to connect with them. For example, when he read a *U.S. News & World Report* special issue on "America's Best Leaders," he followed up directly with those mentioned, sending a brief note commenting on some aspect of the article and then following it up with a phone call to see whether he could make a personal connection.

In his research, David learned that a VP of one of his target companies, Global Insurance Services, was to speak at a Wharton School symposium. As a graduate of one of Wharton's executive programs, David earned an invitation to the symposium. After the VP spoke, he made a point to approach her and engage her in a discussion about her presentation. During the course of this conversation, he mentioned his own background, and the VP was quite interested in his Army experiences. (He found this to be true throughout his search—the concept of leader development within the Army intrigued most people in his field.) David mentioned that he was in a job search, and she agreed to take a look at his resume and offer some suggestions.

David wrote a customized cover letter (included in this package) to the VP and sent it along with both his resume and critical leadership initiatives. He then followed up with a phone call and arranged a meeting. In the meeting, the VP was quite interested in his ideas for nurturing young talent as a key strategy for building organizational strength and stemming the loss of high-potential employees. David's experience with the Army was a major point of discussion.

A few days after the meeting, David followed up with a brief e-mail, sending along a link to a relevant article on leadership development. Over the course of the next two months, he and the VP kept in touch sporadically. She referred him to executives at three other companies in the financial services industry, and he had good discussions with all of them. Although no open positions existed, he felt optimistic that his meetings would eventually yield a solid lead.

He took care to follow up appropriately with each person and stay in touch from time to time.

Three months after their first meeting, the VP from Global Insurance Services asked him to meet with her again. At the meeting she told him that her company had decided to expand its leadership development function, and she asked him whether he would be interested in leading it. Four or five rounds of interviews with senior executives followed, and about six weeks later David accepted the newly created position.

Time from first contact with company to offer: Four-and-a-half months

Total transition time: Seven months

David L. Ramirez

4935 Fountain Street, Houston, TX 77016
Cell: 713-449-7409 • Home: 713-781-0494 • dlramirez@gmail.com

SENIOR EXECUTIVE
Organization & Leadership Development • Global Workforce Learning & Performance

High-impact change leader with extensive experience developing, implementing, and managing global leadership development strategy and programs for one of the world's most innovative and adaptive training organizations.

- Track record of innovation and results during 20 years in strategic leadership development for the U.S. Army.
- Corporate experience leading strategic change initiatives for a Fortune 50 international insurance enterprise.
- Deep expertise in best practices and methodologies to develop Emotional Intelligence (EQ) and specific competencies *proven* to drive results.

Strategic thinker, consistently successful in aligning OD and workforce learning with organizational objectives. Recognized for drive and perseverance in creating high-performance environments where vision and mission are clearly defined and targets for performance are aggressive and rigorously measured.

Expert in building collaborative relationships (internal and external), gaining buy-in for new ideas, and driving strategic programs through complex organizations. Executive with broad administrative/operations/line leadership experience, including multimillion-dollar budgets, staffs up to 150, training for a worldwide workforce exceeding 20,000, and delivery of tested methods to transform strategic decision-making capacity.

EXPERIENCE AND ACHIEVEMENTS

2004–2006   **AXA Group Executive Development Program—New York, Paris, Saigon**

Recruited as part of worldwide search to build bench strength for $84B-revenue AXA and its subsidiary companies. One of 3 from outside the company selected to join pilot class (20 people) of Executive Development Program grooming high-potential executives for global leadership roles. Completed 3-month rotation examining every area of operations and then assumed leadership of performance-improvement projects for one of the company's most profitable groups.

- **Led a strategic change initiative**—after unsuccessful attempts of 3 prior executives—to reform administrative practices within an underperforming $100M Vietnamese subsidiary. Successful results paved the way for divestiture to a Japanese financial enterprise and avoidance of $15M capital investment in infrastructure. (Saigon, 6 months)

- **Conceived global training and development strategy** to reduce excessive (up to 80%) annual turnover in sales force. (New York and Paris, 2 months)

2003–2004   **Director of Performance Development** (Rank: Colonel)
             Army Headquarters—The Pentagon, Washington, DC

Spearheaded strategies and programs to improve human performance within the U.S. Army. Recruited immediately following major staff restructuring to revitalize the organization and bring a fresh approach to performance development. Managed 35 staff (10 direct reports) and led numerous cross-functional teams of executives from all branches of the military in complex project planning and execution.

(continued)

Figure 5.13: David Ramirez's executive resume.

(continued)

David L. Ramirez • Page 2 of 3   Cell: 713-449-7409 • Home: 713-781-0494 • dlramirez@gmail.com

continued   **Director of Performance Development—Army HQ—The Pentagon**

- **Transformed Army's strategy for communicating with key stakeholders.** Repaired relationships and built consensus for groundbreaking approach based on the communications strategies of Fortune 500 companies.

- **Designed and executed a world-class, competency-based leadership training methodology** for top executives (Presidential appointees).

- **Introduced Balanced Scorecard process** to quarterly review/assessment of legislative objectives.

2001–2003   **Senior Operations Officer** (Rank: Colonel)**—NATO Allied Forces, Europe**

Launched and led an accelerated readiness/training program for multinational leaders, developing model that has become the NATO standard. On 24 hours' notice, assumed leadership of a critical training initiative, first assessing need and then developing and rapidly deploying a first-class educational program for leaders from 25 nations. Directed international staff of 150. Subsequently transitioned to operations leadership role for 40,000-person peacekeeping force (UN, EU, NATO).

- **Led design, development, delivery, and evaluation of world-class training model** for up to 1,000 leaders directing an international crisis response team.

- **Collaborated with UN, EU, NGO, and NATO officials** in the completion of crisis-response programs.

- **Implemented best-practice management systems,** including benchmarking and metrics management.

1999–2000   **Director of Administration** (Rank: Colonel)
              Executive Office of Chief of Staff—Department of the Army, Washington, DC

Led transformation of entire practice of leadership development within the U.S. Army. Recruited to lead an overall reform/change initiative driven by the top level of executive management. Managed up to 20 direct reports, a $56M budget, administrative operations, and numerous cross-organizational initiatives to identify and promulgate best practices in learning and development. Established measurable objectives and aggressive stretch goals. Fostered a collaborative environment and built strong relationships across the organization.

- **Designed blueprint for strategic leadership development,** leading a 24-person task force in identifying trends and best practices from top-performing corporations and then translating findings to leader-development strategies.

- **Created new Senior Executive Development Program,** modeled on private sector and in conjunction with Wharton Business School. Negotiated multimillion-dollar contracts with training and development vendors.

- **In response to Congressional mandate for reduction in force (RIF),** applied industry best practices to assist senior management in aligning strategic functions of HQ staff supporting a global workforce of 480,000.

1997–1999   **Manager, Officer Personnel Management Directorate** (Rank: Lieutenant Colonel)
              Army Military Personnel Center—Alexandria, VA

Delivered unprecedented results in the most challenging job in the Army's HR operation, managing the distribution and assignment of 50,000+ commissioned officers to support strategic priorities and worldwide missions. Designed new, collaborative strategy to identify needs and match the flow of qualified officers of the right quality, rank, and skill.

continued   **Manager, Officer Personnel Management Directorate—Army Military Personnel Center**

- **For the first time, delivered what was promised from the Pentagon to the front lines.** Met high-visibility demands from around the globe with an emphasis on customer service and clear communication of process and strategy.

- **Benchmarked best-in-class personnel management practices** and adopted several to better align processes with multiple staffing requirements (Army, National Guard, Reserve).

1995–1997   **Commanding Officer** (Rank: Lieutenant Colonel)
              Tank Regiment—Waco, Texas

Led organizational change while promoting individual development of a workforce numbering almost 1,000 and stewardship of equipment and facilities valued at over $200M. Successful turnaround of training and leadership programs rocketed the organization to best-in-class among 25 similar units within the division.

1986–1995   **Promoted through increasingly responsible training / leadership / HR positions in the U.S. Army.**

EDUCATION • PROFESSIONAL DEVELOPMENT • AFFILIATION

MS, National Security Strategy—National Defense University, Washington, DC
BS, Criminal Justice—York College, York, PA

AXA Group Executive Development Program—AXA Corporate Training Center, New York, NY
Critical Thinking Executive Program—The Wharton School, University of Pennsylvania, Philadelphia, PA
Leadership Development Program—Center for Creative Leadership, Colorado Springs, CO
Member—ASTD (American Society for Training & Development) & Academy of Management

David L. Ramirez

SENIOR EXECUTIVE
Organization & Leadership Development • Global Workforce Learning & Performance

---

CRITICAL LEADERSHIP INITIATIVES

Created a world-class training model and program, incorporating global partners and including world-renowned figures as training leaders, in a matter of months.

Toward the end of a NATO-led military campaign, was singled out for challenging role based my reputation for driving results and extensive background designing training and development programs for groups up to 20,000.

- Rapidly assimilated the challenge and assembled a top-flight team for project planning and execution.
- Created training concept, including action-learning modules and simulations-assisted exercises to ensure thorough grasp of a great deal of detailed historical, geographical, political, and sociological information.
- Recruited experts—political figures, 4-star generals, media leaders, historians, and university scholars—to prepare and present training components.
- Successfully involved representatives of multiple nations in program development, observation, and assessment without slowing rapid progress toward completion in extremely tight timeline.

Impact:
- Validated strategy/program through successful pilot and then expanded on the ground.
- Positioned leaders to successfully execute their challenging mission.
- Our model was adopted by the NATO military council and remains intact today in peacekeeping efforts.

Transformed strategic leadership development of 60,000 officers.

Several years ago the Army launched an initiative to better train leaders for the 21st century, with a stronger focus on strategic decision-making and the development of core leadership competencies down the ranks. I was selected to lead a cross-functional/matrixed team to develop the blueprint for this new approach.

- Researched leading corporations and identified the specific leadership competencies and practices that produced results time after time; used findings to develop leadership-development recommendations.
- Built consensus by championing blueprint to 30+ leader-development schools and operational units.
- Created performance milestones and action plans for pilot programs to be implemented organization-wide.

Impact:
- Pilots have since been launched and are now educating today's and tomorrow's leaders.

Turned around an underperforming unit numbering nearly 1,000, with equipment and facilities valued above $200M.

Revitalized and grew the organization through leader development—for individuals and through the establishment of stretch goals for the organization. Built a high-performance, highly competitive unit.

- Designed blended learning solutions, including action learning, self-directed, electronic, and coaching/feedback methods while benchmarking other Army units to improve training and leadership readiness.
- Instituted rigorous training program, using training simulators to improve the accuracy of 60 crews.
- Introduced best practices that were battle-tested to help people learn at a more rapid pace.

Impact:
- Turnaround rocketed the organization to best-in-class among 25 similar units within the division.
- 360-degree feedback became a catalyst for accelerating organizational change and individual development.

4935 Fountain Street, Houston, TX 77016
Cell: 713-449-7409 • Home: 713-781-0494 • dlramirez@gmail.com

Figure 5.14: David Ramirez's Critical Leadership Initiatives document.

David L. Ramirez

4935 Fountain Street, Houston, TX 77016
Cell: 713-449-7409 • Home: 713-781-0494 • dlramirez@gmail.com

April 30, 2007

Edith J. Simmons
VP Leadership Development
Global Insurance Services, Inc.
2121 Eighth Avenue
New York, NY 10012

Dear Edith:

I enjoyed meeting you at The Wharton School symposium last week and certainly appreciated your presentation! You touched on many of the critical leadership skills that I have worked to instill throughout my career in Human Resources.

As you suggested, I am forwarding my resume and a slightly expanded summary of my most significant initiatives to give you an idea of my background and capabilities.

In addition to an accomplishment-rich career with the U.S. Army, I have recent experience with a major insurance/financial services firm, AXA Group, and have demonstrated a deep skill set implementing meaningful change within large organizations. My expertise and passion is creating high-performance learning environments—where vision and mission are clearly defined, performance targets are aggressive, results are measured, and feedback is sought and used to improve future performance.

As I mentioned, I am seeking an executive role in Human Resources—more specifically, in Organization and Leadership Development—with a Fortune 500 corporation. I possess the full range of executive and operational leadership skills to manage staff, budgets, multiple strategic initiatives, and cross-functional relationships with stakeholders in any part of the world. And I thrive on complex challenges and "impossible" goals.

Because of your vast network in the insurance industry, I will greatly value your ideas and referrals within companies that are a good fit for my skills. I will call you next week to schedule a time to talk.

Again, thank you.

Sincerely,

David L. Ramirez

Enclosures

Figure 5.15: David Ramirez's cover letter.

David L. Ramirez

ELEVATOR SPEECH

I am a Leadership Development executive—what I do is create the strategies, programs, and processes to help organizations build and nurture talent both for immediate objectives and for sustainable growth. My deepest expertise is with very large organizations. I spent most of my career with the U.S. Army, which is recognized as one of the most innovative, adaptive, and forward-thinking organizations in the world in the areas of learning, training, and leadership development. With the Army I had the opportunity to shape global learning strategies, design and lead multinational training programs, and create the foundation for next-generation leader development.

After leaving the Army in 2004, I accepted an executive role with AXA Group, one of the world's largest insurance companies. They had created a new executive development program to build bench strength for their global operations, and I was one of only three people from outside the company chosen for this program. After completing the three-month rotation, I took on a variety of projects related to strategic change and global learning programs. However, my family circumstances changed and I was no longer able to manage the heavy international travel that was essential, so I left the company just a few months ago to look for another executive role.

I want to join a company that is serious about developing leaders as a critical foundation for growth. I know how to get things done in large, dispersed, complex organizations, and I am eager to partner with the executive team to make leadership development an integral component of business strategy.

In my research into potential employers, I learned that your company has a formal Leadership Development program and might be looking for new ideas and leadership for this initiative. In any event, I'd welcome your insights and ideas into my search.

Figure 5.16: David Ramirez's elevator pitch.

Case Study #5: Marguerite T. Osborne (Resume Writer: Jan Melnik)

Documents Included

- Three-page executive resume
- One-page Critical Leadership Initiatives
- One-page cover letter

Unique Challenges

- Targeting specific relocation to the West Coast (San Jose area).
- Lack of key contacts in consumer goods outside her two areas of expertise.
- Perception of limited headquarter opportunities.

Case Study

Marguerite loved her position with Avon—almost as much as she'd enjoyed her successful career with General Mills. Job dissatisfaction was not the reason for seeking a change. In fact, looking at internal opportunities and challenges, she could easily see herself working 10, 15, or more years at Avon. However, after pursuing a long-term, long-distance relationship with a gentleman on the opposite coast, she had become engaged to him more than a year ago. Following long talks, they'd agreed that they would be living on the West Coast following a wedding planned for "sometime in the next 12 to 18 months." Marguerite planned to allow up to a year for a successful, confidential search.

Although Marguerite had effectively used a resume she'd prepared following her very successful career with General Mills, she knew she'd need to "up the ante" in conveying key successes in her relatively short-term stint with Avon. She engaged a professional two months into the process after finding herself immobilized by lack of a clear plan and an up-to-date resume. In addition, she had limited time for pursuing a real job search—in addition to working 60- to 80-hour weeks (including extensive travel), she was spending many of her weekends either as business layovers-into-weekends in San Jose with her fiancé or between her apartment in Manhattan and her home in the Boston area. In addition to her job search, she was cognizant of the many details she'd also need to begin planning: giving up her sublet in the city; selling her home in Massachusetts; and planning the myriad details of a large, formal wedding.

In strategizing with her resume writer/career coach, Marguerite focused on the elements of her next position that were most important to her: the ability to be innovative in marketing direction and planning; the chance to make a real difference to an organization; the opportunity to mentor and cultivate professional growth in subordinates; and alignment in values with a company that appreciated diversity, did "good works," and produced a product/service that added value to the lives of its users.

Marguerite implemented a multipronged plan, relying first on her personal network (as she began mining contacts, she realized her network was bigger than she'd initially thought). She recognized the value of working with professional recruiters and undertook a campaign that resulted in contacting more than 600 target recruiters (retained and contingent) in her areas of interest: senior-level marketing, consumer goods (primary), and soft goods (secondary). She also scoured the *San Jose Mercury News* and the *San Jose Business Journal,* following up with cold calls and letters of introduction whenever there was a glimmer of possibility. In some instances, she forwarded just her Critical Leadership Initiatives coupled with an abbreviated e-mail message. In other instances, she used her traditional cover letter and resume.

Ultimately, it was after speaking with several recruiters that she began to garner interest and interviews that led to several promising leads and one near-offer. However, working with her coach she recognized that her sense of altruism was giving her search a clear new direction. She wanted an opportunity to use her significant corporate strengths in marketing and strategic planning, but to do so in an environment that really mattered to her.

Just as Marguerite identified that an appropriate direction might be the not-for-profit world, in disciplines ranging from public relations and pure marketing to development and fund-raising, one of her recruiter contacts presented a unique public relations opportunity within the development office of Stanford University, ideally situated just outside San Jose, where she would ultimately be living. Marguerite was immediately attracted to the idea of using her innovative marketing know-how for the benefit of an educational institution. Her candidacy was advanced by the recruiter, and a series of many key interviews followed over the next six weeks. Then followed an agonizing three-week lull, during which she kept in close contact with the recruiter as well as several contacts within the "farm" (as Stanford is known).

Fortunately, an offer and full package of benefits was soon tendered. After a short give-and-take negotiation of terms and benefits (including a six-week delay in her start date to allow for her to wrap up details on the East Coast), Marguerite happily accepted and, with great excitement, began to contemplate the details of her new career and new West Coast life.

Time from first contact with company to offer: Three months

Total transition time: Nine months (five months after working with resume writer)

Marguerite T. Osborne

21 Carol Avenue • Allston, MA 02134
(617) 469-2374 • (617) 301-5921 mobile • margtosborne@earthlink.net

Senior Marketing Executive

Providing Consistent Market Leadership to Leverage Exceptional Marketing & Sales Results

Outstanding record of highly focused, strategic marketing and sales leadership. Exceptional executive-leadership skills with talent for establishing and communicating vision, developing strategy, executing tactical plans, and motivating and empowering teams and individuals to achieve remarkable, sustainable results.

- Achieved rapid speed-to-market in successful product launches through hands-on leadership of brand and product development, strategic planning, packaging, marketing, and innovative distribution channels.
- Reputation for consistently creating value and delivering strong sales results.
- Precision focus on identifying and capitalizing on new business opportunities to generate profitable and sustainable growth.

Demonstrated Strengths ...

• Profit & Performance Improvement	• Team Leadership / Motivation	• Strategic Planning
• Sales & Marketing Strategy & Execution	• Collaboration / Teamwork	• Results Orientation
• New Business Development	• Customer / Channel Expertise	• Brand Repositioning

Professional Experience

AVON PRODUCTS, INC. • New York, NY   2003–Present
Director of Marketing, Avon Color, Skin-So-Soft, and Wellness Brands

World's leading direct seller of beauty and related products with $7.7 billion in annual revenues; Avon has largest network of independent sales representatives globally (5 million).

Recruited to lead marketing and sales initiatives for a portfolio of 3 diverse brands generating more than $2.5 billion in sales annually. Quarterbacked transformation of company's heritage brand, Skin-So-Soft (previously 3 share points behind category leader), and propelled it to #1 with a 31% increase in revenues (+$95MM) and a 65% increase in profits (+$38MM). As a result, Skin-So-Soft has become the dominant #1 player in its $1.1 billion category in less than 2 years.

Product Innovation ... Executed launch of Avon! Wellness for Women, the company's most successful single-item launch in 20 years with revenue projections exceeding $300 million annually in 2 years. Avon! Wellness received 3 top Avon awards for marketing and innovation excellence.

- Repositioned Avon's well-established flagship Color brand from focus on purely cosmetic elements to incorporate highly impactful thematic and lifestyle cues that successfully achieved strategic brand rejuvenation across all the brand's SKUs.
- As one of 2 marketing executives chosen for intensive 6-month cross-functional task force, established new go-to-market model integrating Avon! Wellness for Women with Avon Color.
- Spearheaded 10-member team that proposed sweeping changes to Avon's annual business planning process that enhanced overall operations planning, reduced systemic complexity, linked relevant functional areas with planning and budgeting, and improved organizational performance. Recommendations adopted company-wide by Executive Management Team.

(continued)

Figure 5.17: Marguerite Osborne's executive resume.

(continued)

Professional Experience

AVON PRODUCTS, INC. • *continued*

- Selected by President of Avon USA (from a pool of 4,000 stateside associates) as the only director-level manager on a team of 5 senior Avon executives to teach Avon Executive Performance Principles (an intensive 2-day professional development program) in more than a dozen workshops to key U.S. Avon managers over a 24-month timeframe.

Marketing Management ... Increased unaided brand awareness 126% and penetration 23% as a result of new line-sell creative and aggressive trial campaign at top 10 accounts (2004 to 2005).

- Managed team of 4 Brand Managers, 2 Assistant Brand Managers, and 2 Promotions Assistants.
- Direct relationships with 7 communication partners (television/print, media, Internet, CRM, promotions, experiential, and public relations), optimizing process through use of collaborative team approach to build and enhance brand.

GENERAL MILLS • Minneapolis, MN   1995–2003
Director of Marketing, Cereal/Cake/Fruit Snacks Division (1999–2003)

Advanced rapidly to Director of Marketing and assumed leadership role for one of General Mills' most prominent Divisions. Spearheaded all business initiatives for 85 SKUs representing $650 million in annual revenues.

Betty Crocker ... Contemporized General Mills' flagship brand through innovative first-to-market new-product initiatives and a communication campaign to expand brand's appeal to a broader (and younger) demographic. Result: Elevated brand to largest and most profitable in category with sales growth of 29% ($95MM), two 5% price increases, and a 45% reduction in trade dollars.

Fruit Snacks ... Successfully turned around brand that had been experiencing double-digit erosion in sales. Launched aggressive plan to reformulate product, add 2 new SKUs (Fruit Gushers and Fruit Shapes), develop new packaging (Fruit Roll-ups and Fruit by the Foot), and augment distribution with imaginative point-of-sale merchandising. Within 2 years, produced a 22% increase in sales and a 27% increase in profit, making it the fastest-growing brand in the Division from 1999 to 2002.

Marketing Management ... Achieved record-high sales, profit, and market share on top cereal brands for 4 consecutive years.

- Was catalyst in driving complete redesign of the Big G's/Cheerios/Lucky Charms/Chex/Wheaties small multipack business. Garnered senior management support for a significant capital and cost-of-goods investment to handle reengineering of packaging. Result: Sales jumped from $2MM to $30MM in first year (multipack revenues exceeded $200MM in 2003) and the identical variety pack concept has since been adopted by all competitors in the category, resulting in a $350MM multipack segment.
- Led 15-member multifunctional team in development and execution of snack packs. This 18-month packaging project was the largest, most complex capital investment in the Division's history. Milestones: Project launched on time and on budget and delivered $5.5+ million in incremental sales in the first 6 months.
- **Appointed Cochair, General Mills' National Marketing Summit** by President (2002; led 10-member planning team with $800M budget for development and execution of 3-day marketing summit).
- As **Cochair of General Mills' United Way/Adopt-a-School Campaign,** raised record-breaking $500K+ in employee donations that supported Greater Minneapolis charities (2000).

Marguerite T. Osborne

Professional Experience

GENERAL MILLS • *continued*

Marketing Manager, Alternate Channels (1998–1999)

Selected by President for newly created position to lead marketing initiatives for nongrocery channels.

- Developed long-term strategic plan that successfully accelerated growth for all brands in nongrocery channels (delivering 25%+ of Division's sales and profits).
- Launched comprehensive pricing strategies for all cereal and fruit brands in each major class of trade.

Earlier Background with General Mills includes:

- **Associate Brand Manager** for Frozen Foods (Richmond, VA; 1.5 yrs.)
- **Category Sales Development Manager** for Cereal Division (Minneapolis, MN; 1 yr.)

Education and Continuing Professional Development

THE COLLEGE OF WILLIAM & MARY • Williamsburg, VA
- **Bachelor of Science Degree, Business Administration** (*magna cum laude,* 1995)

AVON CORPORATE TRAINING CENTER • White Plains, NY
- Matriculated in Avon's Executive MBA Program, where fewer than 1% of Avon's top executive managers pursue continuing professional education (2004–Present).

Marguerite T. Osborne

21 Carol Avenue • Allston, MA 02134
(617) 469-2374 • (617) 301-5921 mobile • margtosborne@earthlink.net

Senior Marketing Executive: Vice President, Director Level

Critical Leadership Initiatives

Expertise in effectively managing diverse portfolio of business and driving successful marketing and sales initiatives.

As Director of Marketing, currently manage all marketing and sales activities for 3 strategic brands representing $2.5 billion in annual sales revenues. Charged not only with maintaining revenue, but with positioning Division for exponential growth. Challenged the status quo and created a culture that integrates a precision focus on the consumer with a high-performing team that is energized to work synergistically and produce exemplary results.

Results	Throughout career with General Mills and Avon, developed 12 different first-to-market products. Catapulted several underperforming or tired brands to new heights, earning distinctions as "fastest-growing brands in Division" and "recaptured role as #1 in $1.1 billion category."
Key Strengths	I bring tremendous value to the bottom line by applying in-depth knowledge of the marketplace and an emphasis on the consumer proposition. My own brand of leadership embodies critical strengths in the areas of team-building, motivating by example, and effectively communicating vision and direction. I am consistently recognized for my expertise in ideating new concepts for products that are wanted and needed by consumers and then executing a development and delivery solution.

Repositioned a heritage product and strategically expanded brand to generate nearly $1 billion revenue stream, a 31% increase over 2 years.

Identified opportunities to leverage Avon's hallmark product, Skin-So-Soft, by reenergizing popular brand and increasing its revenues by $95 million in 2 years despite aggressive competition, a 5% price increase, and flat budgets.

Results	Product became the largest and fastest-growing brand in its $1.1 billion category and eclipsed the previous #1 player with a 3-point share lead. Expansion of brand represented Avon's most successful single item launch in 20 years. Award-winning product introduction is projected to generate $500 million annually after 2 years.
Key Strengths	I evaluate the market to identify opportunities both at present and in the future. I assess the competitive landscape and company as well as product positioning and make strategic decisions to optimize results. My enthusiastic leadership style is contagious, and I lead with passion in garnering support and building consensus to accomplish a mission.

Increased momentum of signature premium brand through innovative first-to-market initiatives and doubled growth expectations.

Challenged to accelerate market reach of General Mills' #1 brand (Betty Crocker), representing 22% of U.S. profits. This superpremium product already enjoyed fierce loyalty from 3 million customers (75% of whom were in the over-50 demographic). Reshaped product proposition, harnessing internal expertise and leveraging marketing know-how. Executed campaign that communicated contemporized brand and delivered extensive sampling to appeal to a broader audience.

Results	Grew sales and profits 29% ($95 million) since 1999, despite a 6% category decline, two 5% price increases, and a 45% reduction in trade dollars. Boosted from #3 to #1 as largest and most profitable brand in the category, which delivered $320 million annually (2002).
Key Strengths	I am professionally exhilarated by challenges to extract incremental value from already-profitable product lines and turn around sluggish performance in underoptimized brands."

Figure 5.18: Marguerite Osborne's Critical Leadership Initiatives.

Marguerite T. Osborne

21 Carol Avenue • Allston, MA 02134
(617) 469-2374 • (617) 301-5921 mobile • margtosborne@earthlink.net

April 30, 2007

Mr. Reggie Oswalt, President
CPG Products, Inc.
2454 Alameda Boulevard
San Jose, CA 95119

Dear Mr. Oswalt:

Bringing brand leadership, invoking clear and deliverable vision, and energizing everyone from members of the executive management team to associates within the marketing and sales realm—these are just some of the signature strengths that I can deliver to your organization.

By way of this introduction, I am very interested in being considered as a candidate for the position of Vice President of Marketing with CPG. Developing and executing innovative plans that **consistently deliver value** and **produce measurable bottom-line results** are what you can expect from me.

I have earned a solid reputation for adeptly understanding a company's marketing needs and growth requirements and then deploying a multipronged strategic plan that effectively identifies untapped market opportunities, assesses unrealized potential gains, and identifies new customers. The result? *A long-standing track record of record-breaking performance, initiatives that produce profitable and sustainable growth, and significant increases in revenue and market share.* Specific highlights include:

- Increasing market share significantly in established markets and producing incremental revenue streams that have accounted for substantial increases in overall profitability.

- Developing and executing innovative strategic plans that consistently generate double-digit increases in profitability and in absolute sales.

- Track record of exceeding plan objectives and achieving record-high sales, profit, and market share on 4 major brands for 7 consecutive years.

What I believe distinguishes me as a Vice President of Marketing is clear success in developing new business in uncharted territories or within untapped market sectors. My energy is unflagging, and the results I have been able to achieve speak for themselves. I would value the opportunity to discuss how these skills and experiences can benefit CPG, and I look forward to speaking with you. Thank you for your discretion and confidence in considering my candidacy.

Sincerely,

Marguerite T. Osborne

Figure 5.19: Marguerite Osborne's cover letter.

Chapter 6

Gallery of Executive Career Documents

"Imitation is the sincerest form of flattery."

–Charles Caleb Colton

A s we've discussed throughout this book, your resume is as unique as you are. All of your career marketing documents should reflect your one-of-a-kind executive brand, your distinctive accomplishments, and your individual experiences. Yet resumes do resemble each other in their core components, so it can be instructive to look at high-quality examples to see what other executives (and their resume writers) have come up with to present their background and qualifications in a compelling way.

Thus, we present the following "Gallery of Executive Career Documents"—all developed, in collaboration with their executive clients, by professional resume writers who hold one or both of the credentials that we think are the most rigorous in our industry: Master Resume Writer and Credentialed Career Master. When we were looking for top-notch samples to include in this book, we went directly to the handful of professionals who have earned these certifications that designate advanced expertise in resume writing and career management. (A complete listing of contributors with contact information is included in the appendix.)

In the pages that follow, you will see an executive resume and, in some cases, one or more additional career marketing documents for the same individual. As you peruse these samples, notice that although each resume is unique, they all conform to the strategies and recommendations we've explored in chapters 2, 3, and 4. In particular:

- "Who I am" is clearly communicated in a quick skim of the resume.

- Accomplishments are a focal point, easily distinguished, and ample.

- Quite often, context is explained to improve the reader's understanding and increase the impact of accomplishments.

- Formats vary in complexity but never overshadow content.

- Documents balance conciseness and readability with depth—there is enough information to tell the candidate's story.

- Additional documents convey added value and enhance the resume.

When developing your resume and related documents, use these superb examples for ideas, inspiration, and a stimulus to overcome writer's block. Viewing how other executives have positioned themselves will help you as you create highly effective documents for your successful career transition.

The Gallery documents are arranged in the following groups:

- Sales/Marketing/Advertising/Public Relations Executives (pp. 161–173)

- Human Resources Executives (pp. 174–178)

- Engineering and Technical Executives (pp. 179–184)

- Finance and Finance/Operations Executives (pp. 185–194)

- Operations and General Management Executives—Manufacturing Industries (pp. 195–203)

- Operations and General Management Executives—Service Industries (pp. 204–217)

At the top of each page, you'll see the name of the professional writer and an indication of what documents are in that executive's "package."

CHRIS WILLIAMS—EXECUTIVE RESUME (WRITER: LOUISE KURSMARK)

CHRIS WILLIAMS

29 Hillview Street, Waltham, MA 02154
H: 781-295-7812 • C: 617-292-0909 • cwilliams@comcast.net

VP SALES • REGIONAL / NATIONAL SALES MANAGER

Excel in building high-performing sales organizations and transforming stagnant sales to vibrant growth.

Unbroken record of top performance in sales, sales management, and development of national sales force to achieve aggressive goals. Demonstrated proficiency in all areas of executive sales leadership—vision through strategies, tactical plans, compensation programs, communication protocols, and reporting structures. Proven ability to lead start-up, restructured, and existing sales organizations and to create customer-focused, solution-selling culture.

Areas of proven performance:

- Driving long-term vision while attaining short-term financial results
- Turning around underperforming teams and organizations; achieving rapid and sustainable growth
- Developing sales skills/improving sales performance through training, mentoring, and one-on-one coaching
- Creating highly efficient and productive operations

PROFESSIONAL EXPERIENCE & ACHIEVEMENTS

GENERAL REVENUE CORPORATION, Division of Sallie Mae   Boston, MA • 2002–2006
Collections service organization specializing in home mortgage defaults; #1 industry leader with a substantial client portfolio of banks, credit unions, and mortgage lenders in 50 states. Acquired by Citigroup from original founders/private owners in 2003.

VP SALES & MARKETING

Recruited to take sales to a new level; transformed unfocused organization with stalled revenues to a dynamic team that virtually doubled business in 4 years. Invigorated sales team by defining vision and introducing the strategies, programs, and tools to achieve it. Fully accountable for revenue performance and management of sales, marketing, and client service. Led a team of 16 direct/indirect reports.

- Delivered dramatic growth, hitting new company records for sales volume every year:

	Placement Volume	Revenue	Number of Clients
2005	$460M	$36M	985
2003	$341M	$30M	715
2001	$206M	$24M	490

- Achieved stellar results via a lean organization, increasing productivity of sales force 33% during tenure.
- Clearly established brand image and value to drive continuous growth and exceptional client retention.
- Developed trade show strategy and exhibits focusing on returns to customers (in 2004, returned more than $100M to clients); oversaw participation in 60+ trade shows annually.
- Improved communication with the sales force; boosted morale and results through carefully structured compensation plans that rewarded the achievement of strategic business goals.
- Retained to lead sales following acquisition; transitioned rapidly and successfully to new ownership and took on new responsibility for marketing, contract bidding, and client service.

REAL SOLUTIONS, Division of Intercontinental Corp.   Cincinnati, OH • 1988–2002
Industry's leading provider of commercial real estate information—paper/electronic sales leads and analytics, serving more than a million customers in the $3.4 trillion global real estate community.

SENIOR SALES DIRECTOR / NORTH AMERICA, NATIONAL ACCOUNTS, 1/02–10/02

Grew revenues 20% annually, staving off competition through focus on value and service to top-tier national accounts in the U.S. and Canada. Led 75-member international sales organization, creating the sales strategies to achieve aggressive corporate goals and managing plans, programs, contracts, expenses, reporting, trade-show activity, and team performance.

- Retained #1 market position and delivered 20% growth in an increasingly competitive/price-sensitive market.
- Introduced "gold" customer concept that rewarded best accounts while boosting sales penetration.

(continued)

(continued)

CHRIS WILLIAMS   H: 781-295-7812 • C: 617-292-0909 • cwilliams@comcast.net

REAL SOLUTIONS, continued

- Devised new reporting protocols that streamlined reporting processes and delivered more usable information.
- Guided sales managers in setting "stretch" yet achievable goals for sales team.
- Boosted morale of sales managers and field sales force through positive team-building and one-on-one coaching.

SENIOR SALES DIRECTOR / EASTERN U.S., 4/00–12/01

Successfully transitioned "turf" coverage to team coverage, leading streamlined/restructured sales organization to healthy revenue growth. Promoted to lead newly combined Regional and National Accounts sales teams, 7 sales managers, and 78 reps covering the eastern half of the United States. Fully accountable for revenue performance and all sales/management functions, from planning, goal setting, and reporting through team member training and motivation.

- Achieved 10% year-over-year sales growth.
- Created joint regional/national selling initiatives while introducing internal telesales for the first time in company history. Retained nearly 100% of staff during challenging transition and created true team chemistry.
- Introduced new reporting and communication protocols that emphasized joint sales calls and internal partnerships to drive solution selling strategies.

SALES MANAGER, NATIONAL ACCOUNTS, 12/99–4/00

Exceeded 100% of aggressive sales goals, leading 12-member National Accounts team in selling to and servicing large corporate customers in 8-state Northeast region. Managed sales reporting, staff assignments, and expense budgets. Set sales goals, created motivational sales contests, and worked with sales reps to improve selling skills.

- Engaged each member of 12-person sales team, defining individual goals and creating success plans that resulted in top team and individual performance, including #1 U.S. Sales Rep in 1998.
- Negotiated and/or approved all major sales contracts.

SALES TRAINING SPECIALIST, EASTERN U.S., 1/97–12/99

Handpicked to build and lead an elite training organization to introduce a radically different technology-based product line to the regional sales force. Recommended selection of 3 team members; built team concept; defined goals and compensation plan; created team structure and communications protocol. Traveled extensively, working side-by-side with sales reps and coaching/empowering them in new sales strategies for innovative product.

- Achieved unqualified success: New product delivered $10M revenue in 2 years, 2X initial goal.
- All team members were subsequently promoted to Sales Management roles.

NATIONAL ACCOUNTS REPRESENTATIVE, Boston, MA • 1993–1997
REGIONAL SALES REPRESENTATIVE, Buffalo, NY • 1989–1993
SALES SERVICE REPRESENTATIVE, Providence, RI • 1988–1989

EDUCATION

UNIVERSITY OF RHODE ISLAND, Kingston, RI
- BS Business Administration, 1987

COMMUNITY LEADERSHIP

- Advisory Board Member, The Country Club, Brookline, MA, 2005–Present
- Youth sports coach (baseball and basketball), Waltham Recreation Leagues, 1993–2003

DANIEL SMYTHE—EXECUTIVE RESUME (WRITER: ANNEMARIE CROSS)

DANIEL SMYTHE

4 Acouple Street,
Currumbarrah NSW 2589

0420 215 987
dsmythe@bigpond.com

SALES & MARKETING EXECUTIVE

*Exceptional leader and influencer energising follow-through on strategic business opportunities
while driving constant improvement and expansion within a highly competitive industry*

Commercially astute, sales-driven Senior Executive with incisive ability to strategise and execute forward-thinking solutions across business and consumer markets within startup, turnaround, and high-growth multimillion-dollar enterprises. Track record for the research and forecasting of appropriate industry and customer trends, driving rapid expansion in client acquisition/retention across multichannel distribution settings. Possess keen focus on revenue growth, setting and achieving aggressive targets; drive complex decision-making to synchronise with challenging and rapidly evolving market conditions. Skilled at cross-functional leadership and performance management, steering large-scale operational change and advancement.

Professional strengths:

- Business / Sales Forecasting & Management
- Performance & Productivity Improvement
- Negotiations, Presentations, & Consultations
- Key Alliance & Partnership Building
- Innovative Sales/Marketing Program Design
- Multidistribution & Revenue Optimisation
- Product Launch & Market Penetration
- Market Sizing & Opportunity Assessment
- Competitive Product Positioning
- Key Account/Client Management
- Team Leadership & Performance Growth
- Analytical & Conceptual Problem Solving

Professional Experience

HUBBA LAWNCARE PTY LTD   1991–Present
'Iconic' brand company topping $60M in annual turnover.
National Sales & Marketing Manager (1998–Present)
Key leadership role. Fully accountable for devising revenue-generating and performance-enhancing initiatives that have stimulated turnover growth by an outstanding $10M despite being challenged by a drought-ridden, highly competitive, and relentlessly shifting marketplace.

Dealer & Customer Growth

- **Seized 14% market growth** and an **additional 55% dealer business** following launch of Gold Dealer Programme that involved 300 selected dealers being given exclusivity across specific geographic locations:
  - Initiated ongoing retailer product knowledge training, improving sales and marketing of an expansive Hubba product range.
  - Introduced national service/warranty network providing additional retailers with an agent in their local area, thus prompting retailers to eliminate competing products and solely promote Hubba.
  - Improved marketing programme by providing potential buyers with informative and appealing materials to entice product purchase.
- **Grew business 40%** by nurturing and building an expansive client base of loyal and referring distributors strengthened by quality products backed with strong after-sales and warranty support.
- **Recaptured 35% revenues** through rekindling and repairing previously tarnished relationship with major account, Kmart.

Clients:
Major retailers, including Betta, Bing Lee, Bunnings, Good Guys, Kmart, Harvey Norman, Mitre 10, Retravision.

Report to:
Chief Executive Officer

Marketing Budget
$1.5M

Staff:
20 indirect reports
9 direct reports

Continued...

(continued)

(continued)

Dealer & Customer Growth, continued

- **Added 20% to annual turnover** by securing preferred supplier status with 9 major accounts.
- **Retained competitive edge** through regular market feedback from field sales teams, identifying competitor strengths and additional business opportunities, with information collected promptly acted upon.

Product Launches

- **Played pivotal role in the research, creation, and launch of two major products,** including award-winning Razor mower (now 20% of annual turnover) that outperformed existing competitor products, and Tornado mower (now 75% of annual turnover):
  - Provided crucial market/competitor feedback and united a core group of specially chosen dealers to participate in the initial Razor product development/brainstorming sessions.
  - Spearheaded first-ever Gold Dealer National Conference involving 450 dealers to unveil new Razor, with mower later **winning the coveted 'Australian Design Award.'**
  - Relayed market reaction and key findings (from recently launched Razor), exploited knowledge of dealers and focus groups during preliminary brainstorming/product testing sessions, and influenced overall design of the new Tornado mower.
  - Coordinated Hubba's second consecutive National Dealer Conference to present new Tornado mower to more than 400 delegates. Secured overwhelming market acceptance, with stock levels selling out and prompting a 2-month product backorder list.
- **Grew 4-stroke mower sales by 50%** following return of industry-leading Briggs and Stratton engines, through strategic negotiations at same pricing as current (industry-second) vendor.

Sales & Marketing Programmes

- **Championed groundbreaking sales and marketing initiatives that** strengthened brand recognition, amplified market share, and grew revenue/profitability (while competitors continued to suffer steep turnover declines due to climatic difficulties), including:
  - *Gold Dealer stretch target incentive,* reinvigorating achievement of impressive performance targets by offering regular rebate rewards.
  - *National Outdoor Advertising Campaign,* eliciting overwhelming response in brand recognition (despite droughts across many parts of Australia) for new Tornado mower by combining billboards and the catchy slogan "Another reason to pray for rain."
  - *Major press campaigns on a national scale coinciding with major sporting events,* using captivating catchphrases that seized patron attention and prompted further enquiries.
  - *NSW/VIC television campaign with Channels 7 and 9,* generating numerous customer enquiries and **boosting YTD sales by 22%.**

Cost Minimisation & Profitability

- **Sourced boutique production company** that created a high-quality, audience-captivating television advertising campaign with **production investment costs 75% less** than major vendor prices.
- **Cut costs $100K/annum** by eliminating entry model's factory assembly, allowing reduction in packaging size/costs and freight charges without impact to retailer or consumer satisfaction.
- **Reduced annual payroll $200K** by prioritising/redistributing workload within marketing, impacting positively on overall productivity despite having 3 fewer staff members.
- **Elevated corporate profile/branding and productivity** by devising cost-effective sales and promotional solutions that underpinned continuity and standardisation of all marketing communications.

Team Building & Performance Growth

- **Built a loyal team** of highly talented and performance-driven staff by providing an encouraging/supportive setting, leading by example, and continually promoting corporate vision, values, and goal achievement.
- **Instilled an appreciation for goal setting/monitoring,** impacting greatly on team's ability to prioritise/achieve goals in a demanding market.
- **Boosted staff performance and retailer support** by executing innovative incentive programs, including the recent 50th Anniversary "Garden Makeover" consumer promotion.

National Sales Manager (1997–1998)
Drove sales/profitability growth of the Hubba business by crafting strategies, plans, and budgets to sustain both short- and long-term corporate goals, while providing optimum support to the entire Hubba sales team. Led, mentored, and built a loyal and talented team of 7 direct/14 indirect staff.

- **Generated $30M annual turnover** by forging key customer alliances with 9 major account head offices, including Bunnings, Kmart, Retravision, and Harvey Norman.
- **Positioned Hubba for continued corporate objective/budget achievement** by providing crucial market/competitor feedback (in collaboration with marketing department), facilitating ongoing revamping and revitalisation of strategic plans and marketing programmes.
- **Promoted to Sales and Marketing Manager** in recognition of outstanding attention to detail combined with innate passion and knowledge of point-of-sale and promotional collateral that captured customer attention and ultimately buyer spend.

Previous experience demonstrates expertise across sales, marketing, and account management, harnessing market insight with strong client relationships to seize market share and champion distribution and mower growth for Hubba by an outstanding 50%.

Professional Development

Effective Management Development Course ~ Leadership Management Australia (LMA)
Leadership Development Program ~ Mt. Eliza Business School
Fundamental Selling Skills • **Advanced Selling Skills** • **Public Speaking**
~ Australian Institute of Management
Advanced Selling Course ~ Manpower Management

KATHRYN EVANS—EXECUTIVE RESUME (WRITER: LOUISE KURSMARK)

KATHRYN L. EVANS

513-209-2176 • klevans@cinci.rr.com
7745 Highpoint Trail, Cincinnati, OH 45237

STRATEGIC MARKETING EXECUTIVE: Technology-Driven Organizations

Global Marketing Strategies • Brand & Product Management • Market-Focused Product Development

Catalyst for profitable growth: Strategic, analytical, customer- and solution-focused marketing executive with proven success delivering strong results in sales growth, profitability, and account penetration:

- **134%** revenue growth over 5 years
- **40%** to **70%** market share for every product in digital testing equipment portfolio
- **42%** gross-margin improvement in the most challenging technology market in recent history
- **#1** revenue-generating product for 135-year-old company

Expertise in all aspects of marketing and sales strategies, planning, and execution for technology-based organizations. Exceptional track record of building high-performance teams and developing strong relationships and alliances with customers and channel partners. Equal success in launching marketing initiatives for new product introductions and product-line revitalization. Exceptional presentation skills.

EXPERIENCE AND ACHIEVEMENTS

XAVIER TECHNOLOGIES ($700M global test and measurement company)   Cincinnati, OH, 2003–Present

BUSINESS MANAGER / NEW BUSINESS PRODUCT MANAGER
Delivered 42% profit increase during challenging market conditions, driving product strategies and sales efficiencies across entire division. Hired to develop and implement sales and marketing programs to capitalize on new business opportunities. Concurrently challenged to lead initiatives to improve performance of existing multimillion-dollar product line and resolve sales efficiency barriers.

- Developed new business model for innovative technology to generate **$20M** incremental business in 3 years—**$100K** revenue and **$1M+** sales funnel in first 3 months.
- Led a cross-functional rapid-action team in developing and implementing a web-based configuration/quote tool for the global sales team that reduced customer quote times from **3** days to **15** minutes.
- Spearheaded product-line optimization that delivered exceptional profit performance during severe industry downturn:

	2002	2003	2004	2005
Revenue	**$6.5M**	**$5M**	**$5M**	**$5.5M**
Gross Margin	**28%**	**60%**	**70%**	**70%**

GREAT RIVERS COMPANY ($120M worldwide water analysis test equipment company)   Cincinnati, OH, 1998–2003

PRODUCT MANAGER
Transformed business from R&D- to market-driven, reversing declining sales and generating 134% growth in 5 years. Managed product line P&L and led combined marketing/engineering team. Analyzed markets; conceived long-range and competitive strategies; prepared marketing plans, budgets, and sales forecasts; initiated product improvements to meet changing market needs. Established program metrics and consistently held post-program evaluations to identify and institutionalize best practices.

- Delivered steady and substantial revenue growth:

	1997	1998	1999	2000	2001
Revenue	**$7.9M**	**$8.8M**	**$11.2M**	**$13.5M**	**$18.5M**
Growth	**-6%**	**+11%**	**+22%**	**+20%**	**+37%**

- Launched **12** successful new products in 4 years, including 2 products introduced in the Americas through acquisition and successful integration of a European firm.
- Seized leading market share (**40%–70%**) for all products in my team's portfolio.
- Increased profits **15%** through marketing strategies that clearly articulated customer value to command premium pricing.
- Reestablished Great Rivers as the world leader in analytical testing, working collaboratively with sales, key customers, and EPA to produce a "disruptive technology" that overwhelmed the competition.

KATHRYN L. EVANS

513-209-2176 • klevans@cinci.rr.com

GREAT RIVERS COMPANY, continued
- Guided engineers out to the customer, leading to the design of high-profit, value-added products.
- Created a high-performance team. Defined vision, empowered team members to act, and led by example.

WRIGHT SYSTEMS, INC.   Dayton, OH, 1991–1997
(Privately held company, a leader in design of control systems for power generation applications)

PROGRAM MANAGER, 1995–1997

Accelerated product development and tightened cost/scheduling controls by formalizing project management practices division-wide. Promoted to full program management for industrial controls; managed cross-functional project teams in system design, development, and deployment.

- Cut new product introduction cycle times **50%** by implementing a formal project management system.
- Efficiently managed scope, schedule, and budget of multiple projects, resolving technical and business issues with internal and external customers.

PRODUCT MARKETING MANAGER, 1993–1995

Championed new business/product opportunity that set a company record for revenue generation. Provided leadership and direction to an international OEM sales team. Performed market research and developed strategic plans to increase sales, meet profit objectives, and penetrate new markets/accounts. Developed strong customer relationships that led to business opportunities.

- Initiated and closed 5-year contract to supply control systems for a large European power generation company; displaced competitor as vendor of choice. Assumed role of product champion and account manager, repeatedly removing internal barriers and renewing executive support for the project.
  - Generated **$20M** incremental revenue in 3 years and **$100M+** in 10 years.
  - Product became the company's **#1** revenue generator for industrial power generation products.

ACCOUNT MANAGER / APPLICATION ENGINEER, 1991–1993

Grew revenue 58% in 2 years, managing national OEM accounts and actively pursuing new business.

- Increased sales **30%** first year, **21%** second year; consistently exceeded divisional goals.
- Tapped to develop sales training seminars for U.S. and international sales force.

EDUCATION

MS Technology Management   Wright State University, Dayton, OH
BS Computer Engineering / Minor—Mathematics   University of Cincinnati, Cincinnati, OH

Extensive professional development in marketing, management, product management, negotiation, sales.

AFFILIATIONS

Member American Management Association (AMA)
Member American Society for Testing and Materials (ASTM)
Former Member Board of Directors, Electrical Generation Systems Association (EGSA)

THAD VON BRAUN—EXECUTIVE RESUME, CRITICAL LEADERSHIP INITIATIVES, LEADERSHIP TESTIMONIALS (WRITER: DEBORAH WILE DIB)

Thad Von Braun

SENIOR-LEVEL MARKETING EXECUTIVE—CMO

CAREER PROFILE

MARKETING · ADVERTISING · BRANDING · PUBLIC RELATIONS

Strategic & Tactical Marketing

Product Strategy, Development, & Launch

Customer Acquisition, Loyalty, & Retention

Integrated & Cross-Channel Marketing

Brand, Message, & Image Development

CRM/PRM Implementation & Mining

Advertising & Media Planning & Buying

Customer Profiling & Segmentation

Vision, Conceptualization, Strategy, & Execution

Business Development & Market Entry

P&L Management—Business & Marketing

Finance, Accounting, & Budgeting

Strategic Alliance & Relationship Management

Campaign & Turnkey Project Management

IT Strategies & Solutions

Public Relations & Media Affairs

Corporate & Crisis Communications

Decision Support & Knowledge Management

Corporate, Agency & Client-Side Experience
CMO, Partner, Vice President, Management Director, Senior Director—Marketing & Advertising, Brand Manager, Manager of B2B Marketing, Marketing Consultant

Business & Global Perspective
Hold dual Wharton MBA/Master's in International Management. Fluent in German.

Drive Growth, Revenue, Market Share, Brand Awareness, Profit & Value
Conceptualize, design, develop, and execute high-profile, well-targeted marketing strategies, campaigns, and solutions for:

- CONSUMER PRODUCTS & RETAIL
  Procter & Gamble Brands, Beck's Beer, Radio Shack, Bailey's Irish Cream, Streamline, White Castle, Doubleday Book & Music Clubs
- FINANCIAL, PROFESSIONAL SERVICES & PUBLISHING
  NASDAQ, O'Shaughnessy Capital Management, United Credit Counseling, Spencer Stuart, FreedomPoint, Gibbons/Barrons, Bertelsmann AG
- TECHNOLOGY & ECOMMERCE
  Reflect, UnitedCredit, Netfolio, Presiva, SecurityVillage
- TRAVEL & LEISURE
  Wyndham Hotels & Resorts, Discovery Travel, Rosenbluth International
- TRANSPORTATION, ENERGY & PHARMACEUTICAL
  Mobile Oil, Gibbons, Bristol-Myers Squibb

VALUE DRIVERS

MARKETING & MANAGEMENT

Accomplished Senior-Level Marketing Executive

Bring full toolbox of theoretical and practical marketing skills as well as excellent intuition, judgment, timing, and experience in domestic and international channels. Critical link between operations, product manufacturing, marketing, and sales. Acutely tuned to key business drivers, market signals, consumer buying trends, media perception, and public opinion.

Provide creative and managerial direction to high-impact, cost-effective marketing strategies, campaigns, and events that consistently achieve results—rapid market entry, lead generation, revenue generation, customer acquisition and loyalty, differentiation in the marketplace, brand recognition, market penetration, and account penetration.

Strategist, Tactician, Innovator, and Valuable Member of Executive Teams

Consistently successful in making the "impossible" possible. Valuable to companies in dynamic growth, turnaround, reposition, and change phases. Thrive in challenging, fast-paced, entrepreneurial, and intellectually stimulating environments. Pivotal participant in enterprise-level strategic planning, decision-making, and leadership. Seek out, value, and reward professionals with superior qualifications, strong work ethic, dedication, and loyalty.

PROFESSIONAL EXPERIENCE

MARKETING & MANAGEMENT

AdFocus, New York, NY
Chief Marketing Officer (CMO)

2002 to 2006

$90+ million financial services company. Three divisions/several brands. Focus on consumer debt management solutions.

Top-ranking marketing executive on corporate leadership teams, contributing to daily business operations and visualization and execution of future business strategies for three corporate divisions—3Ci Corporation (United Credit Counseling brand), Amerix Corporation (processing and fulfillment business unit), and Apex Corporation (Apex brand).

Held direct accountability for conceptualization, development, deployment, and management of marketing, advertising, messaging, media buying, prospecting, branding, strategic positioning, and customer experience for two brands. Administered and controlled $15 million cross-channel advertising budget and a team of four professionals.

2224 Central Park West #10B, New York, NY 10020 ▪ 212-949-5555 (home) ▪ 914-505-7915 (mobile) ▪ tvbraun@aol.com

PROFESSIONAL EXPERIENCE _____ **AdFocus, continued**

Management & Marketing Successes

- *Influenced and participated in consolidating and rebuilding corporate executive team* from 10+ to four (operations, marketing, finance, human resources).
- *Strengthened message and brands* by bringing cohesiveness to look, feel, tone, and implementation of corporate communications across all channels—TV, radio, print, yellow pages, direct mail, website, PR, telephony, sales process.
- *Reduced broadcast advertising production costs 50% while accelerating time-to-market* for United by developing and deploying a new TV campaign approach focusing on changing/improving customer perception. Rebranded to eliminate confusion and shifted brand focus from offer-driven to empathetic and helpful while maintaining responsiveness.
- *Improved marketing results and ROI* by building, testing, and proving the effectiveness of PRM, CRM, and customer-centric (vs. product-centric) database architecture for new-product development, rollout, and marketing.
- *Slashed cost of customer acquisition in key initiatives at least 30%—as much as 70%—*and boosted customer retention in key initiatives 40% through the combination of remarketing interventions (offline and online) and customer "save" strategies.
- *Improved sales agent conversion performance in key segments 50%* by introducing/blending a new tool mix—inbound teleservices, IVR, database, lettershop, returns processing, email distribution/management—acquired by hiring/managing new external partner conglomerate.

KMG Group—Lansing & Dunrite, New York & Washington, DC   2000 to 2002
PARTNER & VICE PRESIDENT—MANAGEMENT DIRECTOR

Global advertising and marketing services company (division of UK-based LMT Group). Major corporate clients worldwide.

Recruited by top executive to partner in acquiring new clients and directing business operations. Personally developed, sold, and managed direct marketing concepts/campaigns focused on providing best value to end clients based on their unique needs and objectives. Mentored and led a team of three marketing professionals and coordinated activities of eight others in cross-functional roles. Served as relationship manager for several major brands/accounts.

Management & Marketing Successes

- *Credited with personal contributions to stabilizing the Direct Marketing Division* by performing gap analysis of existing operations, implementing strict accountabilities for client profitability, and rebuilding the marketing team.
- *Instrumental in partnering with Chicago office counterparts in acquiring Spencer Stuart account* that propelled division to a great start and proved to corporate parent that team could win and run a business, be an asset, and be an easy working partner. Teamed with Detroit group in winning White Castle account. Salvaged Bailey's Irish Cream account.

Transglobal Marketing, New York, NY   1996 to 2000
ACCOUNT DIRECTOR (1999 to 2000)/MANAGEMENT SUPERVISOR (1996 to 1999)

Global advertising and marketing services company. Full range of direct marketing solutions to major corporate clients and brands.

Recruited by president. Promoted to senior-level client-side executive position. Held client relationship management and end accountability for major clients and brands—Procter & Gamble, Radio Shack, NASDAQ, Discovery Communications, others. Mentored/led staff of up to 10. Provided indirect supervision to 17 additional creative, production, and marketing support staff.

Management & Marketing Successes

- *Delivered explosive growth for advertising agency—to $4+ million from $700,000—a 42+% year-over-year increase in* fee-based revenue. Brought in separate multimillion-dollar P&G contract on behalf of sister agency, Critical Mass.
- *Credited with winning and building robust P&G accounts* and a piece of business parlayed into agency's (and industry's) portfolio showpiece. These accounts were foundation for Transglobal—the "hot shop"—the place to be, the one clients had to see.
- *Differentiated agency competitively and enhanced client value*—from traditional marketing support to complete outsourced business solutions—by introducing turnkey business model integrating expanded capabilities and service offerings.
- *Contributed to solidifying and protecting agency's position as industry's preeminent thought leader* and world's largest direct-response agency by participating in an enterprise-wide change initiative (including 360° review).
- *Achieved up to 65% improvement in time-to-market* by designing and implementing structured, yet flexible, cycle management process, since adopted by other internal groups/account directors.
- *Developed and deployed complete integrated marketing campaign*—television, radio, print, direct mail, fulfillment—for Discovery Communications within six weeks while meeting/exceeding client expectations.

2224 Central Park West #10B, New York, NY 10020 ▪ 212-949-5555 (home) ▪ 914-505-7915 (mobile) ▪ tvbraun@aol.com

(continued)

(continued)

- *Selected to take P&G into direct-to-customer business*—bypassing the retail distribution fight for shelf space. Key brands included Millstone Signature Blend, Reflect.com, and Presiva.
- *Increased agency reach by winning the national Beck's Beer account*—through development and presentation of innovative brand-building concepts and execution strategies.

PROFESSIONAL EXPERIENCE

Early Career

Simon & Schuster, New York, NY

1994 to 1996

BRAND MANAGER/Good Reads for Kids (GRFK)

Division of one of the world's largest global media and publishing companies—publishing houses, record companies, magazines, and production/printing facilities. Markets products/services to negative- and positive-option bookclub members.

Managed brand strategies and campaigns for $35 million business (U.S./Canada operations). Held P&L and marketing ROI accountability for editorial placement, creative design, production, and distribution for 46+ annual catalog mailings.

Part of team that slashed catalog production cycle time 50%—to 10 weeks lead time from five months. Delivered $1 million in first-year revenue without increasing overhead through positioning and rollout of Good Reads for Kids. Achieved 66% growth in bookclub membership. Detected five high-potential, implementable brand extension opportunities. Identified as high-potential executive and invited to join prestigious and intensely competitive management program.

The Barrons Companies, New York, NY

1993 to 1994

MANAGER—Gibbons

World-class publishing enterprise. Barrons owns Gibbons, a $50 million division publisher covering global commodity market.

Management team member of dynamic organization with high-energy group of well-trained professionals involved in creative and business sides of publishing financial analysis information for global commodities/futures market. Managed product development, research, branding, and general marketing activities. *Credited with contributing to 60% product category profit margin for launch of Gibbons Metals Alert online service.* Prepared and presented cost-benefit and entry analyses for potential M&A targets as Barrons was expanding.

ABC Consulting, Phoenix, AZ

1990 to 1993

PARTNER

Privately held marketing research and management consulting firm providing services to corporate clients entering and/or expanding into the Eastern European marketplace.

EDUCATION, AFFILIATIONS & DISTINCTIONS

MIM—Master of International Management (dual-degree program with Wharton's MBA)
The Wharton School, Philadelphia, PA

MBA—Master of Business Administration (dual-degree program with Wharton's MIM)
The Wharton School, Philadelphia, PA

BSJ—Bachelor of Science in Journalism
New York University, New York, NY

Affiliations & Distinctions

Member:	Direct Marketing Association, Junior Chamber of Commerce, Senator Jr. Chamber of Commerce Int'l.
Recipient:	U.S. Congressional Gold Medal for "Outstanding Community Service"
Designation:	Outstanding Young Marylander, Former Governor Donald Schaefer
Distinguished:	Only Eagle Scout to earn all 124 merit badges in history of Boy Scouts of America
Military Service:	Lieutenant & Search-Rescue Pilot, U.S. Air Force/Civil Air Patrol

2224 Central Park West #10B, New York, NY 10020 ▪ 212-949-5555 (home) ▪ 914-505-7915 (mobile) ▪ tvbraun@aol.com

Thad Von Braun

Addendum to Resume
SENIOR-LEVEL MARKETING EXECUTIVE—CMO

LEADERSHIP PROFILE
GROWTH MANAGEMENT & CULTURE CHANGE

CMO
AdFocus

Challenge	To ensure future growth, improve market presence/share, and optimize long-term profitability, company needed to refocus its marketing activities. Determined two priorities: 1) reduce reliance on cable television for lead generation, and 2) shift business model to improve existing customer acquisition and cultivate new platform/culture focused on remarketing.
Actions	Developed and executed (phased in to control costs and mitigate risk) PRM & CRM strategies and leveraged related solutions, campaigns, and partners for teleservices, database administration, and lettershop fulfillment. Expanded TV broadcasting buying into hybrid-DRTV, syndication, network, spot, and PI. Helped restructure marketing organization into online advertising and online customer-service delivery systems.
Results	➡ Cut reliance on cable TV to 30% from 55% and began process of reducing costs (in an environment of three-year, near-100% increase in TV advertising costs). Increased customer acquisition from Internet by 200%.
	➡ Created marketing campaigns to turn "prospects" into "purchases" in nine customer segments. Reduced lost calls and improved throughput rates to sales agents as much as 75% by enhancing telephony IVR messaging and logic.
	➡ Doubled lead generation from Yellow Pages at 40% better cost-efficiency than cable TV.
	➡ Maintained on-air presence during periods of low inventory and generated an abundance of leads through hybrid-DRTV and syndication.
Analysis	Changed a "can't-do" culture to a "can-do" culture. Strategies and actions—against seemingly "impossible" odds—salvaged the business, retained its market share lead, established effective PRM-CRM model for new-product launches, and created a pathway for future growth.

LEADERSHIP PROFILE
CLIENT FEE REVENUE GROWTH

Transglobal Marketing
Account Director

Challenge	Increase client fee revenues and protect company's standing as industry's thought leader.
Actions	Differentiated company from competition by marketing core competencies and service offerings that were difficult to replicate. Targeted acquisition efforts to start-up companies (high-potential segment during peak in the IPO and dot-com market) seeking and willing to pay premiums for total marketing outsourcing solutions vs. investing in marketing internal infrastructures.
Results	*Delivered 530% growth—to $4+ million from $750,000—in client fee revenue over three years.*
Analysis	Valuable to clients for ability to create needs-specific programs. Valuable to agencies as a consistently top-ranking contributor to business development, customer acquisition, and revenue generation.

LEADERSHIP PROFILE
BRAND DEVELOPMENT & POSITIONING

Brand Manager—Good Reads for Kids
Simon & Schuster

Challenge	Launch and grow a current-member marketing brand in an extremely mature sector.
Actions	Part of core team that set out to understand evangelical Christian market—the heartland of America (virtually a world away from New York City), then tapped into nontraditional communications outlets in home schooling, pastoral newsletters, and PR, and aggressively marketed to niches as they were identified.
Results	*Delivered what was touted as most successful launch of a new bookclub category in 25+ years. The Good Reads for Kids brand generated $35 million in new revenue (1996) to company. Contributed to 66% growth in membership (1995) and effected 13% improvement in sales-per-catalog.*
Analysis	Undaunted by facing an unfamiliar market and unaffected by a general air of pessimism (most said this market was opportunity-barren). Researched, learned, then applied creative energy, marketing knowledge, and branding expertise to help make project a success.

2224 Central Park West #10B, New York, NY 10020 ▪ 212-949-5555 (home) ▪ 914-505-7915 (mobile) ▪ tvbraun@aol.com

(continued)

(continued)

Thad Von Braun

LEADERSHIP PROFILE
LEAD GENERATION & CUSTOMER ACQUISITION

CMO
AdFocus

Challenge	Improve effectiveness of the online channel for lead generation and customer acquisition.
Actions	Represented marketing as senior member on cross-functional management team tasked with building better online "mousetrap." Allocated internal IT resources and participated in sourcing, hiring, and directing activities of external consultants and channel experts.
Results	*Achieved 30% signup and purchase rates from online channel—up 300% from previous years—and created 25% offline spillover from online-generated advertising, without additional offline marketing spending.*
Analysis	Strong IT orientation. Adept at leveraging technology to achieve both marketing and business objectives. By reducing the artificial barriers to interaction and enabling the customer to choose how they wished to buy, we changed our business paradigm. Being vigilant about removing barriers to purchase earns money.

LEADERSHIP PROFILE
CLIENT/CAMPAIGN CYCLE IMPROVEMENT

Account Director
Transglobal Marketing

Challenge	Accelerate time-to-market and improve quality, efficiency, and cost effectiveness of development and production life cycle.
Actions	Rallied and led seasoned, cross-functional team of professionals that shared entrepreneurial orientation and sense of urgency. Conceived, developed, and managed deployment of sweeping campaign, including television, radio, direct mail, fulfillment collateral, and infrastructure.
Results	*Exceeded client's expectations for hitting a category in-market sweet spot by deploying full-scale, integrated marketing and advertising campaign in six weeks.*
Analysis	Never object to taking on the "impossible," regardless of complexities. Senses and skills are fueled when the pressure is on. Consistently able to lead a team and "make it happen."

LEADERSHIP PROFILE
PUBLIC RELATIONS

CMO
AdFocus

Challenge	Utilize public relations to drive lead generation volume at cost comparable to traditional cable television advertising rates.
Actions	Initiated aggressive courtship of high-volume media outlets and high-profile personalities, developed an infrastructure to handle peak call volume, and retained a public relations agency.
Results	Secured four-minute spot on NBC's *Today Show,* generating most leads from any television placement in company's history. Online visits increased 20% during that same period.
Analysis	Proficient in linking public relations strategies and events with traditional marketing and advertising campaigns to optimize lead generation, brand recognition, and, ultimately, sales revenues.

LEADERSHIP PROFILE
MARKETING & ADVERTISING COLLATERALS

CMO
AdFocus

Challenge	Create targeted high-impact collaterals more swiftly and at less cost than a traditional full-service agency.
Actions	Utilized contact network (highly competent freelance creative and strategic talent) to design and produce all required creative advertising materials from TV to inserts to sales collateral.
Results	Exceeded creative needs for all AscendOne brands at 50% of cost of using full-service agency.
Analysis	Over 10+-year career, have assembled, and continue to maintain, a Rolodex of readily available contacts and relationships. Such a list keeps costs down and generates creative, high-quality work.

2224 Central Park West #10B, New York, NY 10020 ▪ 212-949-5555 (home) ▪ 914-505-7915 (mobile) ▪ tvbraun@aol.com

Thad Von Braun

Addendum to Resume
SENIOR-LEVEL MARKETING EXECUTIVE (CMO)

LEADERSHIP TESTIMONIALS

MARKETING · BRANDING · ADVERTISING · PUBLIC RELATIONS

"You are one of the most creative, smart, hardworking and passionate people I've ever worked with. You made significant contributions while you were here. Most notable was your willingness to be bold, creative, and tenacious.... Any success we have with remarketing around here is because of your recognition and pursuit of the approach."

President & CEO, AdFocus

"Your greatest accomplishment at Transglobal was the P&G business that you won and built. They are tough customers; they were looking for something new and innovative in channel and in marketing. One piece of business was parlayed into a portfolio that was a showpiece for the agency, for the creative department, and for our industry... Those accounts were the foundation for Transglobal, the hot shop, the place to be, the one clients had to see in their reviews. You did it; no one else could, and I really believe that."

EVP, Transglobal Marketing

"I thought the prospecting and remarketing system and creative that went with it was outstanding because you developed it from idea to full implementation at a VERY LOW COST. I also thought your work on IVR and call flow was top-notch."

COO, AdFocus

"When you decide something must be done...you work harder than everyone else to achieve the goal. You have vision and creativity, and you have a strong network of external resources. My hope is that you taught us well enough and left a network [for us] to draw on so everything will get done."

Managing Partner, KMG Group

"In my opinion, your greatest accomplishment is how you've influenced the organization to move beyond the status quo, make changes, and strive to grow into a highly functional company—the energy and passion you brought to AdFocus will definitely be missed. No one else has the breadth of knowledge on various topics."

Marketing Manager, AdFocus

"The partnership and team building you created—for a difficult account such as Beck's—that brought together diverse individuals from two continents [was a major accomplishment], and you are good at keeping the team involved and informed. You have an amazing understanding of data."

Director of Production, Transglobal Marketing

"Thad is a very intelligent and driven manager. He identifies with the projects he manages and invests a great amount of energy in them. He is goal-oriented and measures his success by the results, not the effort."

Managing Director, Canada, Simon & Schuster

"You modeled how to be a strong team player (for all levels); very supportive of the company vision (even if you had questions/concerns)... [You] created an infrastructure for marketing unparalleled by predecessors (and challenged our old ways of doing things)... You know what is the right thing to do...[are] extremely bright, able to think strategically and see well 'down the road'...and design a game plan to get there."

Senior Director, Waterman Corporation

"[You are] extremely innovative. Able to find solutions to very difficult company issues... A master at dissecting data and presenting it... Able to take a small amount of data and in a very short time (minutes or seconds, it seems to me) and tell the story the data represents...and use technology to the company's advantage... You know how to think it out and then...convey matters in words that people can understand."

President, Grisham Consulting Group

2224 Central Park West #10B, New York, NY 10020 ▪ 212-949-5555 (home) ▪ 914-505-7915 (mobile) ▪ tvbraun@aol.com

JORGE STEVENSON—EXECUTIVE RESUME (WRITER: JAN MELNIK)

Jorge L. Stevenson

3966 Cape Hope Road ■ Dallas, TX 75201
214.270.3870 ■ mobile: 214.399.6604 ■ stevensonjl@aol.com

SENIOR-LEVEL HUMAN RESOURCE MANAGEMENT PROFESSIONAL ■ CONSULTANT
EXPERTISE: BENEFITS ■ OUTSOURCING ■ M&A ■ PROJECT MANAGEMENT ■ SERVICE DELIVERY

- Accomplished, experienced **HR Professional** with demonstrated ability to drive change, consolidate operations, creatively manage work teams, launch continuous-improvement initiatives, and achieve objectives. Track record of success in motivating and developing staff while optimizing operational results. Expert outsourcing strategist.

- Proven performer who thrives on challenges, delivers results under pressure, and gets the job done—consistently exceeding all expectations. Team player and consensus builder.

Professional Experience

M. DAVIDSON ASSOCIATES ■ Dallas, TX   1995–Present
Principal — Human Resources Officer, 1999–Present

Provide senior-level HR leadership, direction, and project management oversight in managing service delivery to high-profile clients, enacting HR reengineering projects and managing mergers, acquisitions, and rollups worldwide. Key member of executive management team leading successful business development initiatives and implementations.

- Develop and manage accounts generating in excess of $1MM in revenues annually, **consistently exceeding annual revenue goals by 140%.**

- **Direct 6 offices in Northeast Unit; provide overall HR leadership for 1,100 employees.** Provide counsel to Unit Leadership Group in HR, employee relations, and legal issues.

- **Managed pension program consolidation for major merger and acquisition in financial services industry.** Partnered with senior-level executives to identify, design, and accomplish innovative project management plan.

- **Directed successful consolidation of HR function in 4-company rollup for leader in high-tech business segment.** Deployed multipronged program to outsource benefits, streamline multiple payroll methods to one vendor, synthesize audit process, and eliminate redundancies.

- **Managed successful Department of Labor audit; participated in HR Transformation project and certification by Development Dimensions International** (DDI) on attraction and retention.

Principal — Senior Consultant, 1995–99

As Human Resources Operations Consultant, served as Project Manager on strategic and highly visible projects, including **client mergers, acquisitions, and integration processes.** Range of projects included HR administration, organizational redesign, vendor management, process reengineering, and outsourcing.

- Project Manager for HR/Benefits rollup of plans impacting 85 unions and 265,000 employees in aerospace industry merger; orchestrated transition to outsourcing of all benefits, coordinating unique and completely customized plans. **Effectively managed project generating $7MM–$8MM annually over 3-year project timeline.**

- Project Manager/Consultant for large energy provider's HR reengineering initiative. **Managed post-outsourcing organizational design, reengineering of corporate benefits, and internal customer service center creation.**

- Project Manager, Health and Welfare SAP implementation (functional requirements, system configuration, testing) for client's vendor. **Oversaw on-site vendor management of ongoing operations and system development.**

Jorge L. Stevenson   214.270.3870 ■ mobile: 214.399.6604 ■ stevensonjl@aol.com ■ Page 2

SCUDDER INVESTMENTS ■ Ft. Worth, TX   1993–95
Client Manager

- **Spearheaded development of Scudder's first Defined Benefit and Health and Welfare client account and launch of service center;** provided highly focused and directed account management.
- **Leveraged ongoing defined contribution relationship in coordination with implementation of emerging products.** Troubleshot and strategized with project managers to provide seamless integration and avoid silo effect.
- **Created strategy and guidelines for managing financial and administrative implications of divestitures.**
- Oversaw business planning, coordination of resources, training, client reporting, and product/service segmentation.

WINDOC ANALYSIS SOFTWARE SYSTEMS, INC. ■ Oakland, CA   1992–93
Application Consultant / Business Analyst

- **Pivotal player on reengineering team that redesigned administration process in multiple business unit environment with 150,000 employees.** Instrumental in managing successful rollup of 85 residual plans.
- **Project Manager of benefit system conversion;** analyzed plan design features and directives from operation and multiple system perspective; developed functional specifications and system implementation strategy.

ADVEST, INC. ■ San Francisco, CA   1985–91
Assistant Vice President, Human Resources, 1987–91

- **Promoted to manage administration and operations of company's profit-sharing plan and deferred compensation plans.** Supervised staff of 6. Designed and implemented plan documents; oversaw annual audit.
- **Reengineered department to administer benefit programs more accurately and efficiently;** programs included medical, dental, disability, flexible spending accounts, group life, tuition reimbursement, and stock purchase plan.
- **Negotiated contracts.** Maintained legal ERISA compliance and tax requirements.

Special Project Manager, Corporate Finance, 1985–87

- **Managed conversion of internally designed Focus Employee Recordkeeping System** from manually calculated system; oversaw project management and system development from user perspective. Liaison between CFO and computer service division. Ensured accurate implementation; managed audit/compliance requirements.

Education

CONCORDIA UNIVERSITY ■ Irvine, CA — **Master's Degree in Business Administration,** 1989

HARVEY MUDD COLLEGE ■ Claremont, CA — **Bachelor of Science Degree, Business Administration,** 1985

ROBERT BROWN—EXECUTIVE RESUME, CRITICAL LEADERSHIP INITIATIVES (WRITER: LOUISE KURSMARK)

ROBERT L. BROWN

513-294-9972   2309 Miami Trail Drive, Loveland, OH 45140   rlbrown@zoomtown.com

HUMAN RESOURCES EXECUTIVE

Training • Organizational Effectiveness • Performance Improvement

Business-focused HR executive, a leader in delivering strategic learning solutions clearly linked to corporate goals for sustainable performance improvements. Headed training functions for some of the nation's best-known companies in consumer goods and services; consulted for corporations and the U.S. Air Force; managed strategic enterprise-wide initiatives and millions of training dollars.

- **Influential change leader,** building consensus to effectively implement new models, methodologies, and initiatives.
- **Partner with business leaders,** evaluating needs and determining solutions to drive business goals.
- **Expert in educational design and adult learning,** applying traditional, blended, and online best practices.

EXPERIENCE AND ACHIEVEMENTS

EXECUTIVE CONSULTANT: HR SOLUTIONS   Cincinnati, OH, 2005–Present

Launched a consulting practice dedicated to the improvement of human performance to drive business growth and goal achievement. Landed high-profile clients and repeat assignments; highlights include:

- **U.S. Air Force:** Expert resource/advisor to performance analysts within new Leadership Development Center. Coached team on business development, project management, customer relationships, and human performance improvement methodologies. Delivered immediate results:
  - 3-fold increase in number of customers and 4-fold growth in number of portfolio projects
  - $450K annual cost savings projected as a result of a successful leadership development project
- **Cinergy Corp.** ($4.6B publicly traded diversified energy corporation):
  - In accelerated 3-week timeframe, planned and facilitated HR strategic planning meeting for top HR executive, then rolled down to entire department.
  - Initiated e-learning transition, launching project plan for a Learning Management System for 400 employees.

PROCTER & GAMBLE   Cincinnati, OH, 2004–2005

TRAINING MANAGER

Recruited to lead start-up of training function for newly established P&G division (400 employees nationwide). Advocated and gained executive support for comprehensive training strategy rather than "quick-fix" solutions; headed up entire process, from organizational needs assessment through strategy development, curriculum design/development, program delivery, vendor selection/management, and budget oversight.

- **Led evolution from training focus to performance focus,** partnering with and coaching senior management to adopt leading-edge concept, then creating a strategic learning and performance plan linked to business goals. Included a smart decision-making process to align capital investments with highest-value HR solutions.
- **Evaluated and quickly addressed skill gaps** of newly merged divisions.
- **Collaborated with sales leadership on new customer-centric strategy** to reduce competitive price pressures.
  - Researched best-practice sales models and led a cross-functional team in selecting the model most adaptable to new customer-centric culture.
  - Improved consistency and effectiveness of performance assessment and performance coaching.
  - Launched "Solutions Selling" training curriculum that contributed to achieving 125% of sales goal in 2005.

AMERICAN FINANCIAL GROUP   Cincinnati, OH, 1999–2004

HR SENIOR CONSULTANT

Provided strategically focused leadership to training, performance, and human capital solutions organization-wide. Initiated company "firsts" and delivered measurable results in training effectiveness and customer satisfaction.

ROBERT L. BROWN • Page 2 of 2 513-294-9972 • rlbrown@zoomtown.com

AMERICAN FINANCIAL GROUP

continued

Partnered with senior management across business units to identify opportunities to improve business performance through HRD initiatives. Managed a team of 12, with full accountability for project portfolio management, metrics, and evaluation; vendor management; and achievement of customer service benchmarks and specific program goals.

- **Spearheaded top-to-bottom upgrade of AFG's training organization,** delivering a best-practices model that made in-house training department the "vendor of choice" in our shared services environment.
  - Increased customer satisfaction to 88% "completely satisfied"—a 9% increase in 1 year.
  - Contributed to AFG's being recognized as a top-50 training company by ASTD.
  - Earned AFG Chairman's Award for exceptional contributions.
- **Designed and executed program to clearly communicate company's mission, goals, and business model to all employees nationwide.** Video and Leaders Discussion Guide provided information and process to translate corporate strategy to tangible individual strategies for each employee.
- **Launched the company's first leadership website,** leading cross-functional team charged with improving the leadership development process enterprise-wide.
  - Led team in comprehensive evaluation and solution development, involving senior leaders across the company and creating a robust, flexible tool and process for cost-effective, long-term results.
  - Rolled out Leaders@Work website, with development resources linked to clearly defined competencies.
- **Overhauled Leader Development course,** foundational training program for all company managers.
  - Added 11 hours of training while cutting costs, eliminating inconsistencies, and improving customer satisfaction.
  - Implemented self-study, e-learning, and train-the-trainer components that eliminated year-long training waitlist, reduced cycle time to train 4,000 managers nationwide, and allowed workshops to focus on skills practice.
  - New program adopted for use by international business units.
- **Drove several key initiatives to improve learning and development for the field sales organization.**
  - Responded quickly to CEO's new, transformational business model requiring significant change for the field sales force. On an aggressive schedule, designed and rolled out new business model and technology training to entire agency sales force; then designed immediate learning and long-term performance development programs to build newly required competencies.
  - Averted $100K retraining expense by analyzing agents' use of technology and identifying root causes.
  - Designed e-learning training modules to educate field agents and invigorate sales of profitable product lines.

ANDREW JERGENS COMPANY

Cincinnati, OH, 1988–1998

HUMAN RESOURCES ADMINISTRATOR, 1996–1998

HR generalist role for regional facility of 1,200. Managed 4 direct staff, $1M annual budget, and multiple Human Resources functions: Training & Development, HR Policies, Community Relations, and Recruiting.

- **Built bench strength and cut training costs 25%** by launching first Leadership Development Training Curriculum.
- **Cemented an innovative university partnership** to bring leading-edge best-practices training to Jergens.

PRIOR POSITIONS WITH ANDREW JERGENS COMPANY, 1988–1996

Administrative Supervisor, Claims Service Department • HR Associate • HR Assistant

PROFESSIONAL PROFILE

Education	Bachelor of Science in Education, Xavier University, Cincinnati, OH
Professional Development	Performance Assessment Tools and Techniques; Performance Consulting: Blanchard & Robinson Measuring the Impact of Learning: APQC Advanced Instructional Design: Langevin Learning Services
Affiliations	International Society for Performance Improvement (ISPI): National Membership Committee American Society for Training and Development (ASTD): conference presenter, article author

ROBERT L. BROWN

513-294-9972   2309 Miami Trail Drive, Loveland, OH 45140   rlbrown@zoomtown.com

HUMAN RESOURCES EXECUTIVE

EXAMPLES OF EFFECTIVENESS

Launching a New Training Function for a Start-up Division *(Procter & Gamble)*
Driving force behind strategy, planning, and launch of training organization for a new division; transformed initial vision of "training programs" into a strategically focused training curriculum closely aligned with organizational mission and goals. Gained executive buy-in for new strategy through advocacy, education, and persuasiveness.

Guiding Emerging Leaders in Leading-Edge Human Performance Methodologies *(U.S. Air Force / Consultant)*
Introduced team of inexperienced performance analysts to the latest methodologies in human performance consulting as well as strategies to establish themselves as a trusted resource to their internal customers.

Reducing Costs Through Streamlining and Training *(Andrew Jergens Company)*
Developed and managed training and performance improvement project. Consulted with Accounting/Finance Manager to reduce department expenses. Analyzed department's work flow, streamlined operations, and created a cross-functional on-the-job training program. Saved $115,000 in expenses while maintaining department production and efficiency levels.

Leading Process to Reduce Bad Debt *(Andrew Jergens Company)*
Initiated and led effort of Quality Improvement Team to support Regional Controller's debt-reduction business goal. Audited existing consumer collection process; recommended and implemented cross-organizational changes. Produced the largest bad-debt reduction in the company's history, saving $1 million.

Reducing Risk of Litigation *(American Financial Group)*
Led team in developing an employment law curriculum. Addressed company legal liabilities during rapid expansion, which included the hiring of 1,200 new managers. Curriculum adopted by international business units.

Heading Company Effort to Establish Industry Leadership *(American Financial Group)*
Initiated and led education design team to develop and implement an evaluation strategy, which included best practice standards and competencies. Resulted in the identification of process improvements, an employee competency development process, a method for linking design materials to business objectives, and a means to ensure that client training met or exceeded industry best-practice standards.

Developing Innovative Partnership to Benefit Frontline Management *(Andrew Jergens Company)*
Managed training curriculum, vendor, and budget for a regional facility of 1,200. Consulted with executives to initiate Leadership Development Training. Developed beneficial partnership with state university, gaining added expertise and saving $52,000 (25% total training expenditures) by tapping into state grant training funds.

Managing Transition to Smoke-Free Workplace *(Andrew Jergens Company)*
Involved smokers and nonsmokers in selecting a smoking-cessation training vendor and developing employee communication and facilities modification plans. Partnership with employees across all levels of the organization produced a smooth transition without employee complaints.

CAREER HISTORY

Executive HR Consultant (clients include U.S. Air Force, Cinergy)	2005–Present
Training Manager	Procter & Gamble, 2004–2005
HR Senior Consultant	American Financial Group, 1999–2004
Human Resources Administrator	Andrew Jergens Company, 1996–1998
Progressive HR and Management Roles	Andrew Jergens Company, 1988–1996

ANDREA ANTONINI—EXECUTIVE RESUME (WRITER: LOUISE KURSMARK)

Andrea Antonini

1749 Cartridge Trail, Lynchburg, VA 24503
434-324-0171 • andrea@antonini.com

ENGINEERING EXECUTIVE

Product R&D • Continuous Process Improvement & Cost Reduction • Lean Methodologies • Value Engineering Programs

Top performer in engineering leadership roles, delivering operational excellence and sustainable performance improvements through innovation, technology, and best-in-class manufacturing methodologies. Partner with business units and manufacturing operations to execute strategic business initiatives; able to translate customer/market needs into product solutions and establish market differentiation through technology, innovation, and patented products/processes.

Dedicated to utilizing all resources, including technology, to streamline processes, improve product quality, and drive revenue growth. Energized by "impossible" challenges. BSME, MBA.

Executive Endorsements: *"I really believe the lifeblood of a company is new product development, and there is absolutely no doubt...in my mind that you...are developing new and exciting products which will take [the company] to new heights."*— CEO, Dawson-Kent Industries
"Your dedication to innovation, to productivity, and to quality is exemplified in many of the 'extra' things you achieve or the way in which you achieve them."—VP Engineering, DK Engineered Products

EXPERIENCE AND ACHIEVEMENTS

DK ENGINEERED PRODUCTS, Lynchburg, VA

#1 in its industry in the U.S.; $600M subsidiary of Dawson-Kent Industries, a Fortune 500 company

Engineering Director for New Business Development, 2005–Present

Chosen to spearhead new business initiative, leveraging existing technologies and capabilities to meet strategic corporate goals of revenue growth and market-share expansion. Senior executive for the initiative. Develop strategic plan and lead an engineering team in implementing new products into production lines, streamlining and simplifying processes for rapid ramp-up, and providing engineering support to the marketing and sales team.

- Outperformed first-year revenue goal—currently on pace to deliver $7M revenue, 75% above target.
- Jump-started new initiative by personally landing first 2 contracts, generating $500K seed capital.
- Accelerated product launch through a modular approach that reduces engineering procedures. Brought 40 new products online in one year, 4X–5X more than company average.
- Developed a returnable packaging system for small components; delivered 25% cost savings to the customer.
- Evaluated a $3.5M tooling acquisition, prepared cost justification, recommended go-ahead, and modified acquired tooling into existing production systems. Delivered $15MM revenue—more than 3X ROI—in first year.

Director of Research & Development, 2001–2005

In newly created internal consulting/R&D leadership role, led numerous initiatives across all of the company's business groups to improve manufacturing processes, materials, and results. Managed 2 R&D engineers, 1 group manager, and 15 engineering services staff; consulted for the company's Metal, Wood, and Plastics product groups.

Analyzed all areas of plant operations and R&D initiatives, identifying product, waste-reduction, and cost-control opportunities. Devised and executed 3-year prioritized action plan to achieve strategic objectives.

- Delivered millions of dollars in cost reductions—e.g., cut 30% from component manufacturing by eliminating non-value-added processes.
- Drove innovative product development to generate profitable new revenue:
    - Generated $15MM first-year sales in a new market via a new line constructed from composite materials.
    - Invigorated stagnant product line, added 12 new products, and increased profitability 30%.
    - Conceived new feature for industrial markets, delivering $250K incremental annual revenue.

Corporate Director of Engineering and Product Development, 1998–2001

Improved manufacturing performance by implementing Lean methodologies and continuous improvement initiatives.
Directed all engineering projects in 5 U.S. and 2 international plants (Mexico and Canada). Managed $2.5MM engineering budget, $10MM capital budget, and 27 engineering and management staff.

(continued)

(continued)

Andrea Antonini   434-324-0171 • andrea@antonini.com

Corporate Director of Engineering and Product Development, continued

- Achieved $2MM annual savings through an aggressive Continuous Cost Improvement Program.
- Implemented 3P (Production Preparation Process) and led numerous Kaizen and 3P events in all plants.
- Conceived and launched a 3-tier talent-development plan: high school mentorship, college co-op, and the elite Engineering/Management Development Program, a 2-year business-wide rotational assignment combined with an intensive MBA-like program (developed complete curriculum):
  - Transformed company image to the point where the EMDP program has a waiting list at top colleges.
  - Achieved 100% success/retention rate in 5+ years; earned President's Award.

Engineering Manager/Model Shop Manager, 1991–1998

Reduced the cycle times of virtually every activity, managing all model work for the company's 3 product divisions as well as all engineering projects in the Metal Group. Supervised 9 staff.

- Identified profitable product innovation; developed prototype and successfully market-tested idea for composite designs that could be produced 30% below cost of existing materials.
- Developed and implemented several new product designs and features, earning numerous patents and helping company retain its position as a market leader and innovator.

Senior Engineer, Special Projects, 1985–1991

Led numerous initiatives—both cost/process improvements and major capital projects—for all areas of production. Prepared feasibility studies for new production lines; purchased millions of dollars in tooling and equipment; set up new manufacturing facilities; designed and implemented new processes. Project highlights include:
- Coordinated $1.75MM renovation of engineering R&D center.
- Saved $150K through an interplant hardware packaging program (Kanban) to eliminate corrugated boxes.
- Curbed losses from inefficient plant heating, resulting in $75K cost savings.
- Brought custom production shop online under budget in 90 days. Designed flexible tooling and features to accommodate product variances and volume growth—today shop represents $5MM incremental revenue.

EARLY CAREER

Manufacturing/Tooling Engineer, KENYON MEDICAL SYSTEMS, 1982–1986: Evaluated and purchased new technology capital equipment; coordinated vendor tooling purchases for new product manufacturing requirements; managed 5 tool room staff. Served as plant Safety Director.
- Led numerous technology, tooling, and production cost-savings and improvement programs:
  - Parts redesign: $450K savings.
  - New fixture and tool supply control system: $160K savings, lead time reductions for both standard products (60%) and custom items (70%).
  - Maintenance program for wire termination: $60K cost reduction.

PROFESSIONAL PROFILE

Education	**MBA,** Randolph-Macon College, Lynchburg, VA, 1993
	BS Mechanical Engineering, University of Virginia, Charlottesville, VA, 1982
	Advanced Management Continuous Improvement Program / Toyota Production System, 1999
	Shingijutsu Kaizen Training, Japan, 1993, 1998, and 1999
Patents	Awarded 24 U.S. patents (additional 3 pending) for product innovations; more than 50% of patents converted to revenue-producing products.
Affiliation	Senior Member, Society of Manufacturing Engineers
Languages	Fluent speaking and writing Italian; conversational Spanish and French.

MELISSA CYR—EXECUTIVE RESUME (RESUME WRITER: MYRIAM-ROSE KOHN)

MELISSA CYR, Ph.D.
135 Cypress Court
Monterey Park, California 91755
melissacyr@aol.com

Residence: 213-341-7417

Cellular: 213-456-4016

TECHNOLOGY EXECUTIVE/PROJECT MANAGER/DIRECTOR
Advanced Information, Media, and E-Learning Technologies

*Disraeli said that one secret of success was for a person to be ready for opportunity when it comes.
My job is to help you recognize your electronic opportunities without jeopardizing your current business.*

Technology expert/change agent with a 15-year career integrating and understanding the interrelationship between education, technology, and applications development. Delivered world-class customer-support training programs in networked multifunction educational market; led the development of various new technologies from concept, business case, and feasibility analysis through the entire technology development cycle to penetration of educational, publishing, and consumer markets throughout the U.S. and abroad.

Combine strong general management qualifications with outstanding performance leading advanced publishing organizations. Consistently demonstrate strong work ethic, exceptional negotiation skills, and ability to quickly learn and adapt to new systems, processes, and internal business mechanisms. Possess an entrepreneurial attitude.

Achieved phenomenal growth and a strong competitive industry position through combined expertise in:

- Strategic Alliances and Global Partnerships
- Financial Planning/Analysis, Financial Modeling, Budgeting, and Cost Management
- New Market Identification, Development, and Expansion
- Quality, Performance, and Productivity Improvement
- Product Design, Development, and Engineering
- Advanced Quality and Production Methods
- Training, Team Building, and Performance Optimization
- Organizational Needs Assessment, Continuous Process Improvement

ACCOMPLISHMENTS — HIGHLIGHTS

- **Created media technology department** at Heinle & Heinle. Blended content for different types of learning (e.g., visual, audio) with technology at various paces.
- **Slashed cost of technology development 150%** while increasing available technology **300+%.**
- **Transformed content delivery:** Web site now used to instruct, communicate, and expand business.

PROFESSIONAL EXPERIENCE

EXECUTIVE DIRECTOR MEDIA DEVELOPMENT
Heinle & Heinle – Los Angeles, CA

1996–Present

Senior Executive with full P&L responsibility for the strategic planning, development, operating management, and growth of all electronic media departments across Heinle & Heinle, encompassing 30 disciplines and 35 employees as well as a $15 million media development budget supporting $480 million in revenue for the Higher Education, High School, and Professional Training markets. Established procedures, developed business plans, and managed all production operations/control, scheduling, quality, testing, inventory, staffing, and financial reporting.

Lead cross-functional teams that collaborate as a focused unit to achieve aggressive business goals. Promote and train people to be valuable in other departments and to understand marketing/marketing needs. Introduced a series of productivity improvement, process reengineering, cost reduction, and performance management programs that consistently improved production output, product quality, and customer satisfaction. Innovated unique solutions to complex operating problems.

(continued)

(continued)

Developed sourcing relationships worldwide. Built and nurtured relationships with clients and faculty through attention to detail in defining needs and providing service and solutions to meet those needs.

Serve as point person for all interrelated departments. Administer complete project management cycle, from initial design through planning, feasibility analysis, and writing RFPs, grants, and technical documentation. Negotiate and draft all media-related contracts. Author training documentation (conduct QA with reference to content and functionality). Recruit, train, motivate, and retain all media development and project management staff.

Education/Training
Evaluate, conceptualize, and develop e-learning/distance learning strategies for K-12, higher education, trade markets (e.g., DeVry Institute), technology markets (e.g., Adobe, Microsoft), CNN video, Lexis-Nexis, National Geographical Society, PDF. Provide tools to authors to engage readers (e.g., how to create a story in a 3-D world). Lead and motivate editors and authors to take textbook to 2 or 3 other levels. Conduct seminars.

Alliances
Evaluate, acquire, and negotiate alliances for market-driven partnerships and initiatives. Work one-on-one with authors, **Elluminate** (for 24-hour live online tutoring and WebX software), **CNN** (exclusive digitized video rights for all higher education disciplines with Heinle & Heinle). Internal alliances with Production and Human Resources resulted in intranet-based (WebCT) instructional training courses and reference tools.

Publishing Technology
Managed media development of products ranging from assessment, homework, instructor enhancement (ancillaries), e-learning (CBT), and content management to full courseware. Delivery platforms from web-based, CD-ROM/DVD, video, and MP3 to hand-helds.

Task Forces
Chair, Media Council

- Web Site Development
- Standards
- Digital Learning

- Heinle & Heinle Intranet
- Higher Education Alliance/Initiatives

DIRECTOR, ELECTRONIC PUBLICATIONS   1993–1995
BioMedical Institute – Phoenix, AZ

Editor for all electronic/e-learning-delivered medical books, periodicals, journals, and newsletters. Set up database with composition and layout executed on-site, resulting in increased efficiency through streamlined productivity. Directed production of two quarterly journals, the *BNI* and the *BioMedical News*.

Trainer on platform functionality, use, and data management for staff and medical residents.

PROFESSIONAL AFFILIATIONS
Executive Board Member, SIIA (Software Information Industry Association)
Member, E-Learning Guild

COMMUNITY AFFILIATION
Volunteer, Mills Peninsula Hospital, Surgical Unit, San Mateo, CA

EDUCATION
Ph.D., Neuroanatomy and Physiology, Medical College of Pennsylvania, Philadelphia, PA
B.S., Biology, Northern Arizona University, Flagstaff, AZ
Distance Education **Professional Development Certificate,** University of Wisconsin, Madison, WI

ROSALYN ANDREWS—EXECUTIVE RESUME (WRITER: LOUISE KURSMARK)

ROSALYN ANDREWS

864-749-3465 • rosandrews@earthlink.net
2490 San Gabriel Lane, Greenville, SC 29610

SENIOR EXECUTIVE: Technology • Operations • Business Process Transformation • Global Enterprises

Strategist, change leader, and driving force behind technology advances and business improvements that support corporate objectives.

Versatile executive with a career-long record of innovation and results, leading technology and operations for national and global enterprises with challenging computing, communications, and information processing needs. Expert in aligning technology strategies with corporate goals and driving major initiatives through dispersed and complex enterprises. Broad range of complementary strengths, from vision/strategy and tactical execution through communication/presentation and ability to gain support for major change initiatives.

Reliably delivered cost savings, efficiency improvements, cycle-time reductions, and profitability enhancements through leading-edge methodologies including Six Sigma and Crosby. Expanded role to include business development, corporate communications, and involvement in all key business initiatives. Valued member of the senior business leadership team. MBA.

EXPERIENCE AND ACHIEVEMENTS

Avery Allen Insurance Services, Inc.   Greenville, SC, 2000–Present
$500MM TPC administrator for workers' compensation, liability, and property insurance.

VICE PRESIDENT INFORMATION SERVICES

Drove total transformation of Information Services from outdated, inefficient organization to state-of-the-art business partner supporting company growth in all areas. Crossed all areas of the company to contribute to strategic, business-wide initiatives outside the realm of IS. Recognized for outstanding achievement with rare honor of the company's Innovator Award (awarded just once in the last 5 years).

Technology Improvements

- Led a vigorous 18-month turnaround. More than doubled size of staff (currently 100), added new quality assurance capability, revolutionized underlying technologies supporting the business, and led a company-wide change management initiative to gain widespread support for new technologies.
- Led ongoing projects to automate processes and transform highly paper-intensive business to electronic data management. Added capabilities to improve productivity and performance at every desktop in the company.
- Introduced rigorous project management methodologies and reengineered IS systems, processes, and work flows for maximum productivity.
- Key member of IT team that evaluated and ensured 100% compliance with Sarbanes-Oxley requirements.

Strategic Initiatives

- Launched first-in-the-industry web portal allowing clients instant access to account activity and the claims management process. Serves 15,000 clients and attracts more than 15 million visits per month.
- Initiated e-commerce capabilities, integrated with vendor systems for efficiency and tight control of contracts/performance.
- Drove outsourcing initiative, identifying the right processes to outsource and selecting/implementing an offshore partner. Improved accuracy of highly detailed processes while achieving $2M+ annual cost savings.
- As evangelist for new initiatives, commenced company-wide communications program, regularly visiting field offices and presenting at key sales and marketing meetings to connect business operations with technology changes and strategic plans.

Business Development

- Instrumental in generating $80M in new revenue as a core member of strategic business development team. Delivering sales presentations to key accounts, communicated technology capabilities as a competitive advantage.
- Represented the company at trade shows, learning customer needs and relating them to company strengths and technology capabilities.
- Built recognition through published articles and keynote presentations that position the company as an industry leader.

(continued)

(continued)

ROSALYN ANDREWS   864-749-3465 • rosandrews@earthlink.net

Repo Auctions, Inc.   Greenville, SC, 1998–2000
$100M company, pioneering online site for auctioning repossessed vehicles.

DIRECTOR, INFORMATION SERVICES

Launched Internet presence, a key component of the business strategy, and strengthened technology infrastructure to support robust growth with advanced capabilities and operational efficiencies.

Performance Highlights

- Directed development of corporate intranet and Internet website with fully enabled e-commerce capability supporting 600,000 hits per week.
- Overhauled the computing infrastructure to include mainstream operating systems, software development tools, and database components.
- Increased development productivity 30% by implementing standard quality-assurance programs, application-design architectures, and project-management methodologies.
- Consolidated data and order management from 40 remote auction facilities into a single common data center, producing $2M annual savings and ensuring efficient, reliable, 24x7 system availability.
- Expanded technology services to key customers, implementing digital imaging, EDI/EFT, and custom client/server vehicle-management systems to enable attainment of $80M in new sales contracts.

Heavy Equipment Corporation   Birmingham, AL, 1990–1998
A global market leader in agricultural and construction equipment.

Repeatedly asked to take on new challenges in diverse areas of the company—both U.S. and international. Planned and developed or evaluated/purchased systems and technology to support complex business, financial, and communications needs of this worldwide enterprise.

MANAGER, PRODUCT MANAGEMENT SYSTEMS (1996–1998)
MANAGER, PRODUCT DISTRIBUTION SYSTEMS (1995–1996)
MANAGER, FINANCIAL SYSTEMS (1993–1995)
MANAGER, INTERNATIONAL SYSTEMS (1991–1993)
PROJECT MANAGER, CORPORATE SYSTEMS GROUP (1990–1991)

Performance Highlights

- Created 5-year strategic technology plan and gained executive support for recommended investments, including financial and order-management systems for the global enterprise; delivered more than $15M annual savings.
- Managed company financial systems activities in support of $350M company IPO.
- Led development and implementation of automated business process system to manage sale of $3.7B equipment financing portfolio; reduced annual interest expense by 61%.
- Worked extensively in Asian, Pacific Rim, and Australian sales regions and subsidiaries, implementing infrastructure upgrades and new technologies and services. Managed 15 staff in Singapore data center.

Mobil Oil Corporation   Fairfax, VA, 1983–1990

Competed through rigorous selection process to earn entry to year-long management training program covering all areas of process refining. Advanced steadily to new challenges in Engineering, Marketing, Finance, and Information Technology.

SENIOR SYSTEMS ANALYST, U.S. SUPPLY DIVISION (1989–1990)
SENIOR FINANCIAL ANALYST (1987–1989)
GROUP LEAD, FINANCE (1986–1987)
LOSS PREVENTION ENGINEER (1984–1986)
MANAGEMENT TRAINING PROGRAM (1983–1984)

EDUCATION AND PROFESSIONAL DEVELOPMENT

MBA, Finance   Georgetown University, Washington, DC, 1986
BS, Chemical Engineering   Virginia Tech, Blacksburg, VA, 1983
Six Sigma and Crosby Quality Training

JACINTHE-LEE TETREAULT—EXECUTIVE RESUME, COVER LETTER (WRITER: JAN MELNIK)

Jacinthe-Lee Tetreault

21C Marina Place • White Plains, NY 10601
(914) 827-3963 • cell (914) 302-7930 • jtetreault@mindspring.com

Finance Management • Operations Management
Turnaround Expertise • Analysis • P&L

- **Visible and results-oriented Senior Finance Management Professional** with track record of accomplishment reflecting turnaround experience and demonstrated ability to drive change, optimize operations, ensure integrated IT strategies, and achieve balanced and profitable fiscal performance. Skilled in leveraging talent from multiple disciplines with a focus on profitability by establishing effective financial systems/processes.

- Experience directing multidivisional operations and supply chain management in industrial/OEM distribution, transportation, and financial services market sectors. Uniquely qualified in ability to manage both finance and operations with full complement of IT knowledge. Expert analytical and assessment abilities. Reputation for consistently exceeding all expectations.

Professional Experience

MIDTOWN AUTO & TRANSPORT, INC. • Brooklyn, NY   1999–Present
Chief Financial & Operations Officer

Recruited to turn around Midtown's stagnant operations. Within 90 days, fully assessed opportunity and established comprehensive business management plan that effectively rejuvenated service delivery, restored confidence and customer satisfaction, and leveraged Midtown's reputation in industry to position for growth. Defined corporate mission statement and devised implementation plans to complement growth strategies.

- Under new operational management plan, led organizational growth and produced revenue increases across all 4 segments of business (growing from $2.8 million to $3.5 million in 3 years).

- Established separate profit centers for business operations model: <u>Heavy Hauling</u> (New York as well as transport from port to locations east of the Mississippi River) ... <u>Towing</u> (support major motor clubs throughout the state, provide heavy and light towing, and handle emergency recovery) ... <u>Service</u> (repair and service all equipment as well as provide commercial service) ... <u>Plowing</u> (maintain contracts with the State of New York Department of Transportation, commercial sites, malls, and condominiums).

- Aligned resources to support 4 profit centers—both staffing (reassigned and trained wherever possible) and procedurally (established separate sets of books and systems to support each business and provide accurate business management data that enabled effective decision making).

- Simultaneously established P&L for each division; conducted thorough business analysis of each segment, structured accounting, and ensured clean data to enable timely cost analysis and break-even assessment.

- Implemented best business practices for organization, emphasizing leading-edge customer-service strategies and a professional business model with staff of 40 employees across 4 profit centers.

- Instituted performance standards, provided consistent level of service, and attained highest level of customer satisfaction in company's history.

- Increased operational efficiency by 30% through launch of integrated telecommunications/data support network. Concurrently enhanced customer service and marketing initiatives while contributing to self-sufficient business operations.

(continued)

(continued)

Professional Experience *(continued)*

L.G. SAMUELS COMPANY • Pasadena, CA 1996–1999
West Coast Division Manager
Challenged to build new division serving western tier of national operations. Hired team for warehouse facility distributing 2,000+ OEM SKUs for fastener industry.

- With new southern distribution channel, launched business expansion throughout Florida and Georgia, increasing overall sales by 50% with annual sales volume of $2.5 million.
- Significantly increased customer base, attracting business from competitors through innovative marketing and advertising programs.
- Created and implemented hardware distribution research and evaluation of market.
- Designed and launched Total Quality Management program emphasizing exemplary customer service and customer satisfaction.

MILLENNIUM FINANCIAL GROUP • Los Angeles, CA 1994–1996
Vice President, Operations
Recruited to leverage relationships with brokerages and key accounts for start-up company focusing on commodities markets. Grew book of business from $200K to $1.5 million in just over a year.

- Devised and implemented financial tracking systems that directly enhanced organizational competencies and supported a service-driven culture; played pivotal role as core member of leadership team.
- Spearheaded due diligence efforts for several investigations into relationships with key contacts at top institutional clearinghouses in Chicago.
- Increased trading results by 51% through streamlined processes/cost savings resulting from comprehensive review of software package benefits.

ORION COMPARATIVES • San Diego, CA 1992–1994
Vice President, Operations
Hired to lead implementation of operational overhaul for $1 million start-up boutique financial planning company. Produced significant improvements in overall operations through implementation of key performance- and productivity-enhancing measures directly impacting back-office operations.

- Developed and specialized in presenting market-based living trust sales presentations—producing a 35% increase in sales.
- Earned Series 7 license and quickly mastered financial planning precepts.

Earlier background includes 6 years of successful and progressive experience with United Parcel Service (Chicago, IL) while completing undergraduate degree, culminating with promotion to **Supervisor.**

Education

LOYOLA MARYMOUNT UNIVERSITY • Los Angeles, CA
- **Master of Arts Degree, Organizational Management** (2002)

NORTHWESTERN UNIVERSITY • Chicago, IL
- **Bachelor of Science Degree, Business Administration** (1991)

Jacinthe-Lee Tetreault

21C Marina Place • White Plains, NY 10601
(914) 827-3963 • cell (914) 302-7930 • jtetreault@mindspring.com

April 30, 2007

Randall Summerfield
Chief Operating Officer
Superior Products, Inc.
301 First Avenue
New York, NY 10016

Dear Mr. Summerfield

A colleague of ours, David Martinez, thought my skills and background would be an excellent match for the Divisional Finance Manager's position within your organization. Most recently, I was hired to completely turn around overall operations at Midtown Auto & Transport. In a very short period of time, I fully restored the level of service, method of delivery, and overall satisfaction by assessing and then implementing four separate profit centers, each with its own P&L. I effectively led a team of 40 employees across all organizational levels in a culture that supported improved customer service, consistent performance excellence, and a bottom-line emphasis on sustained profitability.

My talent is building outstanding organizations, refocusing teams across multiple disciplines, and ensuring results that consistently exceed expectations. With an extensive network, I know who to call to bring in the necessary expertise to notch up an organization's level of performance. Strong leadership skills, an ability to energize and rejuvenate faltering operations, and a proven track record of managerial success help to define my management style and results. I especially enjoy the challenge of optimizing a company that may not have hit its stride—or may be going through a bumpy period of lackluster performance. Throughout my career, I have been able to play a leadership role in defining mission and strategy, then creating and executing an implementation plan to fully support these initiatives. I am an expert in change leadership and aligning an organization's existing capabilities with its goals.

I would value the opportunity to discuss this opportunity with you to better understand your organizational challenges and determine how my background might represent the right "fit." Thank you for your consideration.

Sincerely,

Jacinthe-Lee Tetreault

Resume enclosed

LILY CHANG—EXECUTIVE RESUME (WRITER: LOUISE KURSMARK)

LILY S. CHANG

780-209-4449   74 Stonehill Towers #4B, Stoneham, MA 02180   lilychang@gmail.com

COO/CFO/GROUP CONTROLLER/VP FINANCE
Industrial & Consumer Products Manufacturing
Kraft—Hartz Mountain—TekToys—Turnaround & High-Growth Ventures

Strategic and hands-on executive, an accomplished change agent with a 20-year track record of revitalizing, restructuring, accelerating growth, and maximizing ROI for manufacturing operations in intensely competitive international markets. Repeatedly delivered rapid and sustainable performance improvements in turnaround and rescue assignments: restored profitability, transformed operational systems, spurred revenue growth, improved morale, and positioned businesses for growth and sale.

Recognized for ability to distill complex issues to fundamentals, create blueprints for growth, and implement systems to guarantee profitability and sustainable competitive advantage.

- ☑ Strategic Planning & Tactical Execution
- ☑ Financial & Operations Analysis
- ☑ Leading-Edge Technologies & Methodologies
- ☑ Revenue & Profit Growth
- ☑ M&A Due Diligence
- ☑ Contract Negotiations

EXPERIENCE AND ACHIEVEMENTS

PROGRESSIVE CHEMICAL, INC., Waltham, MA (specialty chemicals manufacturer and distributor)   2005–2006
COO

Recruited by owner/CEO to take plateaued company to the next level. Transformed antiquated processes, met strict cost-reduction milestones, grew revenues 50% in 18 months, and structured the organization for profitable sale. With full accountability for all functional areas of the company, installed vital internal controls, budget compliance, strategic planning, and employee training; instilled customer focus and addressed performance improvement at every level of the organization.

- ☑ Led the company into 21st-century technology and methodologies, purchasing essential capital equipment and implementing Lean Manufacturing, Six Sigma, ISO 9002, performance benchmarking, and OSHA/Hazmat training (and successfully averting threatened EPA and OSHA actions).
- ☑ Grew revenues from $12MM to $18MM, primarily as a result of increased manufacturing capacity due to dramatic productivity gains—e.g., cut production time for one product by 80%.
- ☑ Slashed inventory, modernized warehouse, and cut labor costs.
- ☑ Secured federal and state grants, tax cuts, and empowerment-zone concessions to fund capital improvements and technology investments.
- ☑ Created a culture of employee "ownership" and pride in work well done.

THE GEFFEN GROUP, Lynn, MA ($70MM materials-brokerage firm)   2001–2005
CFO/COO

Reversed alarming trend of spiraling costs and declining profitability; implemented cost controls and fiscal accountability that supported profitable growth from $12MM to $70MM in four years. Oversaw P&L and all financial, IS, and business operations; also performed as broker, negotiating and arranging transactions between material sources and world-class manufacturers.

- ☑ Captured immediate $250K profit contribution and 28% reduction in operating costs by reviewing and renegotiating numerous supply and service contracts and establishing disciplines for day-to-day business practices.
- ☑ Implemented tight financial controls. Within 15 months, brought all accounts into compliance, improved cash flow, eased bank tensions, and saved $80K in interest payments.
- ☑ Structured sale of company assets for profitable payout to owners.

TEKTOYS, INC., Burlington, MA ($650MM manufacturer of handheld computers and software)   1999–2001

Senior Director, Financial Planning & Analysis

Through top-down business analysis, set the stage for transformational product shift that boosted profit margins 45% and set the stage for future growth. Participated in executive decision-making that steered business toward profit opportunities. Set financial controls and formalized planning processes.

- ☑ Orchestrated reduction in product offerings from 500 to 16, enabling 30% reduction in plant operating costs and profit growth from $8MM to $26MM within one year.
- ☑ Introduced performance benchmarking and pushed accountability to the lowest levels, leading to headcount reductions, commission-structure adjustments, and elimination of inefficient practices.
- ☑ Championed adoption of Oracle-based ERP system to streamline, standardize, and improve the efficiency of company operations in 65 countries worldwide.

CHEMSPEC PRODUCTS, INC., Saugus, MA (manufacturer of chemical specialty products)   1993–1999

CFO/VP Finance

Rescued business on the brink of bankruptcy, achieving profitability, explosive revenue growth, dramatic productivity gains, and recognition as a "Top 100 Fastest Growing Company" in Massachusetts. Began by negotiating with creditors, resolving existing bank-covenant violations, and securing new capital for automation and equipment. Continued to deliver financial, operational, and product improvements that drove sales from $17MM to $45+MM in a brief six-year period.

- ☑ Reversed $290K loss to $1MM profit within seven months.
- ☑ Improved manufacturing productivity 25%.
- ☑ Drove automation initiatives including smooth implementation of Oracle-based ERP system.
- ☑ Revitalized product development; remarketed existing products; realigned sales territories.
- ☑ Introduced contract manufacturing to utilize excess capacity. Established lucrative contracts with S.C. Johnson and Dupont, among others.
- ☑ Identified and negotiated acquisition of manufacturing plant with complementary products that spurred contract manufacturing revenues.

KRAFT FOODS, INC. ($18B food products manufacturer and distributor)   1987–1993

Plant Controller, Manchester, NH, 1991–1993

Selected for a "fix now or close" turnaround assignment with one of Kraft's largest manufacturing facilities. Led team that assessed operations, identified immediate and ongoing cost reductions, established operational controls, and laid the foundation for 12 years of profitable operation.

- ☑ Identified $600K in first-year cost reductions and year-over-year savings in the millions. Improved efficiency, introduced manufacturing line changes, and reduced headcount.
- ☑ Empowered employees and opened lines of communication with union officials to instill ownership.

Manufacturing Cost Manager (Group Controller), 1989–1991

- ☑ Identified cost savings and operational improvements as roving analyst for six Kraft plants.

Manager of Business Analysis and Financial Analysis, 1987–1989

- ☑ Developed business analysis modeling tool to track key management indicators for eight major brands; adopted company-wide.

EARLY CAREER (progressive accounting positions with Hartz Mountain and Chem-Solv)   1981–1987

PROFESSIONAL PROFILE

EDUCATION	Boston University: **MBA,** 1988; **BS, Accounting,** 1981
CERTIFICATION	**Certified Management Accountant,** ICMA, 1996
AFFILIATIONS	Association for Financial Professionals—American Association of Accountants—Institute of Management Accountants

JOHN WATANABE—EXECUTIVE RESUME (WRITER: LOUISE KURSMARK)

JOHN WATANABE

jwatanabe@gmail.com • 203-494-7509
7 Wisteria Drive, Guilford, CT 06513

SENIOR FINANCE & OPERATIONS EXECUTIVE

Global Operations • Revenue & Profit Performance • Business Analysis • M&A Deal Structuring

Track record of integrity, leadership, and results, driving the attainment of business, revenue, expense, and profit targets for Fujitsu global operations and leading an innovative start-up in the Americas. Expert in identifying strategic business opportunities, analyzing value and impact across complex enterprises, and orchestrating implementation, acquisition, divestiture, or other transaction.

Accomplished team builder, business partner, and negotiator who never fails to win consensus. Effective leader of multicultural teams in diverse locales worldwide; fluent in English, Japanese, and French.

EXPERIENCE HIGHLIGHTS

- Created start-up company for the sales and distribution of medical equipment; earned elite certification as business partner of GE Medical Systems.
- As CFO of $3B services segment for Fujitsu, led multinational team in delivering 109% of profit goal.
- Identified, analyzed, and executed $200M in M&A transactions for Fujitsu Corporate HQ.
- Achieved 21% cost reductions as Controller of $800M in Fujitsu internal IT investments.
- Established a regional Finance & Administration function in 5 countries.

EXPERIENCE AND ACHIEVEMENTS

MEDI-SOURCE, INC. | Norwalk, CT
FOUNDER / GENERAL MANAGER | 2004–2006

Led start-up firm from concept to strategic partnerships and revenue generation. Identified business opportunity in the competitive North/Central American healthcare market. Created business plan; negotiated lines of credit; established supplier and technical support relationships with Canadian manufacturer of a new brand of medical endoscopes. Led rapid launch and managed all marketing, sales, finance, and business operations.

- Secured critical marketing/business relationship as a certified business partner of GE Medical Systems.
- Generated revenue within 3 months of launch through aggressive business-building with distributors, hospitals, and clinics in Canada, Mexico, and Costa Rica.
- Earned product trial with one of the largest medical procurement companies in Central America.

FUJITSU | Asia, Europe, U.S.
CFO INTEGRATED TECHNOLOGY SERVICES, Fujitsu Europe | 2003–2004

Ensured profitable performance of $3B revenue business. Established quarterly and yearly targets for the 5 regions making up Fujitsu's European business; approved investment business cases and tracked performance toward defined goals. Managed multicultural team of 15 dispersed at international locations. Provided functional guidance to 5 regional CFOs and built strong collaborative relationships to ensure revenue and profit attainment.

- Nimbly managed moving targets—constantly revised upward throughout the year—and protected the most profitable business in the portfolio to achieve excellent year-end results:
  - 109% of revised profit goal
  - 93% of revised revenue target, 101% of initial target
- Developed road maps for revenue protection and expense reductions to secure the bottom line.

DIRECTOR FINANCIAL OFFERINGS, Fujitsu France | 2002–2003

Delivered profitability nearly 1.5X target as senior negotiator/final authority on all major contracts for a major global account. Reviewed all proposals prior to submission to the customer and directly negotiated terms and pricing on key contracts with the client's senior executives. Worked closely with administrative team that had direct responsibility for the global customer relationship.

- Achieved 105% of annual revenue target and 145% of profit goal.
- Made and kept promise to turn around all proposals within 24 hours—regardless of time zone differences from the Far East to Europe and the Americas. Built reputation for reliability and integrity in all regions worldwide.

JOHN WATANABE   jwatanabe@gmail.com • 203-494-7509

BUSINESS DEVELOPMENT/M&A CONSULTANT, Fujitsu U.S. HQ, New York, NY   1999–2002

Identified, evaluated, and recommended major investments of strategic value to Fujitsu—mergers, acquisitions, and divestitures. Worked in conjunction with major New York investment bankers and business law firms to identify and assess potential transactions; performed business and financial evaluations; submitted deal structure to Fujitsu senior management for approval; shepherded transactions to closure.

- Closed $200M in transactions in 18 months.
- Pulled together diverse functional teams for each project and led through complex analysis and structured decision-making. Established expectations and firmly adhered to original project timelines.
- Also served as Fujitsu corporate M&A contact for Latin American countries.

CORPORATE FINANCE ANALYST, Fujitsu Corporate HQ, Tokyo, Japan   1996–1999

Developed business and financial targets for $16B division, building strong links and constructive dialogue flow with division CFO and Finance team. Prepared and presented financial review sessions and performance evaluations to executive team. Created action plans for expense reduction to boost profitability.

- Using a "no surprises" approach, carefully managed information flow between division and corporate HQ, resulting in consistently excellent working relationships.
- Earned 100% approval rate on all investment business cases reviewed/recommended to Fujitsu CFO.

CONTROLLER, Internal IT Investments, Fujitsu U.S. HQ, New York, NY   1994–1996

Outperformed aggressive cost-cutting goal, reporting to newly created position of CIO in the U.S. and leading initiatives to better manage and control the company's IT investments in North America.

- Strategically focused efforts on projects that made up 80% of total internal IT expense. Interviewed, questioned, and challenged project owners, funding entities, and end users; created a prioritized list of projects for divestiture or closure. Gained executive approval and drove implementation.
- Achieved 21% cost reduction in 2 years vs. 15% target.

EARLY CAREER WITH FUJITSU: Fast-track advancement through increasingly responsible financial and management positions in Asia, Europe, and the U.S.

- Executive Assistant, Europe General Manager of Marketing & Services, Paris, France
- Manager, Performance & Outlook Assessment, Europe, Paris, France
- Program Manager, North American Manufacturing Plans & Controls, Chicago, IL
- Financial Operations Manager, U.K., London, England
- Finance & Administration Manager, Singapore
- Billing Manager, Singapore
- Associate Financial Analyst, Corporate HQ, Tokyo, Japan
- Accounting Analyst, Corporate HQ, Tokyo, Japan

EDUCATION

BS Economics, 1978, University of Michigan
MBA, 1996, Harvard Business School

Fujitsu Executive Education Highlights
- Acquisition Seminar, 1999
- Senior Management Course, 1995
- Advanced Management School, 1990
- Financial Management, Senior Financial Management, Accounting Management, 1978–1983

Dual U.S./Japanese Citizenship

RUSSELL GALIT—EXECUTIVE RESUME, COVER LETTER (WRITER: BEVERLY HARVEY)

Russell L. Galit, CMA

Forest Ridge Drive
Waco, TX 76712

rlgalit@earthlink.net

Office: (254) 712-5428
Home: (254) 748-5447

Senior Corporate Finance & Operating Management Executive

Multifunctional senior executive consistently successful in partnering finance with operations and business development objectives to drive continuous revenue, profit, and market-share growth. Areas of expertise include:

Finance/Treasury/International Cash Management/Foreign Exchange/Investment Management
Strategic Planning and Organizational Leadership ▪ New Business Development/Customer Relations
Acquisition & Integration ▪ Manufacturing Operations ▪ Vendor Negotiations & Relations ▪ IS/IT

MBA & Certified Management Accountant

PROFESSIONAL EXPERIENCE

LTN, Inc., currently WAF Manufacturing, Waco, TX   1989 to Present
WAF Manufacturing acquired LTN in March 2006. WAF Manufacturing is a $250 million manufacturer and worldwide distributor of screening products, industrial mesh products, drawn wire products, and building products.

LTN was a $95 million manufacturer of screening and building products distributed worldwide and was the largest supplier in the industry. Customers included Home Depot, Lowe's, USG, True Serve, and others.

Vice President & Controller, Divisional Officer, LTN
Member, WAF Manufacturing Executive Leadership Team, Integration Team, and 401K Committee

As LTN's CFO, currently participating in strategic planning, integration initiatives, and meetings with IGP Capital, WAF Manufacturing's private equity group. Prior to acquisition, led due diligence initiatives for LTN's private equity group.

Recruited back to LTN (1989) by the former CEO and equity partner to restore financial stability (after a five-year tenure with another company). Promoted to Vice President and Divisional Officer in 1992, interfaced with private equity owners regularly, served as a member of the LTN Pension Committee, and represented LTN before government boards and in legal matters.

Led strategic planning and financial management with general oversight of operations, business development, and sales for the $68 million corporation with 2 divisions supplying products domestically and internationally (60+ countries).

Financial management includes all aspects of annual budget/plan development and management, financial statements, audit, treasury including international cash management and foreign exchange, investment management, banking relations, risk management, pension, and salary administration. Interface with private equity investors. Manage a financial/IT staff of up to 17.

Operational management includes oversight of 4 manufacturing plants, business development, sales, customer relations, exporting, vendor negotiations and contracts, and relations with 700 employees in 4 states.

Leadership Accomplishments

- Currently leading WAF Manufacturing initiative to reduce operating costs by $2 million in first year.
- Led LTN through several stages as it grew from $40 million to $95 million in revenues; launched export operations and expanded into 60 countries; grew international sales revenue from $4 million to $14 million; and rose from #3 to #1 ranking in the industry.
- Formed a Budget & Planning Team to establish annual objectives to ensure continuous revenue and market share growth. Successfully managed achievement of objectives that resulted in $55 million revenue growth. Leveraged continuous budget/plan success to obtain financing and strengthen banking relationship.
- Managed acquisition and integration of an $18 million manufacturing company to complement the LTN product line.
- Integrated information systems of two manufacturing plants into a single system that delivered $280,000 savings within the Finance Department; provided data critical for determining product pricing and securing new business; and facilitated efficiencies throughout the entire organization.

Russell L. Galit, CMA

- Led company through Chapter 11 (1992) after an unfortunate decision by the equity investors to expand into an unrelated product line. The Court recognized the proceedings as one of the quickest to emerge from bankruptcy protection in U.S. history. Successfully managed all banking, customer, and vendor relations.
- Focused business development efforts on high-margin/high-profit products and customers.

Financial/IT Accomplishments

- Established an IT Department to manage development and customization of current operating systems.
- Saved $110,000 annually and provided cutting-edge processes by establishing streamlined electronic systems: Payroll Reporting & Direct Deposit; ACH of Payables and Daily Receipts from bank integrated into A/R system; 401K reporting to Fidelity Investments.
- Slashed financial close time from 6 days to 2 days.
- Instituted aggressive domestic and international collections system and consistently maintained <.07% annual bad debt.
- Developed financial analysis system to determine contribution margins and gross profit by products and customers.
- Structured treasury operations, cash management systems, and investment management strategies.

Manufacturing Operations Accomplishments

- Upon return to company, established inventory controls and eliminated $1.8 million physical inventory loss. Maintained zero-dollar loss 15 consecutive years.
- Developed JIT inventory management system to meet deliveries, improve cash management, and reduce inventory levels by $2 million.
- Developed system to monitor actual vs. standard raw material prices. Resulted in 9% reduction in costs.

Milton Corporation (A Division of Flesher Group, Inc.), Greensboro, NC   1984 to 1989
$69 million NYSE manufacturer of cleaning products
   Accounting Manager—Reported to Controller. Established cost accounting systems; slashed expenses 31%.

LTN, Inc., GE Wire Cloth Division, Waco, TX   1971 to 1984
   Office Manager & Assistant to Controller (1978 to 1984)

EDUCATION

MBA, Johns Hopkins University

   Selected as **Fellow, Johns Hopkins University**

   Selected for **American University Washington Semester Program**—Completed intensive program in Economics and Government.

BS, Accounting, York College of Pennsylvania

PROFESSIONAL CERTIFICATIONS & AFFILIATIONS

Certified Management Accountant (CMA), Institute of Management Accountants (IMA)
   CPA equivalency for managerial finance and accounting professionals working inside organizations.

Institute of Management Accountants

Financial Executives Institute

LEADERSHIP ROLES

Vice President, Board of Governors, Waco Public Library

Board Member, McLennan County School of Technology Authority

Treasurer, Westville Athletic Booster Club (Established budget system for $50K nonprofit organization.)

Board Member & Fund-raiser, Boy Scouts of America, Big Brothers Association

Russell L. Galit, CMA

Forest Ridge Drive
Waco, TX 76712

rlgalit@earthlink.net

Office: (254) 712-5428
Home: (254) 748-5447

April 30, 2007

Charles T. Smith, CEO
Banner Moldings, Inc.
2974 Banner Corporate Drive
Waco, TX 76715

Dear Mr. Smith:

Are you in need of a CFO/COO to grow revenue, profit, and shareholder value?

The manufacturing company I've helped build and lead (LTN Inc.) as VP, Controller, and Divisional Officer was recently acquired by WAF Manufacturing. As a member of WAF's Executive Leadership Team, Integration Team, and 401K Committee, I'm participating in all aspects of the transition, including upcoming meetings with IGP Capital, WAF's private equity group. Prior to the acquisition, I conducted due diligence on this $250 million company.

As a member of LTN's Senior Executive team for more than 15 years, I have held CFO responsibilities and instituted financial, treasury, operating, and technology systems that enabled the company to expand into 60 countries, grow international revenues to $14 million, increase domestic revenues by $13 million, and grow combined revenues to $68 million. Highlights include:

- Formed a cross-functional team to develop and manage an annual budget/plan that was the foundation for the company's growth and success.

- Met regularly with equity investors to establish and review objectives and progress.

- Managed acquisition, integration, and divestiture of plants and companies.

- Built an IT team and led the development of technology systems, electronic systems and processes, and virtual reporting capabilities.

- Established and managed an aggressive domestic and international collections system— consistently maintain less than .07% annual bad debt.

- Developed and implemented an inventory system—eliminated $1.8 million loss in the first year and have maintained zero loss year over year.

- Strengthened relationships with vendors and customers, including Alcoa, PPG, USG, True Serve, and Aluminum Specialties, headquartered in Australia.

Although I am an integral member of the integration team, the acquiring company has a qualified CFO. Therefore, I've decided to begin investigating new opportunities. I'm primarily interested in an intriguing position in a global manufacturing company and would welcome the opportunity to meet with you to discuss the contributions I can make to Banner Moldings.

Sincerely,

Russell L. Galit, CMA

Enclosure: Resume

PETER RUSSELL—EXECUTIVE RESUME (WRITER: GEORGIA ADAMSON)

PETER RUSSELL

3656 Orchard Valley Road
Santa Rosa, CA 95401

peter_russell@yahoo.com

707-595-9979 (home)
707-400-7612 (cell)

EXECUTIVE MANAGEMENT PROFILE

Goal-oriented, strategically focused executive with more than 20 years of experience and a record of consistently exceeding targets in a competitive, low-margin industry. Commitment to achieving strong business growth and substantial market share utilizing methods such as continuous improvement, best-practice sharing, and implementation of tools to gain a competitive advantage.

Leadership strengths: A leadership-by-example approach that includes integrity, high standards, and strong work ethic. Proven ability to communicate with diverse individuals on many levels and to secure the trust, understanding, and confidence of staff. Development of a carefully balanced structure that encourages individual contributions while satisfying business and regulatory requirements.

KEY SUCCESSES

- Played a major role in 6 successful acquisitions, particularly in asset evaluation, new-entity startup, and effective transition of an entity to independent ownership.
- Increased business volume 5-fold while growing headcount only 3-fold. Drove annual revenues from $10 million to $65 million.
- Provided expertise to assist new international acquisitions and partners in improving efficiency, developing operating guidelines, and implementing worldwide system standardization.
- Served on a review committee that selected an Enterprise Resource Planning (ERP) system for global implementation. Managed the company that was selected as the first site for deployment due to its record of outstanding audit results and detailed work-process documentation.
- Played a major role on a 4-month project that involved working with all company departments to develop an integrated supply chain.
- As a member of the corporate Best Practice Team, visited industry leaders focused on expansion.
- Joined the corporate university faculty in 1998.

PROFESSIONAL EXPERIENCE

Forrester Group, San Rafael, CA   1994–2006
President, **Hammerville Products, Inc.** *(1999-2006)*
(A wholly owned subsidiary of the Forrester Group, a division of Regent Enterprises since 2001. Industry leader for 9 years and the low-cost provider of Hammer and Clover products throughout the world.)

Overview

- Managed over 50 employees, including 5 direct reports. Planned and managed an operating budget of more than $5 million and a capital expense budget of more than $100,000.
- Held full P&L responsibility for this high-growth business, with 3 locations and 1,500 customers in 6 states.
- Implemented plans to fill voids profitably without losing presence in the targeted market.
- Consulted with partners upon request, helping them understand and reduce operating expenses.
- Served on the following teams/committees: Product Supply Leadership Team, Distributor Advisory Board, and Promotion Execution Team.

- continued -

(continued)

(continued)

Major Actions & Accomplishments

Revenue & Profit Enhancement:
- Managed operations to consistently exceed plan. Increased revenue from $35 million to $65 million.
- Repeatedly achieved operating expenses that were lower than peers' results. Decreased operating expenses against sales by at least 27%.
- Negotiated major contracts and lease agreements ranging from $85,000 to over $5 million.
- Reduced equipment costs by reviewing lease options, length, and service life. Reduced total delivered costs by leveraging scale with vendors.
- Executed plans on short notice to fill voids profitably in multiple locations, including Denver, Boston, and Vancouver, British Columbia.

Growth & Acquisitions:
- Grew market share in the mass channel from 5 to over 13 through expansion.
- Achieved growth from $10 million to $45 million in the specialty channel by expanding product availability, being the low-cost provider, increasing logistics services, and initiating a coordinated sales and customer expansion campaign.
- Managed the asset evaluation and assimilation of 2 Canadian locations. Acted as interim General Manager of Forrester Canada and restructured the Canadian business from a North American sales region into a stand-alone regional business unit representing over $45 million in annual sales.
- Spearheaded the acquisition of Tacoma/Boise-based Vital Products, which contributed $15 million in revenue for 2004.
- Repaid the equity investment of $1 million in less than 4 months.

Program & Technology Initiatives:
- Acted as Project Manager for the integration of Forrester/Hammerville into the broad Regent Enterprises organization, a complex project that included linking several proprietary computer systems into a fully developed package solution.
- Launched 2 unique service programs that captured a critical advantage for the company:
  Direct Store Delivery: Reduced cycle time to shelf by direct shipment to customers' retail outlets. Serviced over 500 All-Stop stores nationally through the program.
  DC Replenishment: Provided an increased service level to customers and reduced cycle time by moving from Regent Enterprises regional centers to local centers, a radical departure from the traditional method.
- Implemented Key Result Areas to provide a clear, objective picture of business operating trends.
- Acted as site leader for the Baan ERP system selection and implementation in 2000.
- Successfully executed numerous market development initiatives that were tested and documented at Hammerville before rollout approval and subsequent implementation nationally and internationally.

Team-Building, Training/Development, & Leadership:
- Recruited, developed, and retained a top management team for a period of more than 5 years.
- Created and implemented a program to give corporate personnel a greater understanding of distributor needs in a high-volume/low-margin business and to provide training for new members of the field sales organization.
- Successfully completed 12 individual developmental and training programs. Introduced a pay-for-performance program linked to company performance, the individual's contribution, and annual safety results. Consistently raised the standard of performance each year following program inception.

- continued -

Business Planning & Budgets:
- Developed a process to create an Annual Operating Plan and supporting budget for month-to-month business management, as well as daily and weekly reports/procedures for more frequent analysis.
- Created and compiled operating manuals and plans covering all aspects of the business, including personnel, procedures, and systems manuals and a disaster recovery plan.

Regulatory Compliance:
- Provided leadership to maintain compliance with strict requirements set by regulatory agencies, including the Department of Transportation, AIB, QAKE, and OSHA.
- Of 13 AIB audits, 12 ranked Superior and 1 Excellent, and 3 of the last 4 earned a perfect 1000 points. Nine QAKE audits averaged 96.5 out of 100, and 4 of them scored a perfect 100.

Distribution Manager, **Hammerville Products, Inc.** *(1994-1999)*
- Managed sales and operational responsibilities for a multilocation distributorship in northern California, Washington, and Colorado. Hired, trained, and developed the management team.
- Created and executed policies and procedures to manage growth and operations effectively.
- Developed and implemented meaningful benchmarks for the distribution network.

Accomplishment highlights:
- Turned around an initially failing distributorship with locations in San Ramon and Concord; then expanded by launching a start-up in Denver and purchasing an existing business in Tacoma.
- Exceeded annual budget targets by at least 10%.
- Grew the initial $10 million business by more than 35%.
- Developed comprehensive business measurement tools still used by the company worldwide.
- Initiated and managed Best Practice Workshops, a successful program to encourage sharing of best practices by functional managers, in conjunction with Forrester University.
- Repaid the equity investment in 36 months—2 years ahead of schedule.

General Manager, **Kilmont Distributors,** Salem, OR   1990-1994
Managed operations, purchasing, and sales for this regional wholesale distributor of Forrester products and related items, including a regional warehouse in Phoenix, Arizona.

Previous Experience:

General Manager, **Western Industrial Supply,** Denver, CO
Managed operations, sales, purchasing, and finance for this full-line wholesale distributor of industrial supplies, including regional warehouses in Billings, Montana, and Cheyenne, Wyoming.

AFFILIATIONS

Member, Board of Directors, San Rafael Chamber of Commerce

WESTON WALLACE—EXECUTIVE RESUME (WRITER: JAN MELNIK)

Weston M. Wallace
64 Ashleigh Road • Appleton, WI 54912
920.835.4376 / 920.384.2488 mobile • wmwall@sbcglobal.net

EXECUTIVE PROFILE

- Highly accomplished Senior Management Professional qualified for opportunity with growth-oriented company demanding expertise in operations, manufacturing engineering, business development, and new product design as well as demonstrated ability to successfully reenergize and turn around declining operations.

- Responsive to ever-changing business needs and demands; a visionary with effective coaching skills, expert technical knowledge, and strong strategic planning abilities.

- Progressive advancement directly linked to attainment of key business goals; performance- and results-driven in articulating and implementing change while gaining consensus.

KEY QUALIFICATIONS

- Dynamic hands-on manager and dedicated team player—highly effective leadership style.

- Irreproachable professional ethics and integrity—commitment to quality and measurable outcomes; expert communication/presentation abilities.

- Effective analytical and problem-solving skills.

PROFESSIONAL EXPERIENCE

ALLIED METALS, INC. • Milwaukee, WI   **2/2001–Present**
Integrated design/production manufacturer of materials/components for aerospace-based, metallics/nonmetallics, and overhaul service industries.

Vice President, Operations, and General Manager *(Promotion, 7/03–Present)*
Manage full operations in support of $422 million business; oversee team of 10 direct reports. Promoted to act as corporate change agent and introduce/direct leading-edge manufacturing and engineering processes targeting world-class quality and performance initiatives across all areas of operation.

- Spearheaded team effort, managed project deliverables, and achieved ISO9002 and AS9000 certifications.

- Successfully reduced backlog by approximately 70% in 9 months through multiple initiatives (restructured production control organization, deployed build-to-stock plans, used visual metrics on shop floor, and conducted daily management walkarounds).

- Simultaneously reduced outsourced tooling cost by 75% with no increases to internal overhead or department cost structure; identified areas for efficiency increases, launched training initiatives and management focus, realigned resources, and managed to fruition.

- Through precision planning and focus, reduced cost of quality by 15–20% in 10 months with a 50% cost reduction anticipated for FY2006.

- Reestablished credibility with strategic accounts and increased on-time delivery performance with major customers.

- Implemented MRP Phase I in nonmetallics department; plan rollout across all departments in next 12–18 months.

- Currently leading effort to launch low-cost base manufacturing operations in Mexico.

Weston M. Wallace
Page Two

920.835.4376 / 920.384.2488 mobile
wmwall@sbcglobal.net

PROFESSIONAL EXPERIENCE

ALLIED METALS, INC.—*Vice President, Operations, and General Manager* (continued)

- Leading effort to increase company's diversification in its customer base while crafting profitability analysis models to stratify and assess current business units.
- Oversee capital equipment acquisition process for state-of-the-art machinery, tooling, and equipment, managing annual capital budget of $31M.

Director, Engineering and Tooling (2/01–7/03)

- Successfully established infrastructure and project engineering function as well as resource planning model for company targeting major turnaround in its operations; launched strategic company-wide initiatives, setting priorities and properly aligning resources.
- Devised and orchestrated key plan to provide manufacturing engineering presence on shop floor while segregating responsibilities to optimize engineering and production operations.

MIDLAND US AEROSPACE, INC. • **Kansas City, MO**   **1996–2001**
Multisite division designs/fabricates high-tech composites for structural components supporting commercial aerospace/military industries. Annual revenues of $90 million.

Director of New Business Development (Promotion, 4/99–2/01)

Key areas of leadership included strategic and tactical responsibility for developing business and marketing plans, contract negotiations, oversight of competitive intelligence, and ongoing collaboration with R&D to support marketing objectives.

- Identified and marketed underutilized composites machining capability and secured contracted customer valued at $250K in first year with strong profit margin.
- Initiated negotiations and effectively penetrated new business opportunities with several large aircraft divisions of major commercial engine manufacturers; projected an incremental $10–$15 million in annual revenues for Missouri and Mississippi divisions.
- Successfully strengthened relationships with existing customers and identified potential new business opportunities to further penetrate accounts.

Director of Engineering (1996–4/99)

Managed engineering, new business/product development, research, and strategic planning with responsibility for Missouri's high-tech "centers of excellence for technological development" and Mississippi's high-volume, cost-effective production environment. Oversaw senior-level staff of 15; supported $70 million business base.

- Achieved turnaround objective for faltering Iridium Satellite Program through successful reengineering, process-improvement initiatives, and decisive program leadership; met cost objectives and delivered new product exceeding customer expectations.
- Reduced manufacturing costs through process improvements and strategic use of capital ($9 million); simultaneously reduced standard repair and scrap costs by 35% (1996–97).
- Effective management of Mississippi engineering operations included oversight of 5 managers, 55 indirect personnel, a $1.25 million budget, and a $750K research and development cost center.

EDUCATION

KENNEDY-WESTERN UNIVERSITY • Cheyenne, WY
Master's in Business Administration (2000)

VIRGINIA TECH • Blacksburg, VA
Bachelor of Science in Mechanical Engineering (1996)

RACHEL JORDAN—EXECUTIVE RESUME (WRITER: GEORGIA ADAMSON)

RACHEL JORDAN

236 Allendale Road   San Jose, CA 95124   408-999-9999   rajordan@msn.com

SENIOR MANAGEMENT PROFILE

Customer-focused senior administrator and leader with the vision to define strategic direction for an organization and proven ability to translate the vision into reality. Successful experience in initiating and managing organizational change. Effective coaching and team-building skills. Track record of achieving cost-effective operations and completing major projects successfully by establishing and maintaining strong relationships with customers, vendors, and internal departments.

PROFESSIONAL EXPERIENCE

Rowland, Inc., Sunnyvale, CA   1988–2006
An industry-leading designer and manufacturer of pressure-sensitive products, with customers that include Hewlett-Packard, IBM, Cisco Systems, and Applied Materials

PRESIDENT/CEO
Reported to the Board of Directors, with full P&L responsibility and five direct reports.

Leadership & Team Building
- Transformed the company business model from local to global status.
- Spearheaded progress that earned recognition as one of the Bay Area's 75 fastest-growing companies.
- Built and motivated the team that led the industry with 30% growth in 2002. Ranked in the industry's top 10% for profitability.

Strategic Planning & Alliances
- Drove the company to "think globally, ship locally" and focused on providing JIT service through worldwide manufacturing capability.
- Identified and forged strategic alliances with two Canadian companies and one Indonesian firm.
- Executed strategic planning, achieving over 76% of a U.S. niche market for the PCMCIA and multimedia card industry and generating nearly $4 million in total annual revenue.

Competitive Positioning & Profit Enhancement
- Turned around manufacturing operations from a loss situation to profitability. Drove EBIDTA results from $2.5 million in 1996 to $6.6 million in 2002 while growing the company from $6 million to $28 million in revenues and from 110 to more than 300 employees.
- Increased gross profit from 34% on $16.2 million in sales to 40% on $28 million in sales, versus a 32% industry standard.
- Strengthened profits and competitive positioning by creating a manufacturing technique that achieved unique results unmatched by competitors.
- Developed and managed a $1 million annual capital budget. Reduced costs by increasing efficiency.

Sales & Marketing
- Expanded sales by implementing effective marketing programs. Results included the following:
  - Customized direct-mail campaign that produced a 4% response rate on 14,500 pieces
  - Award-winning video on company capabilities
  - Corporate identity creation as a world-class leader
  - Cost-saving seminars enthusiastically received by customers—saved more than $300,000 for one client's main subcontract manufacturer

continued on next page...

Sales & Marketing (continued)

- ◆ Developed an effective lead-generation program using trade shows, seminars, and advertising.
- ◆ Opened U.S. sales offices in San Francisco and Dallas and an international office in Thailand.
- ◆ Established incentive programs to increase sales, including a progressive compensation plan for field sales and a bonus plan for opening new accounts.
- ◆ Played a leadership role in earning multiple industry awards, including 15 for Excellence, Merit, and Distinction in 2001 and two from major industry associations for operating as an "Environmentally Safe Company," 2003 and 2004.

Technology & Quality Improvements

- ◆ Instituted numerous improvements in productivity, efficiency, and performance, including:
  - Computerized order processing
  - Quotes within seven hours on new projects and within one hour on repeat jobs
  - Up-to-the-minute job tracking
  - Email customer communication and customer data links
- ◆ Led the company to achieve a sought-after, first-in-the-industry certification, which enabled the company to obtain 100% of a major corporation's business from 2001 to the present.
- ◆ Implemented critical infrastructure through first-in-the-industry achievement of ISO 9002 certification. Successfully directed the move to a new, larger manufacturing facility.
- ◆ Initiated and managed multiple state-of-the-art technology implementations from 1998 to 2004.

Previous Experience:

Evans Printing Systems, Redwood City, CA
Privately held offset printing company
Progressed to Northern California Sales Manager from positions as Supervisor and Sales Representative.

EDUCATION

Bachelor of Science in Business Administration, Minor in Marketing, Ohlone College, Fremont, CA

AFFILIATIONS

- ◆ The Executive Committee (TEC) member since 1998
- ◆ Graphic Printing Industry (GPI) member since 1989
- ◆ Junior Achievement advisory board member, 10 years

CHRISTOPHER RAWLING—EXECUTIVE RESUME (WRITER: JAN MELNIK)

Christopher D. Rawling

83 Siesta Key Boulevard • Tampa, FL 33602
(813) 315-3840 (res.) • (813) 315-9842 (fax) • (813) 842-9536 (cell) • rawlingcd@comcast.net

SENIOR MANUFACTURING MANAGEMENT EXECUTIVE:
OPERATIONS MANAGER / GENERAL MANAGER

Building and Leading Lean Manufacturing Organizations
Driving Productivity and Positioning for Rapid, Sustained Growth and Market Leadership

Record of targeted, growth-oriented leadership incorporating strategic approaches to optimize lean manufacturing principles, including implementation of Kaizen, one-piece flow, manufacturing cell development. Proven ability to increase profitability, revitalize performance, and drive overall results. Effectively manage P&L and labor relations while maximizing production output and service levels. Exceptional leadership competencies across all facets of organization, from operations and manufacturing management to engineering and new product design and launch.

- Strategic Planning
- Process Reengineering
- P&L Management

- Profit & Performance Improvement
- Restructuring and Turnaround
- Manufacturing & Quality Processes

- Regulatory Compliance
- Strategic Alliances
- Technical Product Development

Professional Experience

GULF COAST ALLOY COMPANY, INC. • Bradenton, FL   1988–Present
Vice President, Operations (1990–Present)

Manage all operations for one of the nation's largest manufacturers and importers of specialty alloys. Directly accountable for manufacturing, laboratory, quality, engineering, product development, tooling, production control, safety (workers' comp/health insurance), and regulatory affairs; company employs 600 across 3 shifts. Support a dynamic customer base composed of 650 active accounts nationwide; strategic accounts include Sikorsky, Pratt & Whitney, Boeing, ATT, and General Motors.

Select Accomplishments ...
- Created strategic plan that increased division sales by 31% over 3 years; sales growth distribution: 60% organic and 40% incremental. Spearheaded research and development team.
- Reduced energy consumption 15% through innovative measures designed with utility and energy providers.
- Produced significant volume of incremental sales through development/installation of innovative technologies.
- Established flexible manufacturing cells.
- Achieved key cost-saving objectives through following initiatives:
  - Implemented JIT delivery and renegotiated terms; result: 9%–14% reduction in material procurement costs.
  - Captured 11% annual material/labor savings through development of manufacturing software system that eliminated nonusable product.
  - Realized 49% first-year premium savings and subsequent annual savings of an additional 5%–9% through conversion of workers' compensation plan to self-insured program; launched Safety Committee and training programs. Total consecutive days accident-free: 3,100.
- Maintain high retention rate among workforce by ensuring constructive work environment, resulting in positive productivity impact.

Director of Engineering (1988–90)

Managed full breadth of manufacturing engineering, facilities, and tooling. Key accomplishments included:

- Identified key projects in area of regulatory compliance and established comprehensive, proactive program.
- Reengineered alternative energy solution, saving 15% annually. Simultaneously reduced heating oil consumption and avoided hazardous waste shipping as well as liability exposure.
- Collaborated with MIS to automate 80% of regulatory reporting process; result: reduced quarterly hours from 400 to 40 and improved accuracy while ensuring regulatory compliance.
- Introduced lean manufacturing—ultimately responsible for generating 12% productivity improvement.

Christopher D. Rawling

Professional Experience *(continued)*

DIGITAL EQUIPMENT CORPORATION • Burlington, MA   1983–88
Manufacturing Engineering Manager (1987–88)

Promoted to direct Manufacturing and Industrial Engineering Groups for consignment and turnkey PC board and computer systems assembly and testing division. Developed and managed Documentation Control Department. Managed engineering staff of 15+ and coordinated technical support instrumental in assisting sales force with marketing of services. Developed labor and material costing for all production quote estimates.

Select Accomplishments ...
- Designed and executed layout of large, state-of-the-art manufacturing facility that increased manufacturing space fivefold.
- Improved operational productivity by 18% through launch of team development programs; ergonomic workstation improvements increased efficiency 8%–20%.
- Streamlined manufacturing support operations by standardizing all processes, systems, and procedures; result: 98% on-time delivery of product.
- Reduced labor/material costs by 16% for product handling changes as a result of key value engineering initiatives. Achieved savings in excess of 22% annually from development of wave solder zero-defects program and through implementation of semiautomatic and automatic component preforming equipment.

Manufacturing Engineer, Special Systems Division (1983–87)

Implemented process equipment and assembly/test procedures for mechanical, printed circuit boards (PCBs), cable, and systems configuration. Managed introduction of new products and process equipment into manufacturing. Directed and trained process engineers in industrial engineering, product costing, and facilities layout.

Select Accomplishments ...
- Managed project team for renovation and layout of 20,000 sq/ft manufacturing and office facility; implementation resulted in significant annual savings.
- Generated a 17% increase in productivity via specific process improvements; key projects successfully implemented: automatic costing system, bar coding, and Electrostatic Discharge (ESD) Control Program.

Education

TUFTS UNIVERSITY • Medford, MA
Bachelor of Science, Industrial Engineering (1983 Honors Graduate)
Alpha Pi Mu Industrial Engineering and Tau Beta Pi Engineering Honor Societies

Continuing Education ... Successfully completed numerous professional management, environmental, compliance, OSHA, and Haz-Mat training courses throughout career.

MILTON HELFER—EXECUTIVE RESUME (WRITER: FREDDIE CHEEK)

MILTON S. HELFER

406 Brebeuf Place, Lynbrook, New York • (516) 555-3792 • miltonhelfer@yahoo.com

SENIOR EXECUTIVE
Financial Services / International Business / Change Management

PROFESSIONAL PROFILE

Proactive manager who turned $35 million loss into $4 million pretax profit in 1 year.

Key player in restructuring and positioning international corporation for dynamic and profitable expansion.

Proven strengths in bridging multicultural differences and developing long-term business relationships with management staffs at Fortune 1,000 companies.

Broad-based experience in financial services and capital markets, including commercial lending, credit analysis, refinancing, loan restructuring, portfolio management, international business transactions, investment banking, and insurance products. Successful track record of maximizing top-line growth, profitability, and productivity. Hands-on leader skilled in developing focused, high-performance teams to execute strategies and meet/surpass objectives. Adept at promoting performance-based culture that emphasizes mutual respect and secures the best outcomes for the organization. Able to communicate strategic vision and energize team members.

Core Skills

- Strategic Planning and Execution
- Business Startup and Turnaround
- Risk Identification and Reduction
- Problem Solving in Domestic/International Arenas
- Portfolio and Asset Management
- Business Development and Deal Making

Accomplishments

- ➤ Reversed $78 million in annual losses and took to break-even in 1½ years.
- ➤ Tripled business to $230+ million and significantly increased revenues in 2 years by spearheading marketing effort.
- ➤ Reengineered processes resulting in $427 million loss avoidance/risk reduction in 1 year.
- ➤ Optimized asset quality of $30+ billion domestic portfolio.
- ➤ Started up and led growth of export portfolio to $1.8 billion in 2 years.
- ➤ Revitalized mature region and drove asset growth from $100 million to $250 million in 3 years.

EXPERIENCE

BLUE SKY CREDIT INDEMNITY, New York, New York   2002–2006

Vice President & Managing Director

Pivotal in restructuring and turning around $150 million domestic operation with 31 offices throughout North America, serving 4,000+ multi-industry customers. Started up and directed risk management/risk underwriting department overseeing $27 billion in credit exposure. Established formalized training programs. Recruited and oversaw 52-member professional and support staff.

- Reduced risk more than $582 million to date while growing export portfolio from zero to $1.2 billion.
- Saved $475,000 annually through renegotiation of information contracts.

Continued...

MILTON S. HELFER

Page Two

- Significantly improved productivity and customer relations by redirecting focus of efforts to critical areas and developing 350-page credit policies/practices manual accepted overwhelmingly by International Board of Directors.
- Researched and analyzed company's performance with a focused interest in positive marketplace events.

CENTURY FIRST BANK, N.A., Far Rockaway, New York   1994–2002

Vice President & Divisional Credit Officer (1997–2002)

Served as senior member of credit committee. Oversaw $2 billion portfolio and developed credit policies and procedures.

- Eliminated $90 million in operating losses by assessing/downsizing underperforming portfolio of newly acquired bank.
- Improved productivity and morale by restructuring commercial division credit department.

Vice President & Team Leader (1994–1997)

Directed marketing and guided banking officers in new business development, portfolio management, and cross-selling of nontraditional products. Managed portfolio and solidified account relationships with average loan outstandings of $100+ million and commitments exceeding $230 million.

- Grew portfolio from $80 million to $250 million and substantially increased revenues.

BANK OF DELAWARE, New York, New York   1991–1994

Vice President & Team Leader

Oversaw rapid growth of assets in mature region from $90 million to $210 million.

- Advanced from Management Trainee through three progressively responsible positions.

SUMMIT NATIONAL BANK, New York, New York   1990–1991

Supervisor, Credit & Collections

Merchant Representative

EDUCATION

Executive MBA, Columbia University, 1998
BS, University of Virginia, 1990

University of Texas, National Commercial Lending Graduate School, With Distinction, 1996
University of Texas, National Commercial Lending School, 1994

SANDRA O'NEAL–EXECUTIVE RESUME (WRITER: LOUISE KURSMARK)

SANDRA O'NEAL

760-294-7705 phone/fax • sponeal@yahoo.com
18534 Via Ascenso, Rancho Santa Fe, CA 92067

SENIOR EXECUTIVE: SERVICE INDUSTRIES
Revenue Growth • Service Excellence • Lean Operations

Entrepreneurial and growth-focused executive, twice building regional services businesses to millions of dollars in revenue and market leadership.

- **Top performance** in Sears partnership, growing the relationship to #1 in service and #2 in national sales volume among 370 contractors across the country.

- **Proven skills** as a team builder and motivational leader able to inspire staff to excellence.

- **Hands-on management experience** in all facets of the business, with notable contributions as a sales leader and finance manager, able to build lean organizations and capture emerging business opportunities.

- **Service orientation** and ability to make integrity and customer service prime differentiators in the market.

EXPERIENCE AND ACHIEVEMENTS

LA BREA MECHANICAL SERVICES, INC.   Encinitas, CA, 2000–Present
President

Launched full-service repair and installation company, growing into a major service arm of Sears retail organizations in 3 U.S. regions. Defined vision/strategy emphasizing integrity and service as competitive differentiators. Grew the business from start-up to $6MM revenue, 38 staff, in 5 years.

In 2005, recruited a new, highly talented executive team (CEO, CFO, CIO) to ignite massive growth (to $200MM by 2007) and position the company for spin-off.

- **Growth:** Built a strongly ethical business foundation with exceptional pricing, quality, and workmanship; achieved lean operations through ROI-focused expense control; and delivered steady revenue growth:

	2001	2002	2003	2004	2005	2006 (proj.)
Revenue	$1.6MM	$2.1MM	$2.5MM	$4.4MM	$6MM	$25MM

- **Strategic business:** Became a prominent and valued Sears partner:
  - #2 in sales volume among 370 nationwide
  - #1 in quality service rating
  - Top 10% in attach rate—driven through partnering and relationship-building with store staff and managers

- **Expansion:** At the request of Sears executives, took over new regions nationally to improve sales, service, and the Sears brand value in those markets:
  - Washington State, June 2005
  - Phoenix, October 2005

- **Service orientation:**
  - Personally requested to provide intensive customer-service training to Sears' West Coast call center.
  - Introduced compensation plan innovative for the industry, paying service technicians salary rather than commission to drive customer-first philosophy.

SANDRA O'NEAL   760-294-7705 phone/fax • sponeal@yahoo.com

O'NEAL INSTALLATION SERVICES   Encinitas, CA, 1984–2000
President, 1992–2000

Assumed ownership of the business, inheriting steep financial challenges and driving a turnaround to more than triple revenues.

- **Growth:** Increased revenues from $1.6MM in 1984 to $5MM in 2000.

- **Diversification:** Launched home-improvement subsidiary and grew to $2.7MM gross revenue in 3 years.

- **Strategic business:** Managed and grew Sears business from start-up to $2MM annual revenues.

Additional Roles & Performance Highlights, 1984–1992

Learned the business from the ground up, advancing to new areas of responsibility to gain expertise and tackle significant business challenges.

- **Finance Manager:** Identified accounting discrepancies and assumed responsibility for the company's financial operations—A/R, A/P, payroll, worker's comp, liability, and vehicle maintenance as well as oversight of 8 administrative staff and 30 field technicians.
  - Overhauled processes, upgraded technology, and eliminated source of significant financial loss.
  - Developed proprietary system for tracking daily cash flow to the penny.

- **Operations Manager:** Oversaw field service and fleet of company-owned vehicles. Continuously sought opportunities to cut costs, improve efficiency, and increase service.
  - Saved $60K annually by redesigning service flow and assigning dedicated truck/driver for appliance pickups.

- **Sales Manager:** Developed new business and managed major accounts, including regional appliance dealers, Lowe's, Sears, and Home Depot.
  - Recognized market opportunity with the arrival of Lowe's in the San Diego market; cold-called to develop first Lowe's business and grew to the company's #1 account.

Active volunteer in the San Diego community.
References provided upon request.

HANS KOHLENBURG—EXECUTIVE RESUME (WRITER: GEORGIA ADAMSON)

HANS KOHLENBURG

302 Esquire Court
Santa Clara, CA 95051

650-941-5612
hans-kohlenburg@yahoo.com

SENIOR EXECUTIVE
Building and Leading Profitable Organizations from a Global Perspective

Astute, high-energy executive with innovative, future-oriented vision and a track record of successful international business launches. Key strengths and expertise include the following:

- Diverse industry experience and a comprehensive global view of business
- Management experience from start-ups to multibillion-dollar enterprises
- Partnering and strategic alliance development
- Strategic and tactical planning expertise
- High-performance team-building & leadership

- Relationship building with outside organizations, including investment banks and law firms
- Key player in several successful business sales, mergers, and acquisitions
- Board-level communication and membership
- Profit & loss (P&L) management
- Fund-raising to grow and expand company operations

PROFESSIONAL EXPERIENCE

PRESIDENT / CHIEF OPERATING OFFICER
DUOnet, Belmont, CA / Berlin, Germany   1999–Present
Spearheaded the launch of this subsidiary of Lunen Aero Defense & Space Company (LADS), a $20 billion global enterprise. Manage all aspects of operations, including offices in the U.S., Europe, Eastern Europe, and Asia.

- Initiate actions to maintain the company's position as a leading provider of secure, effective e-business software solutions for managing relationships with customers, suppliers, and partners.
- Focus current development activities on integration of the company's e-business and security solutions to create a state-of-the-art system for secure enterprise relationship management (ERM).
- Meet semiannually in an executive summit with leaders of other LADS companies to strengthen inter-company communication and collaborate on profitable business enhancements.
- Participate in parent company merger-and-acquisition activities. Assist with negotiations to determine the value of corporate assets.

Accomplishment Highlights:
- Built the business entity from the initial concept to a successful organization with an international presence. Planned and implemented R&D centers in California, Germany, and Sweden.
- Drove the establishment of a global network with more than 60 partners in 14 countries.
- Played a key role in preparations for a successful dual IPO in Europe and the United States. Interviewed major investment banks, including Credit Suisse, Morgan Stanley, and Deutsche Bank.
- Created a joint venture with VeriSign and German Telecomm.
- Led implementation of a stock option plan in the U.S. and Europe.
- Identified several investment, merger, and acquisition candidates and completed investments in two targeted companies.

- continued -

PROFESSIONAL EXPERIENCE
(continued)

CHIEF EXECUTIVE OFFICER / COFOUNDER
Kurtec Interactive Services, Salt Lake City, UT / **Kurtec GmbH**, Bonn, Germany   1994–1998 / 1985–1999
Sold both companies to Deutsche Technike Company, a $10 billion organization.
- Collaborated with partners to establish a company with the goal of "delivering any information to anyone through any device." Focused on minimizing cost and reducing information access time.
- Developed a business model that included products and technology, systems consulting and integration, outsourcing, and electronic publishing.
- Pursued and negotiated contracts with banks, government organizations, and large corporations to obtain R&D funding for development of multimedia software solutions.
- Developed architecture to be independent of the platform and media used, with applications that included ASCII, telephone, and multimedia.
- Created a publishing function to expand the company's operations by purchasing or developing original content for electronic publication.

Accomplishment Highlights:
- Launched the two companies from scratch and built them into profitable international enterprises.
- Secured the first multimedia award in the retail sector in 1989 and achieved full ROI on the project in less than a year.
- Diversified and strengthened the company through a decision to expand internationally in 1991. Within four years, over 70% of consulting and system integration revenue came from outside Germany.
- Negotiated multiple business deals and strategic global alliances with major corporations worldwide, including Digital, IBM, AT&T, and Siemens.
- Established a business venture in Eastern Europe that included deals with Hungary's major telecommunications company and with the leader of a large privatization project.
- Identified and aggressively pursued the potential of interactive TV in its early stages, attracting two major U.S. corporations, both of which deployed Kurtec products in interactive television trials.

AFFILIATIONS
Member, DUOnet Board of Directors
Former Board Member, Kurtec & Kurtec Interactive Services
Former Board Member, The Germanic Group, a worldwide organization
dedicated to promoting the German language and culture

EDUCATION
Master's degrees in physics and math, University of Bonn

CHARLES BROADWAY—EXECUTIVE RESUME (WRITER: DON ORLANDO)

CONFIDENTIAL

CHARLES W. BROADWAY

cwb777blue@aol.com

5600 Carmichael Road, #901-B, Montgomery, Alabama 36000

(334) 245-7960

WHAT I CAN BRING TO SOLAR BROADCASTING AS YOUR GENERAL MANAGER:

- **Expertise** acquired from serving many different types of stations
- **Credibility** won by mastering nearly every kind of position in television sales and administration
- **Unflappability** honed by bringing people and stations to full productivity under very tough conditions

RELEVANT WORK HISTORY WITH SELECTED EXAMPLES OF SUCCESS:

Vice President and **General Manager,** WTVA-TV (ABC), Montgomery, Alabama
Jan 02–Dec 03 (Vista Entertainment), Jan 04–May 06 (Crowne General)

- Revitalized sales department that worked below potential for years. Introduced full accountability. Revamped hiring system. *Results:* **Revenue up.** In one year, **household market share rose 28%.**

- Broke competitors' "lock" on local news. Recruited top but underused minority to anchor unserved prime slot. Refocused other newscast toward women.
  Results: Deepened, **expanded** news **presence.** No new staff needed.

- Capitalized fast on resources new owners controlled. Boosted ratings with shows such as *Jerry Springer* and *Living Single. Results:* Great payoff in our 38% ethnic market. **In-market household share up 23%** in just one year.

- Found production assistant with media sales experience earned in New York. Turned her loose as our new marketing manager. *Results:* **Best marketing** in years.

- Fixed inappropriate management system I inherited. Worked closely with rapidly changing CEOs to streamline personnel costs, redirect news department, and vitalize marketing.
  Results: **Sales up 13%** in first year. Station's "health" improved so fast that new owner made no management changes.

Corporate Media Consultant, Soundview Media Investments, Gulf Breeze, Florida
Jul 99–Dec 01

Soundview Media Investments was formed by two principals from New Vision Television to acquire television stations mostly in the Northwest and Southeast.

- Routinely handled every aspect of highly confidential due diligence on pending acquisitions and prepared station proformas.

Station Manager *promoted to* **Executive Vice President** and **General Manager,** *later* **Vice President** and **General Manager,** WJTV-TV (CBS), Jackson, Mississippi
Jun 96–May 99

WJTV was purchased from the News-Press & Gazette Company by New Vision Television, Atlanta, Georgia.

More examples of performance Solar Broadcasting can use ➤

CONFIDENTIAL

CONFIDENTIAL

Charles W. Broadway   **General Manager**   (334) 245-7960

- Guided managers of our two sales teams. Handled national accounts myself to restore station's credibility. *Results:* **Highest** overall **ratings in 15 years. Revenue up** 15% the first year, as high 28% later. **$931K increase** in 1/98 alone.

- Took risk of airing, **live,** state beauty pageant **to every station in the state,** three years running. *Results:* **Quality consistently high** enough to persuade local stations to preempt network shows.

General Manager, WEVV-TV (Independent, later Fox), Evansville, Indiana
Aug 92–May 96

- *Results:* Annual revenue up 50% each year in the first three years alone. Won Top Three Fox Affiliate in markets ranked 50–100 (1995).

Account Executive *promoted to* **Office Manager,** MMT Sales, Inc., Dallas, Texas
Dec 89–Jul 92

- Managed national accounts for MMT (client stations in the top 30 markets) across five Western and Southern states.

Account Executive, Katz Communications
Jan 86–May 89 (for the Continental Division), Chicago, Illinois
Jan 82–Dec 85 (for Continental, American, and Independent Divisions), Dallas, Texas

- *Results:* Promoted from serving 78 client stations in one division to covering sales for more than 100 stations in all divisions. Market ranks ran from number one to at least 150. Serviced accounts like Ogilvy & Mather; McCann-Erickson; Ketchum-McCloud; Foot, Cone & Belding; and Western International.

Account Executive, WEHT-TV (CBS), Evansville, Indiana
Sep 79–Dec 81

PROFESSIONAL ASSOCIATIONS:

- Secretary and Treasurer, Montgomery Broadcasters' Association
- Montgomery Advertising Federation
- Advisory Board, Alabama State University, Department of Communications. *Sought out by the faculty to advise this university on its curricula and programs.*

EDUCATION:

- Graduate studies, **Finance,** University of Evansville, Evansville, Indiana, 79
- B.A., **Communications,** Washington & Lee University, Lexington, Virginia, 74

Page 2

CONFIDENTIAL

DANIEL O'CONNELL—EXECUTIVE RESUME PROJECT ADDENDUM (WRITER: JAN MELNIK)

Daniel R. O'Connell

157 Tewksbury Lane • Nashua, NH 03060
(603) 454-2381 • droconnell@gmail.com

Vice President • General Manager • Director

Track record as Vice President and Project Manager within general contracting and construction industry reflects a performance history characterized by keen technical expertise complemented by specialties in high-tech mechanical systems; complex, multimillion-dollar renovations without interruption of service; tenant buildouts; waste and wastewater treatment facilities; and heavy concrete.

- Excellent communication skills and ability to motivate results-oriented teams, leading by example; proactive approach with expert organizational and follow-through skills.
- Proven ability to exceed client expectations with consistent focus on ensuring ROI as well as on-time, under-budget completion of all projects.

Professional Experience

THE PRUDENTIAL • Boston, MA   2000–Present
Vice President, Real Estate Services (2/04–Present)
Promoted to lead team of project managers (2 direct staff; 35+ indirect staff), overseeing multiple facilities projects for Summit, NJ; Waltham, MA; Nashua, NH; and Boston, MA sites. Directly manage project operations for headquarters facilities in Boston as well as security at all sites.

Develop and manage a $14 million capital and expensed project budget encompassing 4 million sq. ft. across 3 states housing 11,000 employees; project scope includes improvements to such infrastructure as windows, building facades, and roof replacements; upgrades to elevators and Category 5 communications cables; mechanical and electrical improvements; structural improvement to on-site parking garage; and carpet replacement program implementation as well as ADA and code upgrades. Analyze and formulate priorities and fiscal spending recommendations.

- Carefully ensure asset and real estate investment protection with appropriate balance between short- and long-term capital expenditures and maintenance versus replacement strategies.
- Identified and launched key workflow initiatives that significantly eased transition with procurement division; streamlined paperwork, contributing to more efficient flows and time savings.
- Execute building condition surveys linked to capital needs, enabling long-term planning; currently implementing analysis of roof maintenance/replacement.
- Collaborate effectively with alliance partners in managing key construction disciplines (mechanical, electrical, plumbing, and architecture); achieved ongoing project consistency and significant savings in capital and time through long-term contracts.

Real Estate Services Project Manager (6/00–2/04)
Successfully managed multiple construction projects throughout company's headquarters complex featuring multiple buildings integrating 5 generations of construction as well as new sites. Key achievements include:

- Accomplished physical separation of Prudential from Mass Mutual in 2 locations, ensuring aggressive deadlines and regulatory compliance issues were achieved in time for sale, including design and construction of new security measures throughout campus and the buildout of a new employee store.
- Integral player in development and implementation of strategic capital improvement plan; following extensive campus evaluation, enacted a 7–10 year deferred maintenance plan that extended resources and provided for maximum utility.
- Oversaw complex City Square $1.45MM VDC room relocation; coordinated construction to ensure seamless move to new facility and provided cross-connection of 24x7 services without disruptions.

... continued

Daniel R. O'Connell

Professional Experience *(continued)*

THE PRUDENTIAL • *Real Estate Services Project Manager* (continued)

- Key contributor to development of preferred vendor program that identified select group of engineers, designers, and construction professionals and ensured optimal yet cost-effective quality.
- Hired design team, issued RFPs, reviewed/approved bids, awarded contracts, and fully oversaw projects from conception to execution to ensure on-time/under-budget completion that consistently exceeded quality expectations.
- Effectively managed team relationships and ensured positive ongoing communications.

SHAWMUT DESIGN & CONSTRUCTION • Boston, MA   1998–2000
Project Manager
Directly supported Construction Manager, collaborating with clients, project architects, engineers, and entire design team from initial project planning and budgeting through the competitive bidding process to construction and successful completion/turnover to client. Ensured quality work was completed on time and under budget.

- Developed well-established reputation for bringing together engineers and design team members with manufacturers, suppliers, and subcontractors, resulting in cost-effective implementation of projects that exceeded functional and architectural design criteria.
- Coordinated all trades and managed subcontractor crews of up to 70 personnel on-site; ensured daily scheduling, production, and deadlines were maintained; effectively managed field operations and personnel.
- Comprehensive construction experience from administration, planning, and scheduling to construction and project closeout.

OBERLIN CONSTRUCTION COMPANY • Providence, RI   1996–1998
Project Manager
Managed wide-ranging responsibilities for design/build construction company; oversaw management of highly complex projects, ensuring superior quality and successful completion within deadlines, to complete specifications, and under budget.

- Directed development of complete project design, scope, and plans, collaborating with architects, engineers, and design professionals; maintained extensive communications/interface with clients.
- Developed and wrote contracts as well as negotiated with contractors/subcontractors.
- Ensured optimal sequencing of construction activity through effective coordination of submittals and deliveries.
- Identified project deviations, wrote and processed Contract Change Orders and RFIs, and maintained overall overhead and profit margins on projects.

DESMOND CONTRACTING COMPANY • New London, CT   1990–96
Project Engineer/Assistant Project Manager
Developed extensive construction/project management expertise on numerous projects. Promoted from Field Clerk to Assistant Project Manager/Project Engineer and Estimator.

Education

WORCESTER POLYTECHNIC INSTITUTE • Worcester, MA
Bachelor of Science, Industrial Engineering *(1990)*
Concentration: Construction Management

Daniel R. O'Connell

157 Tewksbury Lane • Nashua, NH 03060
(603) 454-2381 • droconnell@gmail.com

Select Key Project Accomplishments

- **The Prudential** • Boston, MA
  Project Manager   Successfully managed $7 million home office headquarters' window replacement project, ensuring conformity with historic interests while assuring appropriate asset management; effectively mitigated concerns regarding long-term maintenance.

- **The Prudential** • Boston, MA
  Project Manager   Effectively managed $1.4 million security consolidation project, utilizing technology to provide a single centralized control center in Boston for all sites; significantly reduced staffing requirements, yielding a payback in 1.5 years.

- **The Prudential** • Boston, MA
  Project Manager   Extreme deadline-sensitive building separation to facilitate Prudential/Mass Mutual split ($3.5MM).

- **Barone Investment Management** • Boston, MA
  Project Manager   100,000 sq. ft. high-end tenant buildout, including trading room and technical center ($7MM).

- **Brown University Five College Fire Protection Project** • Providence, RI
  Project Manager   Intense, fast-track fire safety upgrade to five colleges with high-end architectural finishes and complex trade coordination ($2.5MM).

- **Mass Mutual** • Boston, MA
  Project Manager   Administered subcontractor buyout of phased, 21-story tenant buildout ($8MM).

- **Brown University Ebenezer Quadrangle Adaptive Reuse** • Providence, RI
  Project Manager   Assisted in management of pre-construction and establishment of GMP for major campus renovation project ($28MM).

- **Plum Island Animal Disease Control Center Sewer Treatment Facility** • Plum Island, NY
  Project Manager   Pilot plant using phagmitis reed plants for disinfection.

- **Nantucket Sewer Treatment Facility** • Nantucket, MA
  Project Engineer   Upgrade of an existing plant, coordinating extensive construction activities on an island.

- **Warehouse Conversion, Seabrook Nuclear Power Plant** • Seabrook, NH
  Project Engineer   Refurbished existing warehouse (25,000 square feet) to completely finished office space in a compressed, three-week schedule.

- **Warehouse Conversion, Seabrook Nuclear Power Plant** • Seabrook, NH
  Project Engineer   Conversion and upgrade of warehouses (1, 2, 3, 4, 5, and 8) to finished office space and upgraded warehouse.

JONATHAN BUCHANAN—EXECUTIVE RESUME (WRITER: DEBORAH WILE DIB)

JONATHAN BUCHANAN

ENTERTAINMENT & LEISURE DEVELOPMENT SPECIALIST
COMMERCIAL ASSET MANAGER & DEVELOPER

EXECUTIVE PROFILE

Twenty+ years of senior-level management and consulting experience with world-class, complex, large-scale, one-of-a-kind, mixed-use land and real estate development projects valued in the hundreds of millions of dollars.

Notable Projects Include:

- Town Centre at Aston, Aston, GA ($300 million)
- WELCO Arena and BCB Center Renovations, Flanders, VA ($275 million)
- The Bay View, Barstock, DE ($125 million proposed/$300 million planned)
- National Science Hall (NSH), Llanview, SC ($200 million proposed)
- The Gates Racecourse, Pacifica, WA ($150 million proposed)

Areas of Expertise:

Site Selection & Predevelopment	Strategic Planning	Marketing Methodology	Budgeting & Monitoring
Public & Private Partnerships	Integrated Project Development	Market Acquisition Strategies	Concept Strategies
Revitalization & Renovation	Acquisition Due Diligence	Public & Private Financing	Real Estate Investment
Economic Development	Financial Performance	Place-Making	Lifestyle & Entertainment Centers
Highest & Best Use Analysis	Development Advisory Services	Zoning & Entitlements	Networking & Sourcing

PERFORMANCE DRIVERS

● **Versatile Manager & Consultant**
Skilled in complex interactions and relations within multiple horizontal/vertical uses and mixed product types. Often retained to manage challenging projects. Guide projects from viability evaluation and concept development through corporate/government approvals, entitlements, site plans, permits (from URPs to PUDs), public/private financing and partnerships, design, construction, and lease-up. Keen focus on simultaneously balancing supply and demand of multiple project components.

● **Quality & Profit-Driven Steward**
Grounded in the principles of real estate with a thorough understanding of risk/reward ratios. Committed to delivering high-value, profitable projects that meet goals *and* contribute lasting quality of life and environmental impact, creating healthier markets, productive business conditions, and solid community relations.

● **Resourceful Solutions Provider**
Look for solutions opportunities in every challenge and creative ideas from self, team members, and consultants. Adept at quantifying issues, scoping sources, and using extensive network to locate resources. Involved in cutting-edge projects that do not conform to norm and that require resourceful thinking and persistence. These range from unanchored specialty retail (Town Centre at Aston), to location-based entertainment (LBE) for a horse track's surplus real estate (The Gates Racecourse), to an international science museum (National Science Hall).

● **Strategic Planner & Thinker**
Implement project strategies required to manage short-term issues while pursuing long-term objectives. Used these skills to achieve zoning approval for Town Centre at Aston, achieve a museum site for the National Science Hall, and gain governmental approvals after PILOTs for IHE were rejected.

● **Efficient Self-Starter**
Accomplished in activities and order of attack for complex projects, usually hitting achievable deadlines for even the most complicated projects. Require limited supervision, getting a job done quietly and efficiently. Currently running multifaceted Inner Harbor East project with nominal client interface. Typically manage two to three efforts concurrently. While managing BCB Center renovations and WELCO Arena development, oversaw The Gates concept development and NSH pre-development.

● **Egoless Mentor & Team Builder**
Lead through example, for results, not glory. Articulate objectives and work tirelessly to achieve them. Motivate participants (especially young talent) through consistency, persistence, and constant communication, an important skill for Town Centre at Aston, with its multifunction interdisciplinary team and a high-octane, performance-driven culture.

3056 Great Neck Road, Mableton, GA 30126 ● cell: 770.295.2007 ● fax: 770.709.2309 ● jbuchanan@yahoo.com

(continued)

(continued)

SENIOR-LEVEL CONSULTING MANAGEMENT EXPERIENCE

BUCHANAN, INCORPORATED: GREAT ROCK, VA; SILVER LAKE, GA; DEVILLE, MA   **1990 to Present**
● **Consultant/Principal**

Development advisory/management firm specializing in high-density mixed-use commercial projects blending lifestyle, entertainment, retail, restaurants, and other uses. Clients include Struever Bros. Eccles & Rouse, Inc. (SBER); Simpson Sports & Entertainment Development; Benton Broadcasting System; National Science Hall; The Enterprise Development Corporation; Montgomery County, MD; The Gates Racecourse; and many others.

Major projects include:

The Bay View, Barstock, DE ($125 million developed to date/$300 million planned)   6/02 to Present
Master developing three city blocks and providing development management services on 900,000 sq. ft. mixed-use building. Developing optimum program and managing design to achieve construction cost objectives, integrating cost-saving opportunities, preleasing office/retail, preselling hotel, obtaining public financing incentives and public approvals ranging from site plans to urban renewal plans to planned unit developments.

- Attained TIF and PILOT approvals by Barstock Development Corporation only five weeks after rejection. Total tax incentives equaled $57 million in potential tax savings—$22 million from PILOT and $35 million from TIF.
- Achieved site plan, URP, and PUD approvals. Increased building heights (180 feet to 300 feet) and densities (18%), allowing project to begin construction based on current design.
- Developed project schedule to meet accelerated construction start and tenant requirements. Drove design from constructability perspective, allowing for accelerated construction schedule.

National Science Hall (NSH), Llanview, SC ($200 million proposed)   10/99 to 4/02
Acted as National Science Hall Real Estate Planning and Development director developing NSH, a museum-sponsored proposed state-of-the art international science and technology center originally programmed for 365,000 sq. ft./$200 million. Through negotiations and interaction with public, program was phased, with first phase at 250,000 sq. ft./$150 million.

- Facilitated positioning of Museum to have capacity for project, elevating NSH to become one of top-five goals for Llanview Chamber of Commerce, key to building public-sector momentum.
- Planned, advised on restructuring and repositioning museum operations for political constituencies (to meet expansion from 53,000 sq. ft. to 250,000 sq. ft.), coordinated with Llanview Art Museum to develop/share "museum park" site and with city/county officials to obtain public funding, and facilitated private fund-raising campaigns and marketing to international community.

The Gates Racecourse, Pacifica, WA ($150 million)   3/99 to 2/00
Reported to Chief Executive Officer of The Gates. Provided development advisory services to owners who had ceased racing because of declining gaming revenues. Project was used as stalking horse to change Washington gaming laws in early 1999. Once laws changed, motivation for project shifted, and operation was sold.

- Assembled team, produced pro forma demonstrating financial viability, and delivered plan to carve 100 acres from 340-acre horse track for LBE ($150 million value entertainment/retail center) to coexist with horse operations.
- Orchestrated design charrette to accelerate planning process; identified and engaged horse track operations designers to coordinate retail/racing interface; and identified, interviewed, and evaluated various LBE providers for site compatibility.

WELCO Arena/BCB Center Renovations, Flanders, VA ($275 million)   5/96 to 03/00
● **Vice President of Development, Simpson Sports & Entertainment Development Corporation** 1/98 to 03/00
● **Consultant (through TRG)** 5/96 to 1/98

Reported to President, Simpson Sports & Entertainment Development (a Benton Broadcasting System, Inc., subsidiary). Provided development management services for WELCO Arena, a $250 million/20,000-seat multipurpose sports/entertainment project. Initially managed site selection, identifying/evaluating five sites and negotiating with formidable and resistant owners, including Flanders Journal Constitution, State Bar of Virginia, Federal Reserve Bank of Virginia, and Norfolk Southern Railroad.

In 1998, retained as 75% part-time VP reporting to SSED President. Concurrently oversaw $25 million retail renovation of BCB Center and Omni hotel, to mesh visually and operationally with arena. Components included obtaining all approvals, managing design and internal/external improvements, remerchandising retail (ultimately doubling rents), upgrading BCB Studio Tour, redesigning/tripling size of Simpson Store, and initiating concept development for new destination attraction (to be constructed) for BCB to complement the other daytime uses. Completed without disruption to 24/7 broadcasting.

3056 Great Neck Road, Mableton, GA 30126 ● cell: 770.295.2007 ● fax: 770.709.2309 ● jbuchanan@yahoo.com

CONSULTING EXPERIENCE, BUCHANAN INCORPORATED/WELCO ARENA & BCB, CONTINUED

- Achieved senior-management project approval, an important step as renovations increased BCB's visibility, improved public's perception, and doubled retail rents by moving retail environment from business to tourist. Completed on time/on budget.
- Oversaw arena's food service setup ($15+ million revenues). Orchestrated food concessionaire selection process for premium and general concessions vendors. This was one of the first times general concessions operations functioned as a food court during nonevent times. Creative food service enabled arena to achieve among the highest per-unit sales in the country.
- Focused on branding opportunities and capitalized on media impressions showcasing BCB/WBS brands. Managed all retail/entertainment, including BCB Studio Tour renovation, Simpson Store expansion, and initial concept of Benton Experience, a second studio tour. Directed creation of arena's "Team Store" and Cartoon Network cobranded team store.
- Orchestrated/negotiated "high-impact" site selection, strategically accepting early losses to garner long-term gains. Facilitated public/private partnership, culminating in $65 million in public bonds sold prior to potential change in public financing laws and $130 million in private bonds backed by City of Flanders credit. Met extensive MBE/WBE goals (30%/6%).
- Comanaged team-building that successfully executed WELCO Arena from third-party perspective. Set up organization to manage BCB renovations, including architects, owner's rep, and contractor, working through Simpson departmental "project ownership" conflicts.

Oasis Mall, Livingston County, DE ($600 million proposed)   10/96 to 4/97
Partnered with MRA International to provide market verification study of a proposed 2 million sq. ft., $600 million mixed-use project in Duchess, DE (called the Oasis Mall), envisioned as a version of Mall of America.

- Evaluated potential and managed market verification study, developed essential conditions for success, and positioned County to pursue $150 million in public subsidies for project. Project ultimately died for lack of private financing.

SENIOR-LEVEL MANAGEMENT EXPERINCE

LBK PARTNERS, CLAYTON, FL   1999 to 2000
● **Principal and Managing Partner**

LBK Partners invested in small-scale land development opportunities and provided development advisory services to major landowners and institutional investors for large mixed-use projects/developments and for acquisition portfolio due diligence analyses. In first year, generated annual fees up to $500,000 and serviced over $50 million in real estate property.

Oversaw Clayton Office and development director. Obtained entitlements, managed consulting teams and master planning, prepared pro formas, identified/pursued public financing opportunities, prepared private placement memorandum to raise project equity, marketed sites, and pursued new business opportunities/sourcing.

- Built office to $500,000 year-one fees from $0 by astute management of business procurement and client relationships.
- Provided master planning/development advisory services for 3 million sq. ft. mixed-use Clayton project and 280,000 sq. ft. Clayton telecommunications renovation. Successfully managed troubled 1,000-acre PUD master planning/entitlement process. Supported Hartsburgh home office in master planning/entitlements of additional sites.

BRISTOL PROPERTIES, INC., A SUBSIDIARY TO BRISTOL, PLC, BALTIMORE, MD   1992 to 1994
● **President**

Bristol Properties, Inc., was a start-up subsidiary to Bristol, PLC, at the time the world's number-two construction materials firm. It has since been swallowed in a hostile takeover.

Recruited to develop start-up business plan and manage North American entitlement, development, and disposition activities across 3,000 U.S. and Canadian acres, with one asset in mix with a $5 billion value potential. Evaluated sales opportunities, site delivery costs, buyer pursuit/identification, and real estate takeover opportunities as part of hostile takeover of another company. Participated in core business management activities. Reported to President of Bristol Properties, UK.

- Developed firm's start-up business plan. Assessed site marketability and entitlement/capital development needs. Created implementation business plan—a road map for placing real estate in play as market recovered.
- Provided reality check by auditing real estate holdings. When recruited, was told that company's real estate portfolio was valued at $200 million and was readily marketable with no required improvements. Put audit in play that indicated $60 million actual value, requiring annual $3 million to $4 million, five-year effort to create a solid revenue stream.
- Delivered risk/reward assessment of a limestone quarry to landfill conversion, an important factor in valuing Steetley's hostile takeover attempt.

(continued)

(continued)

SENIOR-LEVEL MANAGEMENT EXPERIENCE, CONTINUED

LATHAM/CLARKE FRANCES, ASTON, GA   **1985 to 1989**
● **Senior Development Director, TOWN CENTRE AT ASTON**

Firm developed Town Centre at Aston, one of the nation's premier suburban mixed-use, unanchored specialty centers. Co-managed daily project activities to design, construct, and lease 1.2 million sq. ft. mixed-use project—514-key Hyatt Regency Hotel, 550,000 sq. ft./office, and 240,000 sq. ft./retail ($300 million total project cost).

Managed (as number-two project lead) day-to-day development team and activities, including building and managing all development, consulting, and office leasing teams, and directing all marketing/PR/event management planning/execution. Concurrent with project, periodically evaluated acquisition of alternative development properties in other parts of East Coast.

- Created Town Centre at Aston, an industry leader in entertainment-enhanced, mixed-use development. Participated in team's assemblage and managed follow-through/implementation details. Outstanding long-term results included new demand, new community lifestyle, office rents (at stabilization) of $4/sq. ft. above market, and a market-leading hotel.

- Directed all marketing/PR (print and media) and event planning for multievent, three-month grand opening to put project on map. Crafted destination appeal and seasonal events, creating traffic and building property's perception as an "event" location. Repeat traffic translated into retail sales and events gave aura of Town Centre as the "place to be."

- Created foundation for new uses. Conceived idea of ice rink for events (with portability to test market demand). Rink was so successful that it was converted to a permanent rink and entertainment pavilion.

ASTON LAND CORPORATION (HANNIFORD LAND DEVELOPMENT CORP. SUBSIDIARY), ASTON, GA   **1984 to 1989**
● **Vice President Commercial Marketing and Development**

Firm managed disposition, marketing, and promotion of all real estate in Aston (including Aston Town Centre).

Directed sales strategies, purchaser identification, pursuit, and land sale negotiation. Managed master planning for Aston Town Centre. Oversaw development and master planning of six-building, 360,000 sq. ft. Cameron Pond Office Park.

- Constructed RTC Phase I business deal, attracting and attaining corporate approval for joint venture between Hanniford (their first 50-50 real estate JV and three years in the making) and Latham/Clarke Frances. Venture put wheels in motion for Aston Town Centre development while allowing significant owner control.

- Master planned Aston Town Centre; assembled/managed planning team and internal master planning "task force." Created flexible, evolving, market-driven, economically feasible project plan still being implemented today.

- Entitled last significant tract of land in Aston—RTC 500-acre study area for 8.5 million sq. ft. development. Crafted and negotiated flexible entitlements (in tough political environment) and managed community participation process. Positioned owners to capitalize on market opportunities for next 10+ years.

- Sold $80+ million in commercial land in '80s. Negotiated/closed many land sales with developers and corporations. Saw increase in values ($1.50 to $2.00/sq. ft. to final sale at $20/sq. ft.), providing core development/sale income to owner.

- Managed significant commercial marketing of Aston, including Aston Expressway campaign that enabled hitting 150% of projections in six months and driving awareness of Aston's accessibility and heightening interest in land holdings.

EDUCATION & PROFESSIONAL DEVELOPMENT

Georgia School of Technology & State University, Dawson, GA
- **MBA–concentration in Finance, 1974**
- **BS–Business Administration, Public Administration, 1971**

Memberships: Urban Land Institute, International Council of Shopping Centers, National Assoc. of Office & Industrial Parks.

Professional Activities: Founding member of ULI's Entertainment Development Council, serving since 1995 formation and currently functioning as Vice Chair at Large. Served on ULI's Small Scale Development Council. Charter member, Northern Virginia NAIOP Chapter.

Attendee and speaker/panelist at conferences: Annual/semiannual Urban Land Institute (ULI) and International Council of Shopping Centers conferences/conventions (since 1983). Periodic special-purpose conferences on Developing Entertainment Destinations and other topics. ULI Entertainment Development Conference (eight since 1995). ICSC Annual Convention (since 1998).

Awards: Aston Town Centre received Northern Georgia NAIOP award for "Best Large-Scale Mixed-Use Project" in 1992 and was selected as a Finalist for 1995 ULI Awards for Excellence.

3056 Great Neck Road, Mableton, GA 30126 ● cell: 770.295.2007 ● fax: 770.709.2309 ● jbuchanan@yahoo.com

Appendix

Additional Executive Resources

If you need more help putting together your career marketing documents or finding career opportunities, the professionals and Web sites in this section are excellent resources.

EXECUTIVE RESUME WRITERS/CAREER COACHES

Here is complete contact information for writers whose work appears in this book.

Georgia Adamson, CCM, CEIP, CPRW, JCTC, CCMC
President, A Successful Career
180 W. Rincon Ave.
Campbell, CA 95008-2824
Phone: 408-866-6859
Fax: 408-866-8915
E-mail: success@ablueribbonresume.com
www.ABlueRibbonResume.com
www.asuccessfulcareer.com

Jacqui D. Barrett, MRW, CPRW, CEIP
President, Career Trend
11613 W. 113th St.
Overland Park, KS 66210
Phone: 913-451-1313
Fax: 801-382-5842
E-mail: jacqui@careertrend.net
www.careertrend.net

Freddie Cheek, M.S.Ed., CCM, CPRW, CRW, CWDP
Cheek & Associates
406 Maynard Dr.
Amherst, NY 14226
Phone: 716-835-6935
Fax: 716-831-9320
E-mail: fscheek@adelphia.net
www.CheekandCristantello.com

Annemarie Cross, CEIP, CPRW, CRW, CCM, CECC, CERW, CWPP
Advanced Employment Concepts
P.O. Box 91
Hallam, Victoria 3803, Australia
E-mail: success@aresumewriter.net
www.aresumewriter.net

Deborah Wile Dib, CPBS, CCM, NCRW, CPRW, CEIP, JCTC, CCMC, Certified 360Reach Analyst
President, The Executive Power Group (Advantage Resumes of NY/ Executive Power Coach)
77 Buffalo Ave.
Medford, NY 11763
Phone: 631-475-8513
Fax: 501-421-7790
E-mail: debdib@ExecutivePowerGroup.com
www.ExecutivePowerGroup.com
www.advantageresumes.com
www.executivepowercoach.com

Beverly Harvey, CPRW, JCTC, CCM, CCMC, MRW, CPBS
President, Beverly Harvey Resume & Career Services
P.O. Box 750
Pierson, FL 32180
Phone: 386-749-3111
Fax: 386-749-4881
E-mail: beverly@harveycareers.com
www.harveycareers.com

Myriam-Rose Kohn, CPBS, CPRW, CEIP, IJCTC, CCM, CCMC
President, JEDA Enterprises
27201 Tourney Rd., Ste. 201M
Valencia, CA 91355
Phone: 661-253-0801
Fax: 661-253-0744

E-mail: myriam-rose@jedaenterprises.com
www.jedaenterprises.com

Cindy Kraft, CCMC, CCM, JCTC, CPRW
President, Executive Essentials
P.O. Box 336
Valrico, FL 33595
Phone: 813-655-0658
Fax: 813-354-3483
E-mail: cindy@cfo-coach.com
www.cfo-coach.com

Louise Kursmark, MRW, CPRW, JCTC, CEIP, CCM
President, Best Impression Career Services, Inc.
Toll-free phone: 888-792-0030
Toll-free fax: 877-791-7127
E-mail: LK@yourbestimpression.com
www.yourbestimpression.com

Jan Melnik, MRW, CCM, CPRW
President, Absolute Advantage
P.O. Box 718
Durham, CT 06422
Phone: 860-349-0256
Fax: 860-349-1343
E-mail: CompSPJan@aol.com
www.janmelnik.com

Don Orlando, MBA, CPRW, JCTC, CCM, CCMC
President, The McLean Group
640 S. McDonough St.
Montgomery, AL 36104
Phone: 334-264-2020
Fax: 334-264-9227
E-mail: yourcareercoach@aol.com

MOST POPULAR EXECUTIVE JOB BOARDS

The following list was provided by Mark Hovind of JobBait (www.jobbait.com),
who specializes in direct-mail services for executive job seekers; he gains this
information through his membership in IBN (http://interbiznet.com), a source
of Internet news and analysis for the recruiting industry. Sites listed in bold type
are strictly for six-figures-and-up positions, whereas the others more loosely
term themselves "executive" sites.

Note that this list was current as of early 2006, but of course Web addresses can change.

Executive Site	Type	URL
TheLadders	Six-figure	www.theladders.com
CareerJournal	Executive	www.careerjournal.com
ExecutivesOnTheWeb	Executive	www.executivesontheweb.com
SixFigureJobs	Six-figure	www.sixfigurejobs.com
exec-appointments	Executive	www.exec-appointments.com
Execunet	Six-figure	www.execunet.com
MBA-exchange	Executive	www.mba-exchange.com
eKornFerry	Executive	www.ekornferry.com
execSearches	Executive	www.execsearches.com
Heidrick & Struggles	Executive	www.heidrick.com
RiteSite	Six-figure	www.ritesite.com
Futurestep	Executive	www.futurestep.com
Netshare	Six-figure	www.netshare.com
MBAJungle	Executive	www.mbajungle.com
SpencerStuart	Executive	www.spencerstuart.com
ExecutivesOnly	Executive	www.executivesonly.com
ExecutiveRegistry	Six-figure	www.executiveregistry.com

Index

Q–R